John Capgrave's Lives of St. Augustine
and
St. Gilbert of Sempringham,
And a Sermon.

Original Series
No. 140.

O my wel beloued in our lord god ŋ. nicholas
mayster of ye order of sympryngha   Bysby-
whech ordre is entytled on to ye
name of seynt gilbert / ffrer /   John
a mong̱ certeyne left sende to   Capgrave

nerens as to oþer dignyte: desiryng clennesse
to your soule and helth to your body now
with me feile dyues was notyfied on
to me þat ye lyf of our fader seynt augustyn whech yat / translat in to our tunge
at instans of a certeyn woman was brougt
to your presens whech lyked you wel as u-
is told saue ye wold / stylul adde yto alle
yoo relygyous þat lyue vndyr his reule
But to þis / ansuerd yat it was not my chary
ge but if men like for to knowe ye mateer
diffusely yei may lerne it in a smal ythfu-
at tumbyng ye ser be fold myn opposicion
whech symon inphap / wil sette in englysh
in ye lyst ende of ynd work than aftur ye
had red ye lyf of seynt augusty ye sayde
to on of my frendes yat ye desired gretly
ye lyf of seynt gilbert schuld be translat
in the same forme Thus mad ye instance
to me and / graunted both your peticion for, þ9a
/ wold not frustrate hym of his mediacion
To ye honour of god and of all seyntis ye
wil the begynne yis tretys namelych for the
solitaryo fame of your relygyon whech un-

John Capgrave's Lives of
St. Augustine
and
St. Gilbert of Sempringham,
And a Sermon.

EDITED BY

J. J. MUNRO, F.R.Hist.S.,

EDITOR OF 'ROMEUS AND JULIET,' 'THE
SHAKSPEARE ALLUSION BOOK' AND AUTHOR WITH
DR. FURNIVALL OF 'SHAKESPEARE : LIFE AND WORK.'

LONDON:
PUBLISHED FOR THE EARLY ENGLISH TEXT SOCIETY
BY KEGAN PAUL, TRENCH, TRÜBNER & CO., Ltd.,
DRYDEN HOUSE, 43 GERRARD STREET, SOHO, W.
AND BY HENRY FROWDE, OXFORD UNIVERSITY PRESS,
AMEN CORNER, E.C.

OXFORD
UNIVERSITY PRESS

Great Clarendon Street, Oxford OX2 6DP
United Kingdom

Oxford University Press is a department of the University of Oxford.
It furthers the University's objective of excellence in research, scholarship,
and education by publishing worldwide. Oxford is a registered trade mark of
Oxford University Press in the UK and in certain other countries

© The Early English Text Society 1910

The moral rights of the authors have been asserted

Database right Oxford University Press (maker)

First Edition published in 1910

Published in the United States of America by Oxford University Press
198 Madison Avenue, New York, NY 10016, United States of America

British Library Cataloguing in Publication Data
Data available

Library of Congress Cataloging in Publication Data
Data available

Original Series, 140

ISBN 978-0-85-991886-2

INTRODUCTION

John Capgrave. In his Introduction to Capgrave's *Chronicle of England* the Rev. Francis Hingeston-Randolph expresses his approval of 'the singular honesty and straightforwardness of character, which must have belonged to the writer,'—on the model, may be, of Barham—'Thomas Ingoldsby, Esq., of Tappington Everard'—who speaks in a note to his *Blasphemer's Warning* of 'Honest John Capgrave, the veracious biographer of "English Saints".' To this eulogy, enounced under the authority of Bale, who writes of Capgrave's 'thunder against the wanton and arbitrary acts of prelates'—inaudible thunder to us in these after days—to all of this, Dr. Furnivall, with scripture authentic, in his Forewords to Capgrave's *Katharine* (xv, xxii), protests in fervent opposition. 'Capgrave, being an Englishman, was of course by race and nature a flunkey, and had an inordinate reverence for kings and rank,' says this Edwardian Elizabethan in his whole-hearted way. For the Augustinian friar had meted out unstinted praise to Henry IV, who 'gained the crown, by the providence, as we believe, of God'; had registered his encomium of that felicitous shatterer of heretics, as he termed Henry V, the victor of Agincourt; and had declared himself the devoted servant of his lord, that weak and pious youth, Henry VI; but as Pope says :—

> Manners with fortunes, humours turn with climes,
> Tenets with books, and principles with times,

and so, when Edward IV of York is crowned, the virtues of Lancaster are forgotten; he, in his turn, enters 'by Goddis pro⁻

vision¹, to redress the evils begun by Henry IV; and Prior and Provincial Capgrave dedicates his _Chronicle_ to him. Like the nameless foe of Browning's Brother Lawrence,¹ Capgrave hated with an intensity almost ferocious, but reserved his hatred for the heretic. To his virulent attack on Wyclif, 'the organ of the devil, the enemy of the church, the confusion of men, the idol of heresy, the mirror of hypocrisy,' he turns again in our own text with libidinous insinuation (31/15). He approved of the torture and destruction, even at the stake and the gallows, of those whose nice tenets were not his own. Throughout his _Chronicle_ we may see exhibited an intense love of the marvellous, and an amazing credulity in accepting legendary material, nowadays mostly relegated to the realm of myth and wonder.

But let us not forget that in many of these things he was but of his time. Long generations of controversy, turmoil, and bloodshed were yet to pass before man could allow his neighbour freedom to think, to speak, to live. We are yet but emerging, in Capgrave's day, from the long middle ages, when the roseate dawn of the Renascence is only discernible on the horizon; and little indeed of its light steals into our Lynn scriptorium, and falls upon our black-lettered page. Round about us are war, rebellion, executions, the fall of a dynasty, heresy, hunger, drought, pestilence, and angry thunder. Wonders are and have long been in the air, and find record in our books of history; the heavens fulminate, and stars fall. Some time before 1361, the storm beats down men, beasts, trees, and housing, and the devil appears in man's likeness; in 1361 itself, the sun is eclipsed, rain like blood falls, and a cross of blood moves in the air, and finally falls in the sea at Boulogne; while at the same time in France, England, and elsewhere, two mysterious castles appear, black and white hosts issue therefrom and fight; and all at last, castles and hosts, melt into thin air, and vanish.² These things are in our histories.

Small wonder then that this first among the lettered men of his day abuses Oldcastle and vilifies Wyclif; looks out somewhat severely on this strifeful England, and labors in saintly legend; sees much of the marvellous and supernatural in history, and

---

¹ _Soliloquy of the Spanish Cloister._
² _The Brut or The Chronicles of England_, ed. Brie, 1908, vol. ii, pp. 313, 314.

changes in these changeful times from the old patron to the new. Yet he loved England, too; rejoiced in the beauty of her green and fertile lands, in the grandeur of her cities, in the 'wonderful and angelic splendor', both in countenance and in costume, in courage and vigor of mind, of her people.

Capgrave's biography has already been briefly sketched by Hingeston-Randolph in the *Chronicle*, and told at greater length by Dr. Furnivall in the *Katharine*, and is given in the *Dictionary of National Biography*. Our volume can add very little to the information given in these three productions. *The Life of St. Augustine* is not dated, but must have been finished little prior to the *Life of St. Gilbert*, from the fact that Nicholas Reysby's notice of the former led him to request the latter (61/6), and the *Gilbert* is dated at its conclusion, 1451. The Sermon is dated 1422, and Capgrave tells us he preached it the year before his opposition at Cambridge. His Latin *Concordia*, written for the Abbot of St. James's in Northampton and perhaps identical with the *De Sequacibus Augustini* mentioned by Bale,[1] is referred to in the Sermon, as is also the English *Augustine* and the *Gilbert* (146/5, 6, 34, 147/27). *The Life of St. Norbert*, composed for Abbot John Wyngale of West Dereham, was written in 1440 (*Introduction*, p. xi), and is also mentioned in the Sermon (147/34). The Sermon itself was written down at the end of the *Gilbert*, according to a promise made at the beginning to do so, in 1451 (61/13). It mentions, moreover, the appropriation of Peterston to Walsingham, which took place in 1449.

The Life of St. Augustine. This life was written by Capgrave at the request of an unnamed gentlewoman born on St. Augustine's Day. The writer tells us it was translated 'treuly oute of Latyn'; in the *Gilbert* he speaks of it as 'translat in-to ouᵣ tunge'; and in the Sermon he refers to it as 'þe book whech I mad to a gentil woman in Englisch'.

It looks at first sight as though Capgrave had merely translated an older Latin text, as he did in the *Life of Gilbert*; but no Latin life corresponding to our text has been discovered, and as Capgrave never refers to 'myn auctour', and always alludes to himself as handling the material, I incline to conclude that he is himself the

---

[1] *Chronicle*, pp. 323, note 3, 326.

original composer, and that his reference to translation from Latin signifies his use of Augustine's books, from which he translates whole passages. He speaks, in the first person, of knowing an old copy of the pseudo-Aristotelian *Predicaments* (4/3), and refers once more to his knowledge of the book (11/28). He cites his own supposition regarding *De Beata Vita*, speaks in the first person concerning the name of Augustine's sister, and refers to himself, all in one half-page (5/2, 9, 16). He decides to limit his description of the contents of *De Beata Vita*, and of Augustine's complaint at the death of Monica (24/15, 33/33). He refers to his reading in Augustine's books, and to his opinion regarding regular and secular Augustinian canons (34/6, 44/17), and he makes insinuations against the followers of Wyclif. While it is still possible that a Latin life may have been used, I incline, for these reasons, to the opinion that Capgrave is the composer.

The first twenty-four chapters of the life are based on the *Confessions*, and xx, xxi to some extent on Sermons. The remainder of the life, except the conclusion, is based on Augustine's Sermons and on *De Civitate Dei*, and others of his books; or is an account of the composition of the Saint's writings, *De Immortalitate Animae*, *De Quantitate Animae*, &c., and of the invasion of northern Africa by the Vandals, and the Saint's death. Some of the material to be found in the *Confessions* is not used. Of Augustine's youthful studies of classical poets, and thefts from his parents' table, we hear nothing (Book I). Of his consultation of astrologers (Book II), of Monica's desire to see Augustine wed (Book VI), of Vindicianus and Firminus, of almost the whole of the beautiful seventh Book, no mention is made. The attention given to Augustine's writings and to the frustration of heretics is greatly due, if the work is original, to Capgrave's theological propensities and extreme orthodoxy.

Hermes, in the text (12/19), is Capgrave's misreading of the original Hierius. References to the Augustinian text are given in the Notes.

Capgrave himself wrote a Latin *Vita S. Augustini*[1]; it is improbable, as he does not mention the fact, that this could have been his original for the English text.

---

[1] *Katharine*, xv.

Life of St. Gilbert. This life was written for the nuns of Sempringham, who could read little Latin, for their perusal in vacant times. It is founded on the Latin life of the Saint written at the direction of Roger, Gilbert's successor, and dedicated to Hubert, Archbishop of Canterbury. This life exists in two manuscripts in the British Museum, Cotton Cleopatra B. I, and Harley 468; and in one Bodleian MS., Digby 36. Of these MSS., the Cotton, of the thirteenth century, is the oldest, and from it Dugdale printed long passages in the *Monasticon*, vi. II. pp. v*–xxix*, after p. 945, suppressing the detailed account of the miracles, and the fuller account of the insurrection of the lay brothers. Passages from the Cotton MS., printed by Dugdale, are given in the Notes, to show how literally Capgrave followed it in the main. He reserved to himself the right to add, however, anything he learnt from the Gilbertine monks, or anything pertinent to the matter which occurred to him (62/26). An instance of this ‘ pertinent ’ addition occurs in p. 63, in which Capgrave recounts the merits and fusion of Norman and Saxon, and his acquaintance with John, Lord Beaumont. He breaks in again later, p. 91, l. 23, and p. 103, l. 19.

The Sermon. Capgrave's text can only be regarded as an abstract of his original sermon, preached in Cambridge, the year before his opposition, 1422. He refers in it to other works written since that date, *The Life of St. Augustine, Concordia, The Life of St. Gilbert, The Life of St. Norbert*, and to the appropriation of Peterston to Walsingham, 1449. He also alludes to two famous theologians, Hugo and Richard de St. Victor.

The contents of this sermon were known from an account of it given in Harley MS. 980, p. 231 (see notes, p. 159). The Harley account describes the abstract as from ‘ vii sermon.’

Manuscripts.

1. *Additional MS*. 36704. This manuscript is in Capgrave's own hand, with his characteristic orthography, and contains the author's corrections in the text. It appears to be holograph. It does not, however, contain Capgrave's peculiar monogram, ⁊, which Dr. Furnivall discusses in his Introduction to *The Life of St. Katharine* (p. xiv), and which occurs at the end of *The Life of*

St. Norbert in the Phillipps Collection at Cheltenham. Nor does it contain the characteristic 'Feliciter', which also occurs at the conclusion of the *Norbert*, and of the *Exodus*, and of the Corpus MS. of the *Liber de Illustribus Henricis*. The monogram itself is not infallible, nor is the 'Feliciter', for both of these were liable to be copied by scribes.[1]

Additional MS. 36704 is $8\frac{1}{4} \times 5\frac{3}{4}$ inches, and contains 123 folios of paper. It is bound in oak boards covered with vellum, and is fastened, when shut, by two leather straps and clasps. It was formerly impressed on its front with a coat of arms, evidently a shield quartered, which it is now impossible to identify.

The fly-leaves 1–4 *b* and 122–123 *b* are from an early fifteenth-century MS. of the Digest, containing Lib. xlvi, tit. 1.

On the fly-leaf, fol. 2, is a cypher: 'Cpnstbbbt sfmfl sprfl Thpmf', which reads: 'Constabat semel sorel Thome' (*Brit. Mus. Cat.*, 1900–5, p. 192).

On the fly-leaf, fol. 3, is written: '*M*agister Johanne*s* Capgraue *conventus* Linn fecit istum li*brum* ex præcepto vni*us* generose.'

On the fly-leaf, fol. 4 *b*, in a late hand is written: 'John Cap-grave A Monke of Bury translated this Booke out of Latin into English. Nº. 25.'

Folio 120 is signed: 'Andrew Fountaine, Sepr 25 1817.'

Fly-leaf, fol. 121 *b*, is inscribed: 'Reydun Joh Kewe & Matild*is* uxor Joh. Payn. Tunsted *pro anima* Alicie Curteys Will*elmus* Pays & q*uibus* tenetur (?)' (*Brit. Mus. Cat.*, p. 192).

Fly-leaf, fol. 122 *b*, is signed: 'R. Barn.'

From fly-leaf, fol. 123, has been erased: 'Liber sancte . . .'

The capitals are illuminated in red, and the numbers of the chapters and initial capitals are also in red. Evidently the text was first written in black, and small letters were sometimes put to indicate the chapter capitals, and small Arabic figures were put in the margin to indicate the chapter numbers. Then the illumination in red was done, and as the writer read through his text he made corrections in his red ink. Sometimes he missed a page in illuminating.

---

[1] The monogram, apparently, was so copied in All Souls MS. 17, the *Guide to the Antiquities of Rome*. See *Katharine*, xxiv-v. The monogram might, of course, be affixed by an author to a scribe's copy, as a warrant of authorization.

The manuscript was purchased for the British Museum at the Fountaine Sale at Sotheby's, June 11–14, 1902, where it was numbered Lot 167.

2. *Cotton Vitellius*, D. XV. Of this manuscript only seven small fragments were saved from the Cotton fire of 1731. These are now mounted on paper and constitute folios 29–35. I have been able to identify all of them, and find them somewhat disarranged. They run as follows :—

Cotton.	Additional.	Our Text.
29	48 *b*	p. 64
29 *b*	49	p. 65
30	49 *b*	p. 65
30 *b*	50	p. 66
31 } misplaced 31 *b* }	59 *b*–60	p. 78
	60 *b*–61	p. 78
32	56–56 *b*	p. 73
32 *b*	56 *b*–57	pp. 73–4
33 } reversed 33 *b* }	89	pp. 111–12
	88 *b*	p. 111
34 } reversed 34 *b* }	90	p. 113
	89 *b*	p. 112
35 } misplaced 35 *b* }	50 *b*	p. 66
	?	? (illegible)

From this it will be seen that two fragments are reversed and two misplaced.

The Cotton MS. was inferior, of course, to our original. In monosyllabic words, so far as we can tell, it has the Capgravian avoidance of *gh* spellings for O.E. *h* before *t*, gives *myth* for our *myth* on 32 *b* and 33 *b* (our 73/33, 111/14), *nyth* for our *nyth*, and *þoute* for our *þoute*, 33 *b* ; but has *tawht* for our *taute*, 29, and *ryghtfull* for our *rithful*, fol. 31.

The Life of St. Norbert. On p. 147 of our text, Capgrave remarks of the Premonstratensians that they 'be-gan in Fraunce vndir a holy man þei cleped Norbertus, . . . and be-cause þat I mad his lyf in Englisch to þe abbot of Derham þat deyid last þerfor as now I wil no lenger tarie in þat fundacion.' Capgrave's own MS., dated 1440, with his characteristic orthography and avoidance of the *gh* spelling, and with his monogram, is in the

Phillipps Collection at Cheltenham, having been purchased at Sotheby's in 1861 at the Savile Sale for £150. To my friend, Dr. H. N. MacCracken, who was at Cheltenham working on his valuable Lydgate Canon, I am indebted for the following account of it.

The MS. is a quarto in vellum, in oak boards covered with vellum; it has 58 folios,[1] with xxxvii chapters, and 5 stanzas to a page. The numbers of chapters are marked in the margins, and the chapters are separated by capitals in color.

The first folio is illuminated. In the letter ' J ' (see below) is a monk in black, kneeling, presenting his book to a monk (abbot?) in white, seated.

On fol. 1 is written: Newington. fadbrooke.

12 : Richard Clarke est verus possessor huius libri.

13 _b_ : [a note of Sums.]

26 : Rev. Ai. Hubbard.

27 _b_ : france barnard.

44 : Epping Essex. ffordman Newington his booke 1670.

50 _b_ : Indenture made yere. . Edw. sent Jan 23. [year not stated.] There are other scribblings.

The following are the first four stanzas of _Norbert_ :—

> Joye, grace, in pees, loue, feith, & charite,
> Euyr rest up-on ʒour goodly religio_us_ breest,
> To whom þat I, with moost humylite,
> Euyr recomende lowly as ʒouꝛ preest.
> And þouʒ I be of rymeris now þe leest,
> ʒet wil I now, obeying ʒouꝛ comau_n_dment,
> Put me in dau_n_geꝛ in þis werk pr_e_sent.
>
> Who schal þese dayis make now ony þing,
> But it schal be tosed & pulled as wolle?
> Su_m_me schul sey aꝉ þis is flateryng;
> Su_m_me of charite schul preise it at þe fulle.
> Now lete he_m_ rende, lete he_m_ hale & pulle,
> Swech man_er_ puple, for I haue my_n_ entent,
> So I plese him þat ʒaue me comau_n_dment,

---

[1] Sotheby's Catalogue says a folio and 59 leaves. See Dr. Furnivall's Forewords to _Katharine_, xliv.

To make þis werk of þat noble with,
Norbert called, wich, with ful hye grace,
Made a ordͬ þat schewith now very lith
Of good ensaumple to men in euery place.
Ȝe noble men, if þat ȝe list to race,
Or rende my leuys þat I to ȝou write,
Ȝe may weel doo it; I schal ȝou neuer wite.

In ȝouͬ correccioῆ put I þis materͬ,
ffor I wil sewe & translate þis story.
And wele I wote ȝouͬ hertis be so cleͬ
So ful of charite with-outen trechery;
Ȝe will not put on me no vyleny
But I deserue it, and þat schal I nowt,
As I hope, neythir in speche ne þowt.

These are the last two stanzas :—

Go litel book, to hem þat wil ye rede
Sey you were made to þe abbot of Derham [1]:
Fast be Stoke it stant, witȝouten drede;
It is to lordes and gentilys all in sam,
And eke to for men a very Iulianes ham.
The abbotes name was called at þat tyde,
The good Ion Wygnale, þat neuer wold him hide

ffor no gestis, but rather he wold hem seke.
The freris name þat translate þis story
Thei called Ion Capgraue, whech in assumpcion weke
Made a ende of all his rymyng cry,
The ȝer of Crist our Lord, witȝouten ly,
A thousand four hundred & fourty euene.
Aftyr þis lyf I pray God send us heuene.
ffeliciter.

[1] 'This is, of course, not Durham, but West Dereham, on the Stoke or Wissey, three miles from Stoke Ferry in Norfolk, where an abbey of Premonstratensians from Welbeck had been founded in 1188. East Dereham, famous for Borrow, Cowper, &c., is some distance from Stoke, and on another stream. There was a monastery there too. H. N. M. ffeliciter !'

Other characteristic lines written down by Dr. MacCracken are:

Fol. 3.   On-to our Lord rith þus men may suppose, etc.

On-to my counceles witȝ whech I enspired þe, etc.

Turne aȝen lest þat þou be schent.

9.   Was wroutȝ in þat cuntre rith for heP̃ sake.

In all this we have the genuine Capgravian manner and orthography: the plural and genitive in *is, ys,* and *es*; the avoidance of *gh* spellings for O.E. *h, with,* wight, *lith,* light; the forms *puple, ordP̃, witȝ, wroutȝ*; the curled final *r*; the final *e* for *is* or *y* in *humylite, charite,* &c.; the only unusual form being the *wich* of l. 16. For the 'ffreP̃ I. C. among*is* doctouris lest' of the *Gilbert,* 61/3, we have the author, 'of rymeris now the leest,' l. 5, and the same care in giving the book's date, and the name of its receiver and 'commander'. Above all there is the monogram, with the 'ffeliciter'.

The unusual import of the opening stanzas calls for some remark. The author puts himself in danger in his work: for no work is done at this time, 'but it schal be tosed and pulled as wolle.' Some will say his book is flattery. But he does not mind, so long as he pleases him who commanded it. And if certain 'noble men' list to raze or rend his leaves, they may do it; he will never blame them. He leaves it to them, and thinks their hearts are charitable enough, and lacking in treachery enough, not to do him any villainy unless he deserves it; and that, he hopes, he shall not, either in speech or thought.

All this looks as though Capgrave's book was not certain of a very favourable audience whither it was going. Possibly those 'noble men', the good monks of Dereham, were not inclined to welcome the life of their Norbertus by an Austin friar of Lynn, and had rather that the 'litel book' had been composed in their own scriptorium.

The Language of the MS.

The value of our MS. is that it is holograph, definitely dated, and definitely located as to its origin in Lynn, Norfolk. In these respects it is as decisive a record of Middle English as the

Ormulum (Bodl. Junius MS. I). It was written when the ver-
nacular was appreciably making headway in supplanting Latin as
the language of the erudite and official—a process, nevertheless,
not to be accomplished for many a day,—when standard English
was developing from the East Midland speech. It precedes the
establishment of the Caxton Press at Westminster—the chief
instrument of standardization—by some twenty-five years, and
it was written by the most learned prose-writer of the time.

By Capgrave's time the breakdown of the Old English inflexional
system was complete, and its office was filled by numerous preposi-
tions, &c. The nouns, with a few minor exceptions, were reduced
to a single declension based on the O.E. strong masculines. The
old dative singular in *e* had disappeared, only two regular forms
remaining in the singular, the nominative, and the genitive in *is*
(*ys, es*). One general form alone remained for the plural, *is* (*ys, es*).
The breakdown of the inflexional system with the disappearance of
unstressed final *e* had annihilated all trace of grammatical gender.
Several nouns, specified hereafter, remained uninflected in the
genitive singular, some few had no ending in the plural, and a few
form the plural by mutation or by the addition of *n*. Proper
names were sometimes uninflected.

Capgrave never uses ʒ for O.E. *h* before *t*, as in *kniʒt*, no
trace of this sound remaining in his speech. ʒ is used initially
for *y*, as in *ʒe, ʒer, ʒet, ʒaf*; for a sibilant replacing the *thorn* in
the third person singular present of some verbs, *hatʒ, vsetʒ*, and
tellʒ, with syncopation of *e*, and for the thorn sound in *with—witʒ*;
and for *z* in *ʒel*, &c. Its use in *þouʒ* is probably to distinguish
the word from *þou*.

The *thorn*, þ, is written with an open top like *y*, *th* being used
generally after a stop, for capitalization, and at the end of
words.

For the guttural stop Capgrave uses *g*—*gestis, gessed, gilty*,
where modern spelling has *gu*. *g* also serves for the *j* sound, *gelous,
gayler, gendres*, &c.

For O.E. *cw*, French *qu*, and rarely for O.E. *hw*, Capgrave uses
qw. For O.E. *hw* in *who* (*hwa*), &c., we have generally *wh*, as in
modern English. Modern *how* (O.E. *hu*) is spelt *who*.

th is used for the *thorn* where an initial capital is required;
often for the thorn also at the end of words, *vnneth, both*, and

sometimes in the middle, *anothir*. *th* also replaces *ht* at the end of words in which the O.E. *h* is lost, as *lith, rith*, the spelling alternating with *lite, rite*.

This latter use of the *th* does not indicate that any trace of the old pronunciation remained in Capgrave's speech. Firstly, the *th* spelling alternates in the old *ht* words with *t* or *te*, as noted above; secondly, it so alternates in words, which had no *h*, *profith*, *profite, parfith, parfite, parfit*.[1] The device of employing the *th* for the *ht* spelling is found also in the Northeast Midland *Havelok* (Oxford Laud MS. 108). Here such forms as *brouth, nouth, douther, rith, nith, lith, knith* are common. *cht* and *ct* forms are also abundant; but *th* is used for final *t* in such words as *leth, woth, neth* (let, wot, neat). For the *te* ending to old *ht*, we have *aute* ryming with *laute* (*aute* possessed, *laute* caught, received). This looks to me as though the O.E. *h* sound tended to disappear fairly early in Northeast Midland. (Laud MS. 108 sometimes suffers from its editors in connexion with these spellings. Emerson, for instance, *Middle English Reader*, 1909, consistently transposes *h* and *t*, and reads *riht, niht, mouht* in his text, and makes *auhte* and *lauhte*. He also destroys the *th* ending where it is used for *t*, printing *let, wot, net*. Kluge, *Mittelenglisches Lesebuch*, 1904, consistently retains the *th* forms, but has *au*[*ch*]*te*, *lau*[*ch*]*te*.) Other instances of the early disappearance of O.E. *h* spellings are given by Dr. Furnivall in the Forewords to *Katharine*, and are found elsewhere in the Midland dialect, *nyt* ryming with *syt* (night, sight) in *The Debate of the Body and the Soul*; *lyt, lythe, rythe* (light, right, Emerson, 117, 118) occur in *Gild of St. William of Norwich*; and compare the *broute* of the Digby MS. of *The Harrowing of Hell* ryming with *biþoute*, ll. 5, 6.

An intermediate form to the *th* and *te* endings of the old *ht* words is seen in the *siȝth, untiȝth*, &c., of the *Debate*, the *knicth, knict, ricth, nicth* of *Havelok*, the *þouȝth, briȝth*, &c., of *Adam Davy's Five Dreams about Edward II*, and in other texts. That the *gh* and *ȝ* forms were sometimes wrongly used is seen in the *yghe, lyghe, dyghe, syghe*, &c. (eye, lie, die, saw) of the *Pearl*;

---

[1] 'These two words,' says Dr. Bradley, 'are poor evidence, for -*fiȝt* represented a French intermediate stage between -*feot* and -*feit*.'

in the *clouȝt, ouȝt* (clout, out) of the *Debate*; and in the *whyȝte* (white) of the *West Midland Prose Psalter*, &c.

cc is used for *tch* in *cacch, fecch, wicches, wecch, wrecched.*

Nouns.—The genitive singular is formed in *is* (*ys, es*), the plural in *is* (*ys, es*).

To these forms there are common exceptions :—

(*a*) In the case of O.E. neuters, with unchanged plural forms, *schep, vnch* (from O.E. *ynce*), *þing, wepun, ȝere, god* (goods).

(*b*) In the case of words retaining the plural in *n* from O.E. weak declension : *eyne, hosyn, schon, childyrn* (also *childyr*, O.E. *cildru*).

(*c*) Those forming the plural by mutation : *toth, teth* ; *man*, gen. *mannes*, pl. and gen. pl. *mennys* ; *foot, feet.*

(*d*) Certain words from the French, ending in a sibilant and unchanged in the plural : *sciens, vers, passe, insolens* (126/8) ; or ending in a vowel, *vertu* (67/6).

(*e*) A few words unchanged in the genitive singular : *fader, moder*, though we find also *faderis, moderis*. Proper names are sometimes uninflected.

(*f*) Anomalous : *peticyoñ*, plural (61/17).

The infinitive present of the verb is sometimes used as a noun, as *tary* (113/16). A number of Anglicized Latin words in the text come from Capgrave's originals : *fluctuatioñ, vomite, rectractationes, transumpciones, disceptatioñ*, &c. *Statua, subucula, acrisia*, and *orarium* are quoted as Latin words. *Idus* and *nonas* (see the word in note, p. 158, and glossary) retain their Latin forms.

Verbs.—The verbs in Capgrave are rather irregular in their forms. The present and past indicative are as follows :—

	Present. Weak and Strong.	Past. Weak.	Strong.
S. 1.	—	*id* (*ed*)	—
2.	*ist* (*est*)	[*idest*]	—
3.	*iþ* (*ith, eth*), *th, etȝ, ȝ*	*id, t*	—
Pl. 1, 2, 3.	— *en* (*in, yn*)	*id* (*ed*)	[— *e*]

The third person singular contains the greatest variety of forms. The commonest ending, *ith*, is often found as *eth*, and these, with

b

syncopation of the vowel, appear as *th*, as in *comth* and *lith*. In such forms as *væetʒ* and *tellʒ* we have the supplanting of the thorn by the ʒ, mentioned above. *Tell* provides the whole variety, and one form in which the thorn is represented by a dental : *tellith, telletʒ, tellʒ,* and *tellit*. Other interesting spellings are *hatʒ, makitʒ,* and *þoutʒ* (used, however, for the past, with *þout*, for the singular and plural). The *en* ending for the plural forms in the present tense are common : for the first person we have *lakkyn* ; for the third, *defenden, obeyen, proferen, beren,* &c.

For the imperative of the second person singular we have the *here, forgif, entyr, lete,* &c. of p. 33. The ordinary *eþ* ending for imperative of the second person plural is seen in the *beth* of 16/3 and 52/10 ; but *praisen*, 77/22, gives the unusual *en* ending.

In the third person of the past tense of weak verbs the *id* is weakened to *t* after the liquids : *delt, dwelt, filt, sempt,* &c. The past participle was sometimes likewise *clipt, girt, filt*. *Teld* and *seld* appear for *told* and *sold* in the singular third person.

Infinitives in *en* (*in, yn*) are very common in Capgrave, as *aretten, asken, crien, fytyn, girdin, hydyn, pleten, heyne,* &c.

The present participle is formed in *ing* (*yng*), with numerous examples of *and*, generally characteristic of more northern texts. Examples are *brennaund, folowand, comand, kepand, herand, stodiand,* and other words all of O.E. origin.

The past participle of weak verbs is formed in *id* (*ed*) ; or exists in shortened forms, such as *alienat, implicat, infect, interrupt* (adoptions of Latin participles), *wasch* (representing the strong form), *rest* (wrested). In the strong verbs the past participle is formed by mutation, and sometimes the addition of the *en* ending, liable to loss of *n* (as *falle*). Relics of the O.E. *ge* prefix are seen in the *i-* of *i-schake, i-qwenchid, i-knowe,* and *i-goo*.

In the hands of Capgrave past participles, due to occasional weakening and use of similar vowels, assume a variety of forms. *Written* assumes *wretyn, writin, writyn, wrytin* ; *wound* has *wounde, wounden, woundyn* ; *found* has likewise *found, founde, founden* ; *held* has *hald, halden, hold, holden* ; and *done* has *do, don, doo,* &c.

Pronouns.—As the inflexion of adjectives has disappeared in Capgrave, the adjectival pronoun is not distinguished in the plural from its singular form. There is no example of the weakening of *þu* into *tu* by assimilation, but *of hem* seems in one case to be compounded into *on* (7/7). The personal pronouns are inflected thus :—

	First Person.		Second Person.	
	S.	Pl.	S.	Pl.
N.	*I*	*we*	*þou*	*ʒe*
Ac. and Dat.	*me*	*us*	*þe*	*ʒou, ʒow*
Gen.	*my, myn (myñ)*	*our (ouŕ)*	*þi, þin (þiñ)*	*ʒour (ʒouŕ)*

my is sometimes used before a vowel-beginning word, as *my auctoŕ* (125/30). *þin* is used before vowels, *þin entente*.

The third personal pronoun is as follows :—

	M.	Neut.	F.	Plural.
N.	*he*	*it (he)*	*sche*	*þei*
Ac.	*him*	*it*	*hir (hiŕ), hire*	*hem* (once *þem*)
Dat.	*him*	*him*	*hir (hiŕ), hire*	*hem*
Gen.	*his, hise*	*his*	*hir (hiŕ), hire*	*her (heŕ), here*

This pronoun in Capgrave is quite regular except for occasional use of *he* for *it*, and the occurrence once of *þem* for the accusative *hem*. Reflexive forms with *self* are common. *himself* occurs for *itself* (97/30). The substantival possessive *ouŕ* is given (18/20).

The relative pronouns are *þat* and *whech* (*qwech*), and very rarely *who* (*Katharine*, 24/116). The genitive *whos* and dative *whom* (*quome*) are commoner. Combination of *whech þat* is also common.

The interrogative pronouns are *who* (rare) with accusative *whom* for masculine and feminine, and a neuter *what*, nominative and accusative. The genitive and dative forms are *whos* and *whome* (*quome*). *eþir, neþir, swech, all, many, on*, &c., are common indefinite pronouns.

The demonstrative pronouns are *þe*, undeclined, and singular forms *þat* and *þis* with plurals *þo* and *þese*.

Adverbs.—The commonest form is given in those based on adjectives, *besily, boystously, dirkly,* &c. These assume *ly*, from O.E. *lice* and identical with the *ly* ending of adjectives from O.E. *lic.* In one case, *namelych* (61/19), however, we have *lych.*

Of the genitival adverb we have several examples: *nedis, onys, twyes, þries, eft-sones.*

Of the datival adverb *seldom* is an example. *seld*, like *rith, scharp, soŕ,* and *stille*, are flat adverbs.

The pronominal adverbs are represented by *who* (how), *whan* (*whanne*), *þo*, and *þan, þanne* (then), and *who*. Other adverbs of place are *þidir* and *ʒondir, þenne* (thence), *whens;* and of time, *whili, sone, sith, til,* and *afore.* Compound adverbs are *sumtyme, vndir-fote, ouyr-nyth, ferforth,* and *often-tyme.*

Adjectives.—No distinction is made between strong and weak adjectives, nor between singular and plural.

(*a*) A number of adjectives are formed from the verb, as past participles like *onlerned, croked,* or present participles like *chater-yng, grucching, folowand,* and *comand.*

The commonest class are those distinguished by formatives.

(*b*) Saxon formatives provide:—

> (*-ful*) *schalful*—for *schandful* or *schendful; wilful.*
> (*-fast*) *stedfast.*
> (*ward*) *homeward*—used, however, adverbially, but adjectival in form.
> (*sum*) *buxum, holsom.*
> (*ly* from *lig*) *bodely, dedly, goostly, fremanly.*
> (*w*) *ʒelow.*
> (*en*) *hethen, wollen.*
> (*ir*) *bittir, fayr.*
> (*isch* from *isc*) *lyuysch.*
> (*y* from *ig*) *besi, heuy, redy.*

(*c*) French formatives provide:—

> (*ous, ious*) *licorous, greuous, obliuious, ambicius.*
> (*al, il*) *gentill, simpil, sotil.*
> (*able*) *merciable, mesurable, delectable.*
> (*ik*) *autentik.*
> (*ant*) *poynaunt.* Noun provided by this adjectival form: *seruaunt.*
> (*ain*) *sodeyn, souereyn.*

(*d*) Latin formatives provide:—

> (*if, ive*) *commendatyf.*
> (*er* from *aris*) *seculer, reguler.*
> (*ary*) *exemplary* (noun in text).
> (*al*) *accidental, conuentual, matrimonial.*
> (*ate*) *desolate, approximate.*

The comparative of the adjective was formed in *er*: *hyer, redyer*; the superlative in *est*: *hattest*. Otherwise *mor* or *moost* is prefixed.

While Capgrave's vocabulary marks the tendency of the time in its incorporation of new words, obsolescent words are numerous. For the *progenitouris* of *Augustine* we have the *forth-bringer* of the *Katharine*. *Morer* and *moring* in our text are used with *encreser* and *encresing*. *buxum* is not yet entirely displaced by *obedient*, nor *heyne* by *exalt*, nor *clepe* or *hite* by *call*. *lowed* and *meked* are both used for *humbled*. Capgrave also gives a number of interesting dual forms: *schone or ellis schyned* (83/19), *cloystir or clauser* (83/28), *witnesses or witnesseres* (110/9), *wasch . . . or ellis water* (112/27), *graue or elles þe sepultur* (119/3), *lendes or buttokkes* (120/2), *preisable or praysid* (136/18), and *signes or ellis myracles* (138/9).

Capgrave has a habit of losing the dentals at the end of his monosyllabics: *and* appears as *an*; *saint* as *sain*; *but* as *be. ragyn* and *euyr-lestyn* loose final *g*. *of hem* appears to be compressed into *on* and *aught* to be reduced to *or*.

And lastly a word of thanks. When the Globe editors dedicated their *Chaucer*, and Robert Steele his *Huon of Bordeaux*, and others at home and abroad, too numerous to mention, their books, to Dr. Furnivall, they made some expression of the debt we all owe to this friend and guide and pioneer. I am grateful to him for advice and help on many difficult points in this book. To Dr. Bradley I am also grateful for instruction on various grammatical points where I should otherwise have gone wrong.

J. J. M.

Seven-Kings,
February, 1910.

LIVES OF
ST. AUGUSTINE AND ST. GILBERT

LIFE OF ST. AUGUSTINE

[Capgrave's Prolog.]

GRETE reule to aƚƚ lerned men was sette be Seint Paule in St. Paul said he was debtor to all men, wise and unwise,
þe first capitle Ad Romanos, where he saide þat he was
dettouꝛ on-to wise men and onwise. Wise men clepid he men
4 gretly lerned, and onwise, simple ydiotis, to whom longith þe
blisse of heuene, and of whom ouꝛ Lord Ihesu spak in þe gospeƚƚ,
and seid þat heꝛ aungellis see euyr þe face of þe Fadir whech is in
heuene. To þese both þe holy aposteƚƚ saide he was dettouꝛ, to
8 paye ech of hem aftir þat he sauoured. And þouȝ I þat write now but Capgrave, in-dued with learning, dares only say he is debtor to un-learned men.
þis be a man sumwhat endewid in lettiruꝛ, ȝet daꝛ I not take
up-on me for to be dettouꝛ on-to hem þat be endewid in sciens
moꝛ þan I, but I daꝛ sauely seye þat I am detouꝛ to oþir simpil
12 creatures þat be not lerned so mech as I. Wherfor my dettis wil
I pay of swech tresouꝛ as I haue in possessioñ, with moꝛ esy
labouꝛ þan euyr I receyued hem. The cause of þis writyng whech
meued me moost now will I telle. A noble creatuꝛ, a gentiƚƚ This book was written at the request of a gentle woman
16 woman, desired of me with ful grete instauns to write on-to hiꝛ,
þat is to sey, to translate hir treuly oute of Latyn, þe lif of Seynt
Augustyn, grete doctouꝛ of þe cherch. Sche desired þis þing of me
rather þan of a-noþer man be-cause þat I am of his profession, for
20 sche supposed veryly þat I wold do it with þe bettir wil. Sche
desired eke þis lif of þis Seynt more þañ of ony oþir[1] for sche was
browt forth in-to þis world in his solempne feste. Than wil I, in who per-suaded the writer with sundry re-tributions.
þe name of ouꝛ Lord Ihesu, beginne þis werk, to þe worchip of þis
24 glorious doctouꝛ, and to þe plesauns and consolatioñ[2] of þis gentil
woman þat hath so willed me with sundry [r]etribucione[s] ǁ þat Leaf 5, back.
I coude not disobeye hir desiꝛ. This glorious name Augustinus is
mad comendable a-mongis ouꝛ auctouris for iij þingis. On is for The virtues of Augustine.
28 þe excellens of þe man. The secund for þe brennyng loue of
charite with whech his hert was fyred. The þird for þe noble

---

[1] MS. *part of a word commencing* b *crossed out.*
[2] *corner of leaf faded.*

1

The excellence of Augustine and of his name.

ethimilogie whech longeth to þe name. Ethimilogie is cleped
in gramer þe trewe exposicioñ of a word. As touching þe first,
þat is to sey, þe excellens of þis Seint, it acordith ful wel on-to
his name, for þis word Augustus was first ȝoue on-to þe emperouȓ 4
Octauiane, as to þe moost honorable and excellent prince þat euyr
regned in þe empiȓ. For it soundith in ouȓ langage as a morer
of þe lordchip, and þis same Octauiane engrosed ner al þe lordchip
of þe world oņ-to þe empiȓ of Rome. So sey we of þis glorious 8
doctouȓ þat he berith þis [1] name for excellens aboue all oþir.
Therfor þe oþir doctouris be likned [2] on-to þe sterres and he on-to
þe sunne, as it is pleynly conteyned in the epistil red in his feest,
wheȓ he seith þat lich as þe sunne schynyth in heuene, so schynyth 12
he in þe temple of ouȓ Lord. As touching þe secund diuision, þat
is to seye, his feruent loue whech he had on-to ouȓ Lord, þis
acordeth eke on-to his name. For Augustus is þat month in
heruest whech is þe hattest month and moost ripening of frutes 16
þorw-oute all þe ȝere. So þis man, brennyng in charite, wrote
on-to þe cristen puple swech swete exhortaciones of loue þat he is
cause [3] next God, daȓ I sey, þat many a soule hath ripeȓ frutes of

His book of 'Confessions.'

deuocioñ be-cause of his labour. Off þis brennyng charite whech 20

Leaf 6.

þis noble clerk ‖ had is spoken be his owne mouth in þe ix book
of his Confessiones, where he seith þus of him & his felawis neuly
conuerted on-to God : Thou Lord, he saide, hast hitte ouȓ hertis
with þe hote arowys [4] of charite, and eke we receyued þi wordis 24
in-to ouȓ hertis as þouȝ þei had be scharp 'arowys. Eke touching
þe ethimologie of his name, it berith witnesse of his grete excellens,

The etymological significance of the name 'Augustine.'

for þis name, as auctouris sey, is compownyd of augeo auges, þat
is as mech to sey as to make þing moȓ þan it was; it is eke 28
compowned of ana, þat is as mech to sey as a-boue; it is eke
compowned of astim, whech is as mech to sey as a cite. So for
to putte all þese parties to-gidir [5], þe name of þis glorious Seynt is
þus browt on-to þis reson, a morer of þe cite a-boue, a gret 32
encreser of þe blis of heuene, for he was cause whil he lyued with
his tonge and aftir his deth with his bokis þat many a soule is
ledde þe rith weye to heuene.

[1] b *crossed through.*
[2] kilned *in text crossed out and* likned *written in margin.*
[3] *corner of leaf faded.* [4] MS. harowys, h *dotted underneath in red.*
[5] ast *in MS. crossed through.*

[CHAPTER I.]

Of þe cuntꝛ & þe town where he was bore. cap*itulum* I.
cap. 1.

AT ouꝛ beginnyng ȝe schul undirstand þat þis world is departed The three divisions of the world are
4 in-to iij parties, and it was þus departed as ouꝛ auc-
touris seye be ouꝛ fadeꝛ Noe.   For in þe flood were saued [1] he and
his iij sones, and to þese iij sones was aꝉ þe world departed.
Thei þat cam of Sem were sette in þe est side of þe world, cleped
8 now Asia.   Thei [þat] cam of Iaphet were sette in þat partye of 1. Asia; 2. Europe; 3. Africa.
þe world cleped now Europa.   And þei þat cam of Cam were
sette to dwelle [2] in þat partie wheeh is cleped Affrica, where ‖ þis Leaf 6, back.
glorious man was bore.   Asia is in þe est side of þe world, and it
12 *conteyneth* as mech in space as do þe othir too parties.   In þis The countries of Asia;
Asia stant Ynde and Pers, Mede, Mesopothamia, Surry, Araby,
Capadoce, Comagene, Palestine, Iude, Galile, & many mo prouynces.   Europe *conteyneth* Scithie, Nussie [3], Hungarye, Achay, of Europe;
16 Macedony, Dalmacy, Ytaile, and aꝉ þe Duche tonge, with France,
Ynglond, Spayn, & many moo.   Affrica hath *principali* þe
prouynce of ȝeugis where grete Cartage stant.   It hath eke and of Africa.
anoþir prou*nce* clepid Tripolitane, Getuly, Byȝance, Numedye,
20 Mauritania.   In þis Numedie stant þat cite where Seynt Austyn At Hippo in Numidia
was bischop, cleped Ypone, and in þis same Numedie stant þat Augustine was bishop;
same cyte cleped Tagatens*es*, where þis doctouꝛ was bore, sum-
what upward moꝛ on-to Cartage.   Thus haue I schewid ȝou in at Tagaste he was born,
24 what partie of þe world [4] he was bore, [4]—nowt in þe Greke tonge
ne in þe Latyn tonge, but in þe Barbaꝛ tonge.   Neuyrþelasse
we rede of hym þat whan he cam to lerne dyuers sciens, whech
were þan most in Greke tonge, þat he hated þe Greke letteris
28 and loued weel þe Laty*n*, be whech inclynacioñ we vndirstand
þat þat same langage in wheeh he was bore was moꝛ approximat where the language was
on-to þe Latyn tonge þan on-to þe Grek tong.   For, in very more akin to Latin than
treuth, he had so grete knowlech of both tongis þat aꝉ his bokys Greek.

---

[1] *final* d *inserted above.*   [2] *corner of leaf faded.*
[3] *So in* MS.   [4-4] *In margin.*

Augustine
wrote in
Latin and
translated
Aristotle's
' Categories,'
and the
he mad in Latyn, and oute of[1] þe Greke tonge he hym-selue translate in-to Latyn a grete book whech Aristotle mad, cleped his Cathegories, for I wot who hath þis book of ful eld hand. This is seid[2] to my entent to proue þat he was bore a-mong*is* 4

‖ hem þat speke þe Barbar̃ tonge. The Barbar̃ tonge is eue*r*y tonge

author knows
of a copy in
an old hand.
in þe world whech is fer fro þe iij principall tong*is*, Hebrew, Grek, & Latyn.

[CHAPTER II.]

Off þe progenitouris and þe kynrod of þis ma*n*.   c̃^m ij.   8

OF his progenitoures þus we rede þat þei were not of þe despect laboureres in þe puple, but born of good and rich kynrod aftir þe fame of þe world, for þis man aftir her̃ deth had sufficient possessioñ for to lyue by. And he him-self seith in his 12

and sent him
to school in
Carthage.
Confessiones þat whan he was sent to skole to Cartage, because þei herd sey þat her̃ child had a grete corage to lernyng, þat he was[3] founde as wel and with as grete cost as ony[4] lordis son þat went to skole. This myth not be do with-outen þat þei had 16 substau*n*s of possessioñ. The name of his fader was clepid

Patrik, whech was a hethen man on-to þe tyme þat he schuld deye, for þan, be labour̃ of his modir, he was mad cristen man, and so deyed newly baptiȝed. His modir hith᷒ Monica; sche was a 20

His mother
was Monica,
a Christian,
who had
other child-
ren besides
him.
cristen woma*n* fro hir childhold, and norchid in þe best condiciones and moost plesau*n*t to God and to ma*n*. Sche had moo childyrn þan him, as it semeth be his writing in his Confessiones. And þouȝ þat he telle not her̃ names þere, we haue sout hem 24

In his book
' De Beata
Vita' he tells
of his brother.
He was born
on St. Brice's
Day.
oute of oþir of his bokis. For in þat book whech is cleped De *Beata Vita*, þere tellith he of his broþir whech at þat festfull day was[5] with him and with his modir in an hoth*ous* whech þei clepe a stewe, þe day of his birth. Fore he was bore on Seynt Brices[6] 28

day, as þat ‖ same book makith mencion, and custumably he used whil he was paynem to make a gret fest on þat day, but aftir

---

[1] *a character crossed out.*   [2] *corner of leaf faded.*
[3] *þei crossed out and he was written in margin.*   [4] *n crossed out.*
[5] *in margin.*   [6] *corner of leaf faded.*

he was mad bischop he turned þis bodely fest[1] in-to spiri*t*ual
talky*n*g, and as I suppose þis bok was mad þat first day þat he
mad þis chau*n*ge or he was bischop, for his moder was at þis fest
4 and sche deyid befo*r* þat he was preest.   This ma*n*nes name of
whom we talk of her, whech, as we saide, was his bro*þ*ir, was
cleped Nauigius.   He spekith here eke in þis same book of too
cosynes of his ; on of hem hith Latridianus, þe othir hith Rusticus.
8 Thei both were at his feest, of whom he seith þat þei were trewe
cristen but *n*ot lettered.   He had a sistir, but I haue not herd hir
name, and to hir he wrote a book whech he cleped þe book of
cristen ma*n*nes lyf; it begy*n*nyth þus : Et eg*o* pecca*t*or.   The
12 rubrich be-fo*r* þe bok is writyn þus : The book of Seynt Augustin,
þe bischop, on-to his sistir, a widow.   Eke he had a-noþir cosyn
þat hith Pat*r*icius, as his fader hith, and þis man was on of þe
chano*n*es þat lyued with him in þe þird monsterie aftir he was
16 bischop.   In þe þird monsterye, seid I, for be-cause þat he mad
iij,—on or he was preest, a-noþir whil he was preest vndir bischop
Valerie.   And who long he dwelt þe*r*, and who dwelt þere with
him, schal be touchid aftir whan it comth *in* his place.

Marginal notes: Augustine must have written this book before he became bishop. His brother's name was Navigius and he had two cousins, Latridianus and Rusticus. The author does not know his sister's name, but he dedicated a book to her. His cousin Patricius was a canon in his third monastery.

[CHAPTER III.]

20   Of þe condiciones of his fade*r* and ‖ his modir. capitulu*m* Leaf 8.
terciu*m*.

O F þis mater spekith þis glorio*us* man in þe ix book of his
Confessiones, whe*r* he seith of his fader þat he was of nature
24 ful frendly and goodly and redy eke on-to ire as many men be,
kynde and fre of hert and sone meued to malencolie.   This holi
woman weddid o*n*-to hym, whan sche had aspied his hasti con-
dicio*n*, sche had swech goue*r*nauns in hir dedis and swech moderacion
28 in hir wordes þat he coude neuyr cacch no hold to be wroth with
hir in a*ll* his lyf.   Sche wold, if he excedid, as Augustin*us* tellith,
abide til his i*r* were goo ; þan wold sche reherse on-to him þe euel
a-vised wordes whech he had spoke, or þe onresonable werkis
32 whech he had do.   Sumtyme it happed þat sche sat a-mong oþir

Marginal notes: The character of Augustine's father, and of his mother. How gently she rebuked her husband, reproved other wives, and by her example

---

[1] MS. estyn *with* yn *crossed out.*

taught them to lead better lives. matrones of hir knowlech, of whech wome*n* su*m*me had merkys in her face whech he*r* husbandis had mad only for þei wold speke a-geyn wha*n* he*r* husbandis we*r* wroth, and þan wold þese wome*n* say on-to Monicha : We haue grete wondir of þe and þin husband þat þou bri*n*ggist neuyr no merk of his strokys, ne non of us haue herd þat euyr þe*r* was ony strif be-twix 3ou too, not-withstand þat he is an irous man and hasty as ony dwellith among*is* us.   Sche wold answe*r* on-to hem on þis mane*r* : Iff 3e haue mynde[1] of 3ou*r* tables matrimonial þat we*r* mad be-twix 3ou and 3ou*r* husbandis at

Leaf 8, back. 3ou*r* weddy*n*g, ‖ 3e wold not þan haue me*r*uayle whi þat I suffir my husband, þou3 þat I haue wrong.   For þere is it writyn þat þou3 wyuys[2] and husbandis be o flesch and o blood, 3et ar wyuys[3] put in swech mane*r* of subieccio*n* þat þei be bou*n*de to do dew seruyse on-to men ; wherfor, as me þinkith, þe best seruyse þat þei may doo is to kepe pes in houshold and suffir wrong rather þan pes schuld be broke.   For hir wordis many of þese women were stered to mo*r* pacie*n*s and leued in more rest þan þei dede be-fo*r*.   The*r* was

Monica's mother-in-law lived with her, and yet there was peace in the household. with hir þe modir of hir husband dwellyng in houshold, and as often is sene þei make sumtyme debate betwyx wif and husband, namely whe*r* 3ong damesellis be with chateryng tongis.   Swech seruau*n*tis were in Patrik hous, but for no tales of hem ne no suspicio*n* of þe elde modir, Monicha was neuyr put in no blame, so redy was hir pacie*n*s, so besi was hir plesau*n*s.   The elde mod*er*, seing þe good disposicio*n* of hir doutir, was compelled be consciens to compleyne of hir seruau*n*tis on-to hir son, desiryng of him þat he schuld snybbe þe maydenes þat þei schuld not be redy to telle swech tales with whech pes mith be broke[4] in Patrik hous.

Augustine tells of his mother's virtues in the orison he Leaf 9. made at her death ; Many mo noble condiciones rehersith þis man of his modir whech as now schul not be touched, for in þe oriso*n*, or ellis, þe compley*n*t, whech he mad aftir hir deth, it schal be talked mo*r* largely aftir þe form of his Confessiones.   ‖ O þing he touchith he*r* gretly longi*n*g to hi*r* comendacio*n* in norching of hir childyrn ; he seith þat sche[5] trauayled[6] for hem neuly a-geyn as often as sche say hem do ony þing whech was a-geyn þe plesau*n*s of our Lord ; þat

---

[1] *inserted above.*   [2] wyuys *written in margin;* wifis *in text.*
[3] wyuys *written in margin;* wifys *in text.*   [4] MS. bebroke.
[5] *inserted in small writing above.*   [6] d *added afterwards.*

is to sey it greued hir as mech whan sche say hir childyrn trespas she was hurt when her
on-to our[1] Lord as euyr it greued whan sche bare hem bodyly. children sinned.

[CHAPTER IV.]

Of þe age of Seint Augustin whech is clepid Infancia. iiij.

4 INfancia is on of þe vij. ages, as our auctores say, whech We usually say that there
    lestith fro þe birth on-to þe tyme þat þe child[2] is come to þe is no sin in infancy, but
age of vij ȝere, and þouȝ it be soo þat we sey comounly þat St. Gregory tells of a
childyrn synne not in þis age, þat is to sey, dedly, ȝet in sum on or child torn by the devil
8 to haue be seyn þe reuers, as Seint[3] Gregorie telletȝ in his Dialoges from its father's arms,
li. 4, þat a child of þis age was sodeynly be þe deuele rawt from and Augustine says he
his faderes armes. Not-withstanding þis or oþir whech myth be too must have sinned in his
rehersed, as we said, comounly childyrn of þis age be clepid childhood.
12 innocentis, for þei lak vse of resoñ for to discerne vice fro vertu.
But of þis age, and of synnes do in þis age, Seynt Augustyn
makitȝ open confession in þe first book of þat mater, wher he seith
þat sum childyr þat can not speke, þei can loke angrily on hem þat
16 greue hem[4], and with handes and teth proferen in maner of a
veniauns. Nowt had þis doctour mynde þat he ded soo, but for
he say oþir childyrn do þus, þerfor supposed he þat he ded soo. ‖
Mech more þing he rehersith of þis mater in his first book of his Leaf 9,
20 Confessiones, whech is now not gretly nedful to be writyn. back.

[CHAPTER V.]

¶ Of þat age of him whech þei clepe Puericia. v.

PVericia also is þe secund age, and þat lestith fro seuene Boyhood is the age of
    ȝere to xiiij ȝere. It is as mech to say in Englisch as þe cleanness. Augustine in
24 age of clennesse, for þis age is not mech defiled with dedis of his 'Con-
leccherie or onclennesse. What defautes þat be in þis age of whech fessions' tells of his sins
our maystir had ful grete consciens, is writin in þe same book. At done then.
þis age, he saith, he was put to skole, and whañ he schuld be bete,

---

[1] *inserted in small writing above.*   [2] *a character crossed out.*
[3] *a single g crossed out.*   [4] hem *inserted above.*

At school he prayed to escape punishment, but did not. He hated study and liked games.

he prayed God þat he myth skape it, but ouꝛ Lord herd him nowt, and þat displesed him, for he knew not þat tyme who profitable it was to his soule to be bete for lernyng. With sad men and eld men whech mad a game whan he was laschid, he was in partie 4 wroth. He lerned lesse þat he schuld or myth a lerne. He loued bettir veyn games þan skole. The smale elementis of lernyng receyued he first in þe same cite where he was bore. His gramer

He learned grammar at Madaura.

lerned he in a cite be-side, whech is cleped Mandauris. He loued 8 bettir, as we sayde be-fore, þe Latyn letteris þan þe Grek, not-withstand þat he lerned first þe Grek letteres. In þis age he had

When he was sick his mother wanted him Leaf 10. baptized, but his father would not agree.

grete [1] sekenesse in his stomake, and euyr was his modir bisi þat he schuld be baptiȝed, but þe fader wold not suffir it. And þis was 12 þe cause, as men ‖ suppose, whi ouꝛ Lord wold not suffir him to be baptiȝed, for it was lesse greuauns to his soule [2] þat þe filth of heresie schuld be in him rather be-foꝛ his baptem þan aftir his baptem. Thus lerned he þe smale scienses, as spellyng, reding and 16 constrewyng in his ȝong age.

[CHAPTER VI.]

¶ Who he was sent to Cartage to lerne gretter sciens. **vj.**

At sixteen years of age he went to Carthage and studied Tullius Cicero, and led a wanton life, at which his father laughed but his mother was grieved.

WHanne he was fully xvj ȝeꝛ old his frendis sent him to Cartage, a grete cite whech helde batayle with Rome & alle 20 Itaile many ȝeres. There lerned he rethorik and eloquens oute of Tullius bokes, and oþir rethoricianes whech weꝛ be-fore him. But in þis first ȝere þat he cam to Cartage, he a-bod litil at his study, but rood to and fro, now to his fader, now to Cartage, for what for 24 euel felauchip þat he was falle in, what for insolens of his wauntown age, he used tauernes and stewis and swech sory gouernauns as þei vse whech haue no men to vndirtake heꝛ defautes. For his fadeꝛ low at his gouernauns & rebuked him of no defaute. But his 28 modeꝛ, with ful sad countenauns, forbade him [3] all suspecious cumpany, and he took ful litil heed at hiꝛ wordis. In þis same

At this time his father was converted

tyme [4] was his fadeꝛ conuerted on-to þe feith, and mad a cathe-

---

[1] *sike crossed through.*   [2] *in margin.*

[3] *written in red in small writing above.*

[4] *written in red in small writing above.*

cume ; a cathecume is as mech to seye as a newe receyuour of þe and became a cathechumen.
feith, for in elde tyme men had certeyn dayes assined be-twix her
conuercion and here baptem þat þei myth lerne wel þe articules of
4 our feith or þei wer bounde þerto. And so schuld men do [1] now,
as I suppose, if þei schuld be bap‖tiȝed at þat age. He schryuyth Leaf 10, back.
him [2] also þat in þis age he ded many insolens, more for vanite
þan for nede, and in special of an appil-tre [3] þat stood fast by his Augustine robbed an apple-tree.
8 faderes vyne on a-noþir mannes lond, of whech he makith grete
consciens, be-cause þat he myth haue had bettir appillis in his
faderes possession, and eke for when he had þese appelles, he ete
hem nawt, but þrew hem on-to hoggis. In all þis vanyte of his
12 lif he happed to fynde a book þat Tullius Cicero mad, þe grete He read Cicero,
rhetorician of Rome, whech book þe maker clepid Hortencius,
be-cause it [4] exhorted men gretly to fle þe vanite of þe world, and
to folow þe noble study of philosophie. This book chaunged his
16 hert gretly, & mad him þat he had not so gret ioye in þoo vanites
as he had be-fore. But for al þat þe book plesed him not fully, for but liked no book without Christ's name in it.
he fond not þe name of Crist in al þis book. This name was
couchid in his hert fro his moder tete, þat what book he red, wer [5]
20 it neuyr so wys ne so wel i-spoke, wer it neuyr so trew, he was not
fully plesed with it but if Cristis name wer þere. Than purposed he
for to rede holy scriptur, but be-cause þat, as Seint Paule seith, He began to read Scripture, but turned from it and followed the Manichaean heresy, and abode in it nine years.
cunnyng with-oute charite makith a man proude, and þis sciens
24 requirith meke disciplens, þerfor þe [6] eye of his mynde was
I-qwenchid with þe grete lith of sotil vndyrstanding whech is
conteyned in scriptur, and þus left he þis holy study. Tho felle
he in-to þe grete errour of þe Maniches, for þei saide þat Goddis
28 son of heuene was not bore of a may ‖ de, ne he had not very flesch Leaf 11.
and blood as oþir men haue, but rather a fantastical body mad of þe
eyr, in whech he semed for [to] deye, but deth was þere non, for very
body was þere non. In þis fals heresie, whech avoideth þe most
32 substauns of our feith, [7] fell he [7]. Many mo heresies held þei whech
were ful perilous to be rehersed, specialy in our tonge. In þis

---

[1] *written in red in small writing above.*
[2] *written in small writing above.*
[3] tre *written in margin and mark of insertion made.*   [4] h *crossed through.*
[5] it *written in margin.*   [6] þ *written again and crossed through.*
[7–7] *in margin.*

heresie abood Augustin ny ix ȝere, inqwiring and sekyng groundes
and treuthis, or ellis resones, for to defende þis heresie, but he fond
non.

[CHAPTER VII.]

¶ Of the sorow þat his modir had for his [1] errour.   ca^m. vij.   4

Monica was
greatly
grieved at
Augustine's
heresy, but
God com-
forted her by
a vision,
HIs modir, whan sche herd þat he was falle on-to þis heresie,
sche wept and sorowid more hertly þan women do þat folow
her childyrn to þe graue, and witȝ many menes and many exhortaciones was bisi nyth and day to bring him fro þis mischef.   In 8
all þis tribulacioñ and weping, our Lord [2] wold not suffer hir to
go fully desolat, but schewed hir a consolacioñ be an aungel in hir
sleep.   Sche poutȝ þat sche stood on a fair tre, planed al rith lich
a reule, and a fair ȝong man stood be-side hir with rich cloþis and 12
a mery chere, whech inqwired of hir what was þe cause of hir
weping.   Sche answered on-to him with ful heuy cher [3] : The
losse of my son Augustin, I wepe.   Tho þe ȝong man bad hir be of
good coumfort, and loke wel a-boute hir, for þere þat sche was hir 16
son schuld be, as he seide.   Tho loked sche, and say Augustin hir
Leaf 11,
back.
son stand in þe same reule ‖ where-as sche stood.   The wise woman,
and vsed to swech reuelaciones, took of þis a gret coumfort, vndirstanding herby þat sumtyme sche schuld se him standing in þe 20
which she
imparted to
her son,
who tried
unsuccess-
fully to
convince her
that she mis-
construed it.
same feith where þat sche stood.   Aftir þis not longe sche comound
þis visioñ with hir son, and seyd [4] on-to him þat sche hoped for to
se him a trewe cristen man or sche deyid, for þis consolacion had
sche fro heuene, and þis voys proporcioned to hir ioye, wher þat 24
þou art þere schal he be.   Nay, quod Augustin to his modir, ȝe
vndyrstand þe wordis a-mys ; he seide, þere þat I am þere schulde
[5] ȝe be [6].   Nay, son, nay, quod sche, I vndirstod ful and noted his
wordes ; he seid not, þere þat he is þere schal þou be, but, þere 28
þat þou art þer schal he be.   Thus was þe woman in her consolacioñ stabil [6] and coude not be led oute fro hir trewe beleue with
no sophisticacion þat hir son coude make.   Sche receuyed a-noþir

---

[1] *a character crossed through.*   [2] *in margin.*
[3] *c added afterwards.*   [4] *ont crossed through.*
[5-5] *in margin.*   [6] *added in margin.*

consolacioñ be an holy bischop þat was gretly lerned in holy
scriptuɍ and gretly excersised to lede men fro errouɍ. To þis
man went sche, oft desiring of him þat he wold speke with hir son
4 and comoun with him in þat heresie, and schew [1] þe fals [1] and þe
onresonable doctrine whech þat heresie susteyned. The bischop
answerd to hir a-geyn and seide: For soth, þi son as ȝet is not
disposed for to be led any bettir weye, for he is neuly come on-to
8 þis doctrine, and mech redyer for to purpos questiones þañ to
receyue ony doctrine. Wher‖fore, be my councel, suffir him for
a tyme & pray to God for him with-oute ony letting, and þou
schal [2] se þat he in his redyng and in his stodie schal aspie ful wel
12 in what errouɍ he is falle, and who many horible þingis þat it
techith. For I was sumtyme deceyued with þe same doctrine and
had ful grete corage to lerne þe noueltes þerof, but þorw þe mercy
of ouɍ Lord, with long redyng of heɍ bokes, I aspied þat it was
16 a secte rather to be fled þan [3] folowid. This answere myth not
suffise to þe woman, so grete desire was in hir hert þat he schuld
speke with hir son, so þat þe bischop was compelled to voyde hir
with swech wordys: Go fro me, woman, go fro me with þis
20 sikyrnesse. It is impossible that a child whech hath so many
teres wept for him schuld perisch. These wordis [4] of þe bischop
imprended sche in hir mynde as þouȝ an aungell had spoke
hem from heuene.

Margin note: Monica asked a bishop to lead Augustine in the right way, but he refused, knowing Augustine would not be led, and dismissed her with words of comfort.

Margin note: Leaf 12.

[CHAPTER VIII.]

24   ¶ What þat he ded fro þe tyme þat he was xx ȝeɍ on-to xxix.
ca^m. viij.

A T þe age of xx ȝere he dwelt stille at Cartage, and þe maystires
þat were redde him, þe book of Aristotle cleped his Cathe-
28 gories, we clepe hem at þese dayes þe Predicamentis. Augustinus
gat þis book of his maystir, and hom to his chambir he went, red
it, vndirstood it, with-oute ony techeɍ. For in the iiij book of his
Confessiones he is a-knowe þat alle þe bokes of philosophie, or
32 gemetrie, or arsmetrik, or any of þe vij sciens whech he myth

Margin note: Augustine studied and understood Aristotle and the seven sciences without a teacher.

---

[1] MS. schewid þe falshed; id *and* hed *crossed through in red.*
[2] a *not clear and afterwards written above in red.*   [3] MS. þat.
[4] MS. This word*is*; *is* added in red.

haue at leyseꝛ, he vndirstood hem, with-outen maystir, ¶ or with-
oute ony techeꝛ.   Aftir he was þus lerned in philosophie and oþir
dyuers sciens, he cam first hom in-to þe cite where he was bore,

and þeꝛ taute he grameꝛ, meruelyng aɫɫ þe cuntre of þe noble 4
reules þat he [1] had founde to redinesse of childirn þat schuld lerne.
Whan he had kept þis exersise longe in his owne cite, tho he
resorted a-geyn [2] on-to Cartage, and þere taute he retorik [3] on the
moost excellent wise.   In þe xxvj ꝝere of his age he wrote iij 8
bokes on-to a rethorician of Rome; þei cleped him Hermes [4]: þese
bokes be intituled De Pulcro & Apto, þat is to sey in Englisch, of þing
whech is fayre and able; þei are not in hand now.   I coude neuyr
speke with man þat sey hem, for his bokes which he mad aftir he 12
was cristen be more in deynte þan þoo whech he mad be-fore.   In

þe xxix ꝝere of his age spak he with Faustus, a grete snare of þe
deuele, for þis man was þe moost famous heretik of aɫɫ þe Manicheis,
but he was ful famous in fayre endytyng.   For he mad a ful cursed 16
book a-geyn oure feith, to qwech book þis same Augustin mad
notable answeres in [5] a grete volume whech conteynyth xxxiij [6]
bokes.   The cause whi Faustus was desired for to cum speke with
Augustin is þis: Augustin had many questiones with þe Manicheis 20
of her feith and of here lawe [7], and aspied so many notable errouris
in heꝛ bokes þat he, ne non of hem, coude make no answeꝛ to his
resones.   Tho seid þei whan þei were concluded with argumentis

on aɫɫ sides þat Faustus schuld come and he schuld make ‖ answere 24
on-to aɫɫ þese motyues.   For Faustus was in swech opinion
amongis hem þat who-so [8]-euer folowid him and was conuersaunt
with him, þei saide þat he folowid no man, but rather the Holy
Goost.   So Faustus is come to Cartage; a-non as he was come 28
Augustin with certeyn of his felawschip went on-to him.   Theꝛ
had þei too grete comunicacioñ of þoo questiones for whech þei

were in trouble be-fore.   And with-inne fewe dayes Augustin
aspied wel what Faustus was, a mery man and a iocunde, a fayꝛ- 32
spoke man eke, but not gretly grounded [9] in sciens.   Tho be-gan

---

[1] *he inserted in small writing above.*   [2] *a word or part of a word erased.*
[3] *gramer crossed through and dotted underneath, and* retorik *written in margin with insertion mark.*   [4] Hermes *inserted in margin.*
[5] *inserted in small writing above.*   [6] iij *inserted above.*
[7] lawe *inserted in small writing above.*   [8] *MS.* sc.
[9] groundes *crossed through in red and dotted underneath.*

Augustin to reherse on-to him þe doutes and þe articules comound
afore & writyn in billis a-geyn Manicheis lawe. Faustus, whan Faustus,
seeing his
he had aspied þe grete cunnyng of Augustin and þe sotil inuec- own
inferiority,
4 ciones whech he mad he durst not dispute with him, but be-for submitted.
hem alle he was fayn to sey þat he coude not answere to þo
motiues. Fro þis day forward had Augustin no deynte in her Augustine
was then free
bokes whan þat he say her grete maystir and here prince coude from sects.
8 not[1] satisfie his resones. Thus lyued he[2] with suspense mynde, in
grete doute what secte he schuld hold or what wey he schuld take.
Al þis is touched in þe v. book of his *Confessiones.*

[CHAPTER IX.]

¶ Who Augustin aftir þis went to Rome. cᵐ. ix.

12 CErteyn frendis þat he had at þat tyme, seing þe grete desir of His friends,
knowing of
lernyng in him, ȝoue him councel þat he schulde go to his revels at
Carthage,
Rome, and þis was her cause. For at Cartage both he and his sent him to
Rome.
disciples were lettid gretly with felauchip and reuel, and as þei
16 herd sey, and summe ‖ of hem knew it be experiens, at Rome was Leaf 13,
more liberte ȝoue on-to skoleres and more quiete þan was at back.
Cartage. This same desire þat was in his hert was the dispen-
sacion of our Lord. For our Lord[3] knew ful[4] wel where he schuld
20 be conuerted and what tyme, and had ordeyned be-fore þe menes
and þe ministres and þe places, as he wold dispose. Thus he disposed him fully for to saile to Rome. His modir folowid him to Monica
wanted to go
þe se-side, for sikirly sche wil go with him. And he disseyued with him,
24 hir in þis maner. He feyned first þat þei had no wynd ne likly but he
deceived her,
non for to haue many day, wherfor he desired þat sche schuld goo and sailed
without her.
to hir in a-geyn, and whan tyme cam he wold clepe hir. To þis
wold not sche consent, for fro his presens wold sche not. Tho with
28 grete bisinesse he councelled hire for to a-bide as for þat nyth in a
oratorie þat was consecrat in þe name of Seint Cipriane, for it
was ny þe schip, and sikirly, he told hir, þat þe next day þei wold
saile. Thus deceyued he his modir, for þat same nyth þei pulled

---

[1] not *inserted in small writing above.* [2] he *written in red in margin.*
[3] lord *inserted in margin in red.* [4] wl *crossed through.*

up sail & stale þe schip from hir.   All þat nyth lay sche praying
and sobbing, desiring of ouꝛ Lord[1] þat þei schulde no wynd haue
til þat sche cam.   In þe morow whan sche cam to þe brynk and
say þe schip goo, than wept sche intollerablely[2], and filt þe eres of
God with grete compleintis, and ȝet wist sche not what ioye God
wold cause hiꝛ of his absens.   Thus went sche hom a-geyn and
prayed for him deuly, and he went forth to Rome.   Whan he was

Leaf 14. com þidir he felt ‖ in greuous seknesse & his moder knew not þat,
Augustine
fell ill, but þouȝ[3] he were absent sche prayed for him deuly þat ouꝛ Lord
schuld send her ioye of hir son, for in þis mater sche had moꝛ sorow
for him þan euyr sche had to bryng him forth on-to þe world.
but through
the devotion
and prayers
of his mother
he was made
well, and
taught
rhetoric. Euery day sche offered for him at þe auteꝛ; euery day sche gaf
elmesse.   Twyes on þe day went she to cherch, not for to telle
veyn tales, but for to here tydyngis of ouꝛ Lord of heuene in
deuoute sermones, or elles for heꝛ diuine seruyse that God schuld
accept hir prayeres, whech weꝛ principali for þe goostly helth of
hir son Augustin.   Be hir prayeres Austyn is now rered fro his
seknesse and hath begunne for to do þing for whech he was come,
þat is to seye, to tech rethorik; many disciples be gadered on-to
his skole, and his fame be-gan fast to springe.

8

12

16

20

[CHAPTER X.]

¶ Who Austin eke was sent to Melan to lerne hem rethorik.   x.

Soon,
however,
Symachus
sent him to
Milan to
teach rhetoric
there, and
there he met
St. Ambrose. AT þis tyme þe cyte of Melan, wher Seynt Ambrose was
bischop, sent on-to þe meyꝛ of Rome, whech hith
Symachus, praying him þat he wold sende on-to hem a weel
lerned man for to teche heꝛ inuent rethorik.   And he, with ful
good a-vise, sent hem Austyn, a proued maystir, as he wrote, and
a man of grete cunnyng.   Thus be þe prouidens of God cam
Austyn to Melan, and þere felt in knowlech of Seynt Ambrose þe
bischop[4], a noble man and a holy, knowyn þorw all þe world.
Ambrose receyued Augustin ful faderly, and cherisched him in þe
best maneꝛ.   Augustin went oft on-to cherch for to heꝛ Ambrose

24

28

---

[1] lord *added in margin.*   [2] r *inserted above.*
[3] þouȝ *in margin.*
[4] MS. and *with* nd *crossed out in red and dotted underneath.*

preche, not for [to] lerne ‖ treuthes of ouͬ feith, ne nowt to amende Leaf 14,
þe erroures of his soule, but only to aspie wheithir his fame and his back.
speche acorded. For he was noted þorw-oute Itaile a fayͬ-spoke Augustine went to hear Ambrose's
4 man, and gretly roted in rethorik. Thus went ouͬ Augustin day rhetoric,
be day, only to reporte þe wordis; for þe sentens had he smal
delite; and ꝣet, as he is a-know in his Confessiones, þe wordes of
Seynt Ambrose abiden in his soule magͬ his hed, and were dayly
8 grucching a-geyn swech lif as he had. Happed on a day ouͬ fadeͬ
Ambrose prechid of þe incarnacioñ of ouͬ Lord Ihesu Crist, who
þat for þe special loue whech he had to mankynde he disdeyned
not to take þe flesch and blood of man with aɫɫ þe infirmites, saue
12 synne. Augustin stood in þe puple and sodeyn fere feɫ up-on
him, so þat þe þoutes whech weͬ pryuy with-inne him mad his face and one day his words
pale and his body for to tremel þat aɫ þe puple myth aspie it. turned him to the true faith,
Aftir þe sermon was ended he went on-to Ambrose, and told him
16 of his new chaunge, and who longe he had ben in þe Manicheis
heresie, and who sith þat tyme þat he spak with Faustus þat secte
was ferre fro his plesauns. Whan Ambrose herd þat he had no
trost ne no confidens in[1] þe heresie of þese Manicheis, he þankid
20 God heyly, and be-cause he knew wel þe inspiracion of þe Holy
Gost[2] what Augustin schuld be, he treted him ful fadirly with
swete exhortaciones, þinking with swech menes to brynge him to
þe trew be-leue. Tho Augustin cast in his hert fully to ‖ despise þe Leaf 15.
24 Manicheis heresi, for euyr þe feith of Crist he purposed for to take, but he would
but baptiꝣed wold he not be on-to þe tyme þat he myth know þe not yet be baptized.
treuthis of Cristis feith.

[CHAPTER XI.]

¶ [3] In what maner his moder sowt him.[3] cap. xi.

28 IN þis same tyme Monicha, his modir, took þe se, and put hir- Monica took
selue to grete perel for to se hir son. Hir grete feith and ship after her son.
hope þat sche had in God, hiͬ grete charite þat sche had to
conuercioñ of hir son, mad þe womannes hert bold, and in maner

---

[1] in *inserted above in small writing.*
[2] gost *written in red in margin replacing* God *in text, and a mark of insertion made.*   [3]–[3] *Inserted in margin.*

She calmed
the frightened
shipmen,
and met her
son, who
told her he
had left the
Manichaean
sect.

turned it to a mannes hert, þat not only sche wanted [1] feer or dred
in þe se, but þe schipmen whech weꝛ aferd sche coumforted in þe
best maner, saying on-to hem in þis maneꝛ: Beth of good coumfort, seres, for treuly I had a visioñ fro heuene þat we schul skape 4
þis iornay ful weel. Sche is come to lond and to þe speche of
hir son, and after longe daliauns he told hiꝛ pleynly þat out of
Manicheis skole was he go for euyr, but on-to Cristis skole, whech
sche desired him to come, was he not parfithly entred. ȝet whan 8
sche herd him sey þis sche hopped with ful mery chere [2] þat sche
had o part of [3] hiꝛ desire, for too þingis desired sche, on þat he
weꝛ delyuered fro þat fals heresie of þe Manichees, and þat was
fulfilt, þe oþir þat sche schuld se him a trew Cristen man, and þis 12
sche hoped. With a grete spirith and a merie chere sche cried and

She con-
tinued to
pray for
his soul,

seide: Now beleue I in my Lord God, þat or my soule passe out
of þis world I schal se him a trew Cristen man. Than sent sche
praieres on-to heuene [4] with gretter bisinesse þan euyr sche ded 16

Leaf 15,
back.

þat ouꝛ Lord schuld hast þis mater, ‖ & make brith þe þirknesse
of Augustines soule. Sche loued Ambrose as an aungel of God,
for be him sche wist weel þat hir son was brout þus to swech
fluctuacioñ. Fluctuacioñ calle we heꝛ whan a man is broute fro 20
an euel entent, and ȝet þe same man stand in study wheithir he
schal to þe good wey or nowt. In þis plith stood ouꝛ Austyn.

and made
offerings at
the altars
where saints
were buried,
as she had in
Africa, but
ceased on the
advice of
Ambrose.
Augustine
says she
fasted on
Saturdays,
as was the
custom in
Rome.

The custom of his moder and eke of þe cuntꝛ whilles sche dwelt
in Affrik, was [5] to offer bred and potage and wyne at the aucteris 24
where martires were byried. And þis custom was for-bode hiꝛ
be þe keper of þe cherch at Melane, seying on-to hir þat it was þe
bischoppis wil, Ambrose, þat swech mete and drynk sche schuld ȝeue
to pore men, and to þe memories of the martires sche schuld 28
brynge, he seid, a deuoute soule ful of holy prayeres. Whan
sche herd þis deuoutely sche chaunged hir vse aftir þat informacioñ. Seynt Augustin, hir son, tellith of hire þat sche used to fast
þe Satirday, as deuoute folk ded þan at Rome, and þo persones þat 32
ete and dronk with hiꝛ continually at Melane saide þat it was not
þe vsage þere at Melane, wher-for hir dyuersite was in maner of
a slaundir to þe cumpany. In þis mateꝛ sche took councell of

---

[1] feꝛ *crossed through.*   [2] chere *inserted above in red.*
[3] MS. o part of part of *with second* part *crossed through.*
[4] *final* ne *inserted in red above.*
[5] *inserted in margin in red.*

Seyn Ambrose, and he sette hir¹ þis reule, þat wheꝛ-so-euyr sche
cam sche schuld do aftir þe custom of þe felauchip whech sche
dwelt in. In þis same tyme come too of Augustin grete frendis ^{Augustine's friends,}
4 on-to him², Alipius and Nebridius. This Alipius was bore in þe ^{Alypius and Nebridius,}
same town wheꝛ Augustin was bore, and Nebridius bore fast be
Cartage, ‖ where he had faiꝛ possession, but it likid him bettir ^{Leaf 16.}
to forsake aᴌᴌ þat he had and com to dweᴌᴌ with Augustin.
8 These iij men to-gidir at Melane had grete counceᴌᴌ and grete ^{seek with him}
stody what maner secte þei schuld chese, and what lyf þei schuld ^{what sect they should}
hald. At þese dayes was Augustin xxx ȝeꝛ of age. So aᴌᴌ iij ^{follow, propose to}
were acorded first to chese hem wyues, and all sex dweᴌᴌ in on ^{take wives, and study,}
12 hous, and þei for to stody swech bokes as þei wold haue and do ^{and dwell together.}
non oþir bisinesse. Than was alleggid a-mongis hem what sorrow
þere schuld be if þei acorded not, ³ & specialy for h[er] wyuys, who
þe[i] schuld lyue, if dista[uns] fel betwix³. God ouꝛ Lord had
16 ordeyned a-noþir wey, and for þat cause he put a delay in þat
mateꝛ, for he suffered þe hert of Augustin to be sette on swech ^{Augustine's maid.}
a mayde, and of so ȝong age, that he must nede abyde tyl sche
were able.

[CHAPTER XII.]

20   ¶ On what maner ouꝛ Lord suffered Alipius to be appechid of
theft. xij.

THIS processe telȝ Augustin in þe vj book of his Confessiones
in þis maner. Alipius, he seith, was at Cartage, stodying ^{Alypius studied}
24 in rethorik. It was þe vsage at þoo dayes þa[t] þe rethoricianes ^{rhetoric at Carthage,}
schuld pleten in court for euery cause whech was litigious. This
Alipius, a litil be-foꝛ þe court schuld be hold, walkyd a-lone with ^{and, on a day before he}
his reporting tables in his hand, stodying ful bysily, for it was his ^{should have pleaded,}
28 cours þat day for to plete. Be-neth þat hous where he walked
was housyng be þe ground, in whech dwelt coynoures of siluyr,
and wroute þere ful bisily. Owt of þe strete comth a ȝong child, ^{passed a}
a theef, with an ex in his hand, and went on-to a certeyn roof ^{coiner's house where a boy}
32 whech was cured with leed, and euene ouyr þe coynouris hous ^{was stealing lead,}
he be-gan for to hewe. ‖ The coynouris herd þe noyse and sent ^{Leaf 16,}
up too or thre of heꝛ felauchip to loke what theef was so bold ^{back.}

---

¹ MS. his *with* r *written above in red.*   ² MS. hinn.
³⁻³ *written in margin and part of end words cut away at edge of leaf.*

The boy heard a noise and ran away, and men coming, Alypius was arrested.

þat tyme of þe day and so ny þe dome-place to stele þe metaíl of þe houses.   The boy herd men com with grete noyse; he left his exe þere, and ran hom in grete hast.   Thus com þe men and se no persone þere but Alipius alone; þei [1] se þe led broke, þei fynde þe 4 ex by, and on him þei go aíl and areste him for þis dede.   Alipius, þat was *innocent*, and be-cause of his study took non hed at þe boy, neythir wha*n* he cam ne whan he went, is þus led forth as a theef on-to þe iuge.   Happed a man þat knew him and knew 8 what vertue he was of for to mete him with þese tormentour*is*. He pulled him o side and inqwired of him who þis myth be. A man of swech birth and swech kunnyng þat he schuld be take in swech defaute, he seid, it was grete merueile.   Alipius answerd 12 on-to him and told him þat he was ongilty in þis mateʀ, but he

But a friend tricked the boy into con-fessing the abandoned axe was his,

had mynde þat he say a boy renne fro þe place and leue þere his ex.   The ma*n* caused [2] þat þei turned aíl a-geyn in-to þe same strete, and as it happed, þe same boy stood in þe dore þat had doo 16 þe dede.   This man whech ȝaue [3] so grete fauouʀ on-to Alipius took þe ex in hand; rith þus he seide on-to þe boy: Heʀ haue we founde an exe; knowest þou owt to whom it schuld longe? ȝa,

and so was Alypius saved.

forsoth, seʀ, seide he, þat same ex is ouʀ.   Thus was Allipi*us* 20 wrongfully attached and meruelously delyuered.   God Almyty

Leaf 17.

suffered þis, as Augusti*n* writith ‖ in his Confessiones, for to lerne him whech schuld be aftirward a iuge of me*n*nes soules in þe cherch þat he schuld not deme ouyr sone of signes owtward.   24

[CHAPTER XIII.]
¶ Who he went to Simpliciane.   xiij.

Augustine finally con-sents to become a Christian,

NOW is Augustin dryuyn so feiʀ þat he is fully consentid to go be þe wey of Crist, but be-cause of þe hardnesse of it, he was ful loth þerto.   But ouʀ merciable Lord put a new coumfort 28 in his hert þat he schuld go to an hermyte in þe desert fast by Melan, whech hermyte hith Simpliciane.   Augustin had herd mech þing of him þat he had serued God in ful vertuous lyf, and

and goes to Simplician; the hermit, who dwelt by Milan,

þe fame was trewe in-dede.   This ma*n* Simpliciane lyued in 32 a monastery fast by Mela*n* with othir heremites of holy lyf

---

[1] *final i added in red.*   [2] *final d inserted above.*
[3] *to crossed through.*

at þe costis & expens of Seynt Ambrose. For Seint Ambrose at the expense of Ambrose.
had Simpliciane in so grete reuerens þat he worchipid him as
his fader, and aftir his deth asined on-to his clerkis and his
4 puple to be chose bischop successour on-to him, and so it was
in-dede. To þis Simpliciane teld Augustin þe besinesse of Augustine told him his history,
his hert, in who many errouris he had falle an[d] what dowte
he stood in to what lyf he schuld drawe. The good fader
8 Simpliciane gaf him exhortacion to folow þe meknesse of our and was advised,
Lord Ihesu and despise þe fals delectacionis of þis world. He
rehersed on-to him eke a grete exaumple of[1] þe conuercion of on,
Victorine, a worthi man, a grete rethorician, a famous philisophr, and told of the example
12 whech man for grete sciens had a statua rered to his liknesse in of Victorine,
þe markette at Rome. This same man cam to Simpliciane often-
tyme and inqwired of him many þingis, and oft-tyme wold
say ‖ on-to Sympliciane: Knowe now wel þat I wil be a cristen Leaf 17,
16 man. Simplician wold say a-gayn on-to him: I wil not be-leue it back.
til þat I se þe withinne þe kirk. And Victorine wold þanne in
scorne conclude be maner of an argument: Ergo, þe wallis of þe
cherch make a cristen man. This iteration of wordis was oft- how he was converted to
20 tyme vsed be-twix þese too men, but at þe last our Lord enspired real Christianity.
soo Victorines hert þat sodeynly he seid to Simpliciane: Go we to
þe cherch, for in very treuth, I wil be a cristen man. Thus was
þis worthi man conuerted to þe feith; and al þis told Simpliciane
24 to Augustin þat he schulde folow his steppis. Be þis holy fader
Simpliciane was Augustin brovt on-to þis desire, þat al maner Augustine came thus to
worldly delectacion displesed him, for þe loue of his hert is now despise the world, but
only sette to serue God. He say many men in þe cherch lyuyng had not yet
28 in sundry maner, summe þus & summe þus, wherfor he hatз not chosen his way of life.
chose as зet þe lyf whech he wil lede.

[CHAPTER XIV.]

¶ Off þe comyng of Poncian on-to Augustin and of what þingis
þei talked of. capitulum xiiij.

32 IN þis tyme was Augustin & Alipius dwellyng to-gidyr, for Augustine and Alipius
Nebridius was not with hem at þat tyme. So happed it þat dwelt together,
a man of court whech was dwellyng in þe paleys at Rome whos

---

[1] *inserted above in red.*

andPonciane, their fellow countryman, came to them, name was Ponciane, be-cause he was bore in Affrica, rith as þei were, cam on-to hem to se her welfaꝛ, as þe maner of men is whech be bore in straunge cuntre & dwelle fer fro hom.   He fonde hem sittyng in a hous and be-for hem a bord on whech þei vsed to 4

Leaf 18. pleye certeyn games ‖ to refresch with þe sadnesse of her study. Vpon þis bord lay a book whech book Ponciane supposed had be of sum seculeꝛ sciens whech as þei vsed.   Poncian vnsperd þe bok

and found the 'Epistles' of St. Paul before them. and say wel þat it was a bok longing to cristen feith, whech bok 8 we clepe þe Epistoles of Seynt Paule.   This Ponciane with myry cheꝛ mad in maneꝛ of a þankyng to God þat Augustin his cuntre-man was falle in-to studye of swech holy bokes, for þis same Ponciane had neuly take cristendham and was a stedfast and 12 a trewe cristen man.   Augustin sayde on-to him þan þat al þe felicite of his study was only ʒoue to rede swech bokes.   Tho

They talked of the holy hermits, be-gunne þei to speke of þe dyuers cumpanyes of holy heremites whech dwelled in wildyrnesse, both in Itale and in Egipt, and in 16 special of grete Antonie whos name was ful famous to all þe seruauntes of God, but to Augustin and his felawes it was on-knowyn on-to þat houꝛ.   For whech cause he satte ful stille and herd Ponciane with grete silens.   Ponciane told him who he 20 & oþir thre felawis þat dwelt with þe emperouꝛ went on a day

and Ponciane told how a friend had discovered the 'Life of St. Anthony' in a cave and was converted to hermit-life by it. in-to þe wodis to her disport, and happed Ponciane and his felaw to walk in þe o side of þe wode, and þe oþir too felawes in þe othir side.   On of þese too with whech Poncian was not cam in-to 24 a caue where a heremyte dwelled, whech heremite was up-hap in-to þe cite for to fecch him mete, and fond þere a book with Seynt Antonies lyf; he sat down and red it, and in þe redyng was

Leaf 18, back. sodeynly compunct to forsake þe world.   Thus saide he þan ‖ on-to 28 his felaw : Here in þis same place I purpose me for euyr to serue God, and þis same houꝛ I wil be-gynne.   If þou list not to do as I wil, I pray þe, grucch not my dede.   His felaw answered a-gayn on þis maneꝛ, þat he wold not part cumpany, but swech lif as he 32 hath chose he wil folow, to forsake al þis world and leue þere in solitarie lif.   Ponciane and his felaw sey þe sunne draw fast to inclinacion, sout þese oþir too felawis, fonde hem and hasted hem homward, for þe day was ny at a ende, as þei saide.   Tho told þei 36 her holy purpos on-to hem, what a-vow þei had mad whech þei wold not breke.   Ponciane and his felaw praised heꝛ entent, and

þankyng God of her holy *conuercion*, went a-geyn on-to þe paleys.
Thus dwelt þese men stille *þere* in þat caue, *perseuering* in holy lif,
and to ȝong women whech schuld be weddid on-to hem, be heר
4 exhortacion avowid heר maydenhed to God.

[CHAPTER XV.]

¶ What sorow Augustin mad aftir þis exhortacio*n*. **XV.**

GRETE sorow and horribil ran in Augusti*n* mynde þan�
    whan he had herd þese holy exaumples of þe *seruauntis* of
8 God, whech *seruauntis* ouר Lord God had brout [1] fro þe grete
blaknesse of synne on-to þe faiר white *vertuous* lyuyng. For aֆl
þese exau*mples* had Augusti*n* gaðered in-to þe bosom of his hert,
whech brent him ful sore and mad him a-schamed þat he was not
12 þus disposed.   And whan Ponciane had take his leue & was go,
thoo Augustine with a troubled mynde be-gan ‖ to loke up-on his
felaw Alipius, and with a sobir voys þus he cried : What suffir
we ?   What are þese þingis þat we here ?   These onlerned men
16 rise and sodeynly wynne heuene, and we with aֆl ouר doctryne are
drenchid euene in helle.   Be-cause þei went be-fore us *perfor*
schul we be a-schamed to folow hem ?   Whil Augustin saide þese
wordes Alipius besily loked up-on him, for he pronou*n*sed not his
20 wordis as he was wone to doo.   For nowt only weר þese wordes
expressed with labouר [2] of his tu*n*ge [2], but his forhed, chekis, his
eyne and aֆl his me*m*bres in mane*r* laboured in pronou*n*syng of
þese wordes.   Sodeynly þan� he stirt fro þat hous in whech he
24 had herd þese þingis, and in-to a gardeyn whech was annexid to
þat hous he stert ; Alipius folowid him foot be foot, meruelin*g* soר
of þe sodeyn compu*n*ccion þus neuly com.   Thus þei sat in þe
gardeyn as feר fro þe hous as þei myth sitte, and Augustin be-gan to
28 accuse him-self soר in þe sith of ouר Lord of þe slauth of his returne
to God, and þe grete hepes of synne whech he had vsed he gadered
on-to mynde, whech mad him for to wepe plenteuou*s*ly, and þat he
schul haue þe moר leyseר to wepe, he roos fro his felaw Alipius and
32 went on-to a figge-tre.   Þere he þrew him-selue down vndyr þe tre,

Augustine was deeply moved by the tale of Ponciane's friend,

Leaf 19.

and, with a trembling voice, addressed Alypius.

Then he went into the garden ; his conscience smote him and he wept.

He threw himself on the earth by a fig-tree

---

[1] *broñ crossed through.*   [2-2] *written in red in margin.*

and swech lamentable voyses he þrew on-to heuene : O blissed Lord,
who longe, who longe ? Who longe wilt þou suffir, Lord, þat I go so
ferre fro þi seruyse and differre my *conuercion* fro day to day ?
To-morow, schal it be to-morow ? Why not now, Lord, whi schal 4

not þis same houre ‖ make an end of aH my filth ? Whil he lay
þus with grete contricion of hert and with ful sobbyng voys

uttirryng aH þese wordes, al sodeynly he herd a voys, as þou3
it had ben at þe next hous, soundyng þese same wordes : Tak and 8
rede, take and rede ! Tho be-gan he for þink with-inne him-selue if
childyrn with ony game þat þei vse had ony swech wordes in her
playing, and he coude not þink þat he had herd ony swech. He
þout þan þat þis voys cam fro heuene, 3euyng him a warnyng þat 12
he schuld ope þe bok whech he brout with him fro þe hous on-to
þe gardeyn, and þe first letter þat his eye felle up-on he schuld
rede. Thus ded he, and þese same wordis red he : Non in
comessac*ionibus* & ebrietat*ibus*, non in cubilib*us* & impudiciciis, 16
non in *contencione* & emulacione, *sed* induimini *dominum* ihe*sum*
christum et carnis curam ne fece*ritis* in desideriis [1]. The sentens
of þis texte may be englisched in þis wise : Not in grete festis ne
in dronknesse, not in soft couchis and in schalful dedis, not in 20
strif a[n]d [2] envye, but be clad with ouꝛ Lord Ihe*su*, & fulfille not
þe bisinesse of þe flesch in his desires. He sperd the bok whan he
had red þis and leyd at þe same reson a merk be whech he myth
rydily turne þertoo, for þis same texte put in his [3] hert a lite of 24
swech a grace þat alle þe derk errouris whech he had hold weꝛ

passed a-wey fro him. Tho toke he þe book on-to his felaw
Alipius, and with his fynger or sum othir tokne schewid him
þe clause be-foꝛ red. Alipius red ferþeꝛ whech Augusti*n* had 28
not red, and schewid to Augusti*n* what it was þat [4] folowid. Þus
folowith in þe texte : That man þat is feynt in þe feith, loke

3e be ‖ redy for to receyue. In-to þe hous þei go both ; þere þei

fynde þe blessed woma*n* Monicha, þe modir of Augustin ; þei 32
told hir al þis processe þat sche whech had be in so mech sorow
for hir son schuld haue part of his new ioye. Sche þankid God
with ful humbil hert þat oure Lord had graunted hir hir long
desiꝛ, & mech more þat sche desired, for not only He had brout 36

---

[1] *In margin* Ad Rom*anos* 13.   [2] MS. *ad.*
[3] *s inserted above.*   [4] *t inserted above.*

him[1] to purpos to be a cristen man, but He had stered his hert to despise al þis worldly plesauns.

[CHAPTER XVI.]

¶ Who he left his skole of rethorik only to haue his hert
4 fre to God. **xvj.**

NOW be-gan his hert to be sette stedfastly in ouɾ Lord[2], for þoo vanytees and þoo opinyones in whech he had be-foɾ ful grete ioye, now aɾ þei falle clene fro him, and þat skole whech
8 was a peyne to him þat he schuld leue it, now for to leue it, it is to him ioye. But ȝet him þout for to leue his skole sodeynly and his skoleris desolat, þat it was not best. For þe heruest dayes weɾ ny whan skole is wone to cese; so longe he þout for
12 to suffir hem, þat þei schuld solemply goo fro him. Whan xx dayes were go, for þan entred þe cessacion, whech dayes weɾ on-to him longe for þe grete desiɾ þat he had to serue God with moɾ solitarie lif, than was he dysmittid of his grete labouɾ whech
16 he had in teching of rethorik. And because þat al his desire was for to prey and study solitarily, he left þe cite of Melan, and forth in-to þe cuntɾ he went, in-to a feld þei[3] cleped Cassiate, to a place longing to a worchipful man cleped Verecundus. This
20 Verecundus grauntid him to dwelle þere ‖ on-to þe tyme þat he schuld be baptiȝed. So in þis same place abood he and Alipius, and oþir frendis of his, with his modir, all in o desire to forsake þe delectable onstabilnesse of þis world. And in þis same place mad
24 Augustin dyuers bokes, þat is to sey a book De Achademicis, whech soundeth in ouɾ tonge of on-certeyn opiniones. For Achademia was a town where Plato tawt and all þoo disciples of þat skole held þis opinion, þat no þing is sette in certeyn. This book of
28 Augustin serueth not mech, for he was fayn aftir to make a book a-geyn þis secte, and þat is cleped *Contra* Achademicos. Aftir þis he mad a-noþir book in þat same place, whech he clepith De Ordine, in whech book, as me semyth, he tretith be what
32 order or what forme a man schuld studie. The þird book mad

*Side notes:*
In order to be free to serve God, Augustine gave up his school of rhetoric,

and retired to a field of Verecundus, where he wrote Leaf 20, back.

[1] 'De Achademicis'

[2] (afterwards annulled by 'Contra Achademicos'),

[3] 'De Ordine,'

---

[1] *inserted above.*   [2] *inserted in red above.*
[3] *i added in red.*

and 'De Beata Vita.'
he in þat same place whech he clepith De *Beata* Vita; þat is to sey, of þe blessed lyf. The cause whi he mad þis book is þis. Many men in þis world, specialy þe hethen men, mad a gret feest þat day þat þei were bore. Augustin had vsed þis al his 4 lyf on-to þat tyme. So happed þat day to falle þe same tyme

Why he wrote the latter book, and what it contains,
þat he dwelt in þat possession of the forsaid man *Ve*recundus. And be-cause he wold chau*n*ge þat fleschly fedyng in-to goostly talking, þerfor with his moder and certeyn of his frendis, he mad 8 þat day þat book wheʔ he disputeth what we schuld calle þe blissed lyf. Aħ þe cu*m*pany saue his moder saide it is a blessed lyf a man for to haue aħ þat he desireth. His modir put moo

Leaf 21.
wordis on-to þis diffuncioꝥ. Sche saide ‖ he hath a blessed lif 12 whech hath al þat he desirith, and eke þat he desire no-þing but good þing. Mech moʔ þing is touchid in þis book, speciali of þe knowlech of God, whech þing as now we may not declaʔ.

[CHAPTER XVII.]

¶ Who bisily he red holy scriptuʔ and speciali þe Psalmes of 16 Dauid,[1] & of his baptem [1]. **xvij.**

Augustine became a constant reader of Scripture,
NOW is þe delectacioꝥ of Augustyn only sette in redyng of holy Scriptuʔ; grete swetnesse hath he now in þoo lessones whech kyndeled þe fyre of his hert and mad him to encrese sore 20 in þe loue of God. He mad ful grete sorow þat he had be so bold to berke a-geyn þese holy lett*er*is, whech be swete as hony to þoo soules þat desiʔ heuene, for þei weʔ dewid fro heuene be þe holy vesseles of þe *p*rophetis, and most specialy be ouʔ 24 Lord[2] Iheru and his aposteles. Tho cam Augusti*n* on-to þe

and particu- larly of the fourth Psalm.
Psalmis of Dauid, whech he red w*ith* ful ryp deuocyoꝥ, and specialy in iiij Psalme; þere mad he grete tarying, redyng eu*er*y vers by and by with gret sobbyng of hert, with wepyng and 28 lamentable voys. And whan he cam to þat vers: In pace, in idip*su*m dormiam & requiescam, þan wold he crye: A þou pes, a Lord, þou art þe very pes in whech we schal both slepe and

---

[1]⁻[1] *added in margin.*   [2] *added in red above.*

rest! A-mongis all þese swete consolaciones our Lord sent him Augustine was smitten with grievous sickness in
sum bittirnesse, þat he schuld tast þe loue of our Lord both in
bittyr & in swete. For þat same tyme *in* whech he was come the head and teeth,
4 to þis grete deuocion, he fel in greu*ous* seknesse of þe heed, most
special of þe teth, whech peyne encresed so þat he myth not
speke. Tho ran it in his mynde for to pray þo men whech wer
about him to make a ‖ supplicacion on-to our Lord, þat he Leaf 21, back.
8 schuld of his mercy relese sum of þis peyne. And be-cause he
myth not speke þis for peyne, þerfor he took a peyre tables, and
wroot in þe wax al his desir, þat þei of pite schuld pray for him. and by the prayers of his friends was cured.
And sodeynly, as þei alle sette hem down on knees to pray for
12 him, þe peyne went a-wey. Of whech chau*n*ge he was gretly He asked Ambrose what part of Scripture he should read, and was told to read Isaiah; and did so;
astoyned, for he had neuyr non exp*eri*ens of so[1] sodeyn helth in
al his lyf. Tho sent he lett*eris* to Seynt Ambrose, in whech
lett*eris* he renou*n*sid for euyr all his elde errour*is*, and in þe same
16 lett*eris* he desired of Ambrose þat he schuld assigne him what
book of holy Scriptur was most nec*cessarie* for him to rede, be
whech redyng he myth be mor able and more redy to receyue
þe cristen feith. Ambrose wrote on-to hi*m* a-geyn þat he þout
20 best he schuld rede þe book of Ysaie, þe prophete, be-cause þat
þis book tretith most openly of callyng of hethe*n* men to þe feith.
Augusti*n* red þis book, and þe begi*n*nyng was passyng strau*n*ge
on-to him, for he had not mech vsed þat[2] mane*r* stile, wherfor
24 he leyd þis book a-side as for a tyme, tyll he were mor vsed in but being unused to the style, laid the book aside for a time. He went to Milan for baptism and wrote there 'De Immortalitate Animae.
study of scriptur. Sone aftir þis he went to Melan a-gay[n],
only for he cast him þere to be baptiȝed, and ȝet or he was
baptiȝed he mad þere a book whech is entituled, De I*m*mortalitate
28 Anime. This book tretith who þat a ma*n*nes soule is not dedly
but hath lif for eu*er*. Aftir þe maky*n*g of þis book he was
baptiȝed of Seynt Ambrose, þe ȝer of his age xxxiij, in þe pase-tyme,
in ‖ þe baptisterie whech is halowid to þe name of Seynt Ion Leaf 22.
32 Baptist, all þe cite of Melan standyng aboute, meruely*n*g and
praysing God. And þese too men in þe time of baptising, wha*n* He was afterwards baptized by Ambrose and then these two com-posed 'Te Deum,'
þe p*ri*ncipal sacramental wordes wer said, mad þis ympne whech
þe cherch vsith now, cleped Te Deum. Ambrose be-gan þe first
36 vers, and Augustin þe secu*n*d, and þus þei said it to an ende.

---

[1] *inserted above.*   [2] þe *with* at *written over it.*

All this is
told in the
'Chronicle'
of Dacius.
This witnesseth a seynt clepid Dacius, bischop aftir of þe same cherch of Melan, in his Cronycle whech he mad, þe x. book, þe first capitule.

[CHAPTER XVIII.]

¶ Of his son Adeodate whech was baptiȝed with hym, and of 4 othir also. **Capi*tulum* xviij.**

Augustine
had a son,
called
Adeodatus,
by a single
woman to
whom he was
true.

AUGUSTIN had a son be a sengil woman whech folowid up-on him wheᵽ he went as long as he was hethen, on-to þat ¹tyme þat¹ he and his felawis weᵽ sette in þat purpos for to 8 wedde wyues of good birth, for² aftir þat tyme þe woman sewid him no moᵽ. These be his wordis in his Confessiones, wheᵽ he seith eke þat he had neu*er* no woma*n* but hiᵽ, ne sche no man but him. O child was boᵽ be-twix hem too, whom þei cleped 12

Adeodatus
was a child of
remarkable
intellect,
who, at the
age of
sixteen,
surprised his
father by his
subtlety.

Adeodat*us*, þat is to seye, ȝoue of God, a mal child, a child ful of witte and of vertu, but ouᵽ Lord took him sone oute of þis world aftir he was cristened with his fadeᵽ. His witte was so gret and so sotiᵽ, as Augustin tellit, þat it passed in conyng 16 many³ men of grete age and grete experiens. Augustin his fader had gret m*er*ueyl of him þat a ȝong þing of xvj ȝeᵽ age schuld so m*er*uelously asken questionis, so sotilly⁴ argew. His fader had

Leaf 22,
back.

moᵽ bisinesse for to ‖ take heed at his questiones þanῆ at þe 20 answer*is* whech schuld be ȝoue þertoo. This child, with ful grete bisynesse, laboured to knowe þe trewe wey of God, both in study of sotiᵽ sciens and eke folowing with vertuous lyf. But sone

Soon after his
baptism the
son died.

aftir his baptem ouᵽ Lord took him oute of erde, & sette him⁵ 24 in swech place wheᵽ he is sikir of euyrlasting ioye. This same

Adeodatus
caused his
father to
write 'De
Quantitate
Animae.'

Adeodat*us* caused his fadeᵽ to write þat book whech tretith of þe qu*ant*ite of þe soule, for it is a dialoge be-twix to, wheᵽ on makith int*er*ogaciones and⁶ þe oþir ȝeueth þe answeres. Thus 28 aftir her baptem Augusti*nus*, with his felauchip⁷, leued in ful grete ioye þat þei had receyued so clene a lif, whech lyf was more dere on-to hem þan gold or precious stones.

---

¹⁻¹ *added in red in margin.*   ² *added in red above.*
³ *a character crossed through.*   ⁴ *ag crossed through.*
⁵ MS. hin.   ⁶ *a crossed through.*   ⁷ *ip written in margin.*

[CHAPTER XIX.]

¶ Who Augustin had grete delite in þe song and ympnis songen
in þe cherch of Melan. ca^m. xix.

THUS whan he was confermed in þe feith of holy kirk, al þe
4   ioye and þe hope whech he had in þis world he forsok,
and in þis tyme myth neuyr his soule be saciat or fulfillid of
good desires, most special[1] consideryng who þat ouʀ Lord of His
hie councell had refreschid mankynde with His presens. He[2]
8 be-gan at þese dayes for to vse þe cherch mech, wheʀ he herd
redyng and synging of delectable materes and swete melodies,
whech melody was on-to him a ful grete solace. Ambrose had
þat time mad neuly many ympnys, for all þe temporal ympnys
12 ar ny of his making, as Primo dierum[3] omnium[4], & þoo þat
folow, and þis same bisschop Ambrose mad hem to be sunge
delectabily with consent of dyuers tewnys whech ‖ had not be
used þere be-foʀ. The cause whi þat þese newe songis were
16 be-gunne þus in Ambroses tyme is þis. The emperesse cleped
Iustina was infect with þe venemhous heresie of þe Arianes,
whech held þat þe Fadeʀ and þe Son and þe Holy Gost be not
of o substauns, for þe Son calle þei a creatuʀ mad of þe Fadeʀ,
20 and þe Holy Gost clepe þei a creatuʀ mad of a creatuʀ, þat is
to sey of þe Son. Thei sey ferþermoʀ, þat Crist took flesch and
blod with-outen ony soule. This woman, þus infecte, at instauns
of certeyn prestis whech taute hir þat heresie, hated Ambrose,
24 for he prechid mech a-geyn hem. This persecucion was so gret
þat Ambrose was constreyned to kepe þe cherch both nyth and
day, and mech of his puple abod still with him in tuycioñ of
his person, redy for to deye with her fadeʀ. So for to make
28 hem moʀ lith in heʀ wecch, þis same bisschop ded ordeyn swete
songis and delectable, aftir þe vse of þe cherchis in þe est side
of þe world, þat þe puple þus occupied with swech swete songis
schuld forgete þe heuynesse and þe perel in whech þei stood. Eke

Augustine, thus converted, used church a great deal,

where he sang the hymns of Ambrose.

Leaf 23.

The empress Justina followed the Arian heresy,

and persecuted the church of Ambrose, forcing him and his people to remain in the church night and day.

To make their watch more light, therefore, Ambrose wrote his sweet songs

---

[1] who *crossed through.*   [2] ba *crossed through.*
[3] conditor *crossed through.*   [4] *in margin.*

which are
sung yet in
the church.
whan þis persecucioñ was ended ȝet þe good custom of þese songis
abood stille.   For on-to þis day þe vse of þe cherch is for to
singe his ympnis with mery notes, whech is plesauns to God
and a grete encres of mannes deuocyoñ, specialy whan þei be 4

They made
Augustine
think of the
songs of
angels.
songe deuoutly.   For in þese songis had Augustin so grete delite
þat he herd hem with ful bisy eres, for þei mad him to þink
on þo songis whech aungelles syng in heuene, and in þis same

Leaf 23,
back.
deuocion be alle ‖ his felawes now whech ar newly baptiȝed.   Thus 8
can oure Lord make dyuers bodies lyue in on hous with o soule
and on entent in þe seruyse of God.

[CHAPTER XX.]

¶ Who Augustyn aftir þis took an habite of Sympliciane whech
his heremytes used.   **xx.**   12

Simplician,
who had
helped
convert
Augustine,
gave him a
habit after
his baptism,
black, and
shaped like
a cross,
and girded
with a
girdle.
BE-cause þat Simpliciane with his holy exhortaciones had
    brout Augustin on-to þe feith, þerfor had Augustin grete
recors on-to him, most special aftir his baptem.   For of þis same
Simpliciane took he þe forme of an habite whech his heremytes 16
vsed aftirward, and he eke.   And nowt only þe habite but þe
maneʳ of holy conuersacioñ lerned he of þe same Simpliciane rith
as he sey with his eyne.   The forme of þis habite is touched in his
bokes, wheʳ is seid þat þe habite was schape lich a crosse, and girt 20
aboue with a girdil whech had no barres, and all was of blak colouʳ
þat he schuld neuyr forgete who þat he was hethen sumtyme and
lyued in þe blaknesse of synne.   Off þis informacioñ whech he

This he
mentions
in one of his
sermons.
He writes to
the priests of
Hippo about
his staying
with his
hermits, and
of their
excellence.
receyued of Sympliciane spekith him-selue in a sermone þat he 24
mad and it begynnyth: In omnibus operibus vestris &c.   Thus
he wrytith þere on-to þe prestis whech were gadered be him in þe
monasterye at Ypone, he dwellyng in desert as for a tyme with his
hermytes: What is þe cause þat ȝe grucch for I abood stille with 28
myn heremites all þese estern halidayes?   It plesed me as for
þis tyme to departe fro ȝou and dwelle with hem, whom, as
I haue said often, I haue founden swech as I desire.   Whi are ȝe
troubled?   Be not þei very pore men in Crist, and for his loue 32

Leaf 24.
haue for ‖ sakyn al þis world?   Be not þei very buxum on-to all
my comaundmentis?   And in þe forme of good lyf þei ar fer be-for

ȝow. For þe her good exaumples was I turned on-to þe rith feith. He has always loved them, and by one of their founders, Simplician,
Euyr haue I loued hem, and euyr haue I desired for to folow heꝛ
holy *conuersacioñ.* Be þat goodman Simplician, whech is amongis
4 hem as a foun*dour*, was I broute on-to cristendam and lerned i*n* þe he was brought to the faith.
feith. Wherfor be ȝe not heuy of myn absens. Do thoo þingis
whech are plesau*n*t on-to me, and I schal be with ȝou alt dayes
on-to þe worldes ende.

[CHAPTER XXI.]

8 ¶ Who Augustin went on-to Simpliciane, and Simpliciane
grau*n*ted him xij heremites whech went with hi*m* to Affrik. **xxj.**

A FTIR þis his modeꝛ Monicha desired þat he and sche schuld Monica now wished to leave Italy.
go hom a-geyn on-to heꝛ owne cuntre and leue Melan and
12 alt Itale, for sche had alt hir desire whech sche desired in þis
world whan sche wist þat he was a trewe cristen man. Tho went Then Augustine went to Simplician and asked for men with whom to found a fellowship, and was given twelve of Simplician's holiest men.
he to Simpliciane and prayed hi*m* in most spec*ial* maneꝛ to grau*n*t
certeyn *persones* of his felauchip whech he wold lede on-to his
16 cuntre, as he saide, and leue þere with hem in holy *conuersacioñ.*
Simpliciane was ful glad of his desiꝛ and grau*n*ted him xij þe
moost proued men in *parfithnesse* of alt þat college. So he and
his moder and þese xij, with fouꝛ of his frendis, Nebridius, Euodi*us*,
20 Alipius & Poncian*us*, mad hem redy to go to þe see, wheꝛ þei schuld These, with his four friends, went with him to Africa. Of this he tells in one of his sermons,
schippe. Off þis mateꝛ spekith þis same glorio*us* doctouꝛ in a
sermon whech he mad of iij gendres of mu*n*kys; þus begy*n*nyth
þe *sermone*: Vt nob*is* per li*tter*as, and þus writith he þere: These Leaf 24, back.
24 be þe parfite men to whom I drow mech in tyme of my*n* erro*ur*,
‖ be whom eke I receyued þe lith of my feith, & for þe fame of
her holinesse was I baptiȝed in Crist. For at þe comau*n*dment
of my modeꝛ and desire of my frendis I went on-to þat god fadeꝛ
28 Simpliciane, and desired of him certeyn *persones* of his felauchip, saying that Simplician granted his request so readily because he knew that he wanted to found a monastery in Africa.
þat we schuld leue to-gidyr in þe bou*n*des of charite at hom in my
cuntꝛ. And he, ful faderly, whan he sey me wepe for swem þat
I had whan I schuld depart fro him, grau*n*ted me þe same men
32 whech I desired. But whi, hope ȝe, þat he grau*n*ted on-to me þis
felauchip so redyly? For he knew wel þat my desiꝛ was to edifie
a monasterie in Affrik in whech we schuld dwelle, folowyng þe

steppis of þe apostoles, specially in forsaking of worldly richesse

The names of Augustine's first mouks.
and in chois of wilful pouerte. Of þe men whech I led with me fro Simpliciane in-to Affiik, þese be þe names: Anastasius, Fabianus, Seuerus, Nicholaus, Dorotheus, Ysaac, Nichostrat*us*, i

Of Vitalis he speaks in 'De Verbis Domini et Apostoli,'
Paulus, Arillus, Stephan*us*, Iacobus & Vitalis. Off þis Vitalis speketh he specialy in a book cleped, De Ve*r*bis Dom*i*ni & Apostoli, in þe *ser*mone lxxxiiij whech beginnyth þus : Beati apo*st*oli epi*st*ola, where he tellith þat þis Vitalis was an huscher of gram*er* in Melan or þat tyme whech he cam to þe skole of

how he found a bag of gold, and set up scrolls to find the owner,
Simpliciane. So happed him to fynde a grete bagg of gold þat a marchaunt had lost. And a-non, as he had found it, he sette up scrowes[1] on certeyn gates in Melan, þat what man cowde telle very toknes schuld haue his gold a-geyn. The man cam þat had rith þertoo and told him þe very toknes, & he delyu*er*ed him his

Leaf 25.
gold with[-oute] ony delay. Tho þat ‖ man þat had lost þis mony sey þe treuth of þe fynder, profered him for his labou*r* xx s;

and refused to take reward,
Vitalus wold non receyue. He profered him x s, and þan v s, & euyr he refused it. He þat had lost þe mony was in partye wroth with þe fynder for he wold not take for his labou*r*, þrew

but was forced to, and gave it to poor men.
down þe bagge, saying on þis mane*r*: I lost nowt, take þou al. So was þis Vitalis compelled in partie to receyue þis v s as for his labou*r*, and he a-non gaue it to pore men, kepand to him-selue no part. For þis good dede praiseth Sei*n*t Augustin þis man, and

Of this Augustine writes.
for þis dede writith he here a comou*n* proposicion mech used in þe decrees : Quicquid i*n*uenisti & no*n* reddisti rapuisti. This is to sey in ou*r* tonge : What-so-eu*er* þou fyndist and gyuyst not a-geyn, þou stelist.

[CHAPTER XXII.]

¶ Who Augusti*n* with aff þis meny went to Rome to take þe se in Hostia fast by Rome & whi he taried þe*r*. **xxij.**

Monica was as a mother not only to Augustine but to all his friends,
TO aff þis felauchip þus gadered in fe*r* was Monicha a very moder, as goodly and as frendly to hem aff as þou3 sche had be mode*r* to hem alle, and eke as s*er*uyseable on-to hem as

---

[1] scl *crossed through.*

þou₃ sche had be doutir on-to hem. Fro Melan he went to Rome ^{and served them as}
be Tussie, wher he fond many heremites dwellyng in wodes and in ^{though she had been}
feldis, euene sette in þe same purpos in whech he was sette. Alle ^{their daughter.}
4 þese men for þe moost partie he visite with swete exhortacion of ^{When}
our Lord, with whech both he and þei wer ful vertuously refreschid. ^{Augustine reached}
Than cam he to Rome, and þere herd he mech noyse of þe Manichees ^{Rome he wrote 'De}
whech wer in Rome at þat tyme, teching here errouris ful prytyly, ^{Moribus}
8 be nyth specialy, ‖ for aspying. There at þe prayer of cristen ^{Leaf 25, back.}
men be mad too bokys. On hith De Moribus Manicheorum, the ^{Manichaeo-}
oþir hith De Moribus Ecclesie Catholice. This is to sey in Englisch, ^{rum' and 'De}
of þe maneris of Manicheis, and of þe maneris of hem þat be in þe ^{Moribus Ecclesiae}
12 cristen feith. In on of þese bokes tellith he þat þe Manicheis held ^{Catholicae,' in one of}
her skoles be nyth, and þedir cam both men and women, and all ^{which books he tells how}
sodeynly aftir þe lesson, þe lith schuld be blow out and þan schuld ^{the Mani-chaeans held}
þei pley, as Wiclif disciples played, Sistir me nedith. In þis cyte ^{their schools by night}
16 eke, or he went ouyr þe se, mad he þe book of whech we spoke ^{and played 'Sister me}
be-fore; it is cleped þe book of þe quantite of þe soule, whech is ^{needeth,' like Wyclif's}
mad¹ be maner of a dialoge be-twix him and his son Adeodatus, in ^{disciples.}
whech book many sotil þinggis ar touchid whech long not to þis
20 maner of wryting þat is cleped narratyf. In þis same cite and ^{Here also he wrote 'De}
þis same tyme eke mad he a notable book þat is cleped De Libero ^{Quantitate Animae' and}
Arbitrio, þat is to sey, of þe fre choys þat a man hath to good or ^{'De Libero Arbitrio,' also}
to euele. This book was mad in maner a-geyn þe Manicheis, for ^{against the Mani-}
24 her he determineth a-gayn hem þat all euele spryngith of þis fre ^{chaeans.}
choys, for þei seid þat euele was coeterne with God; so þei put to
þingis coeterne, on called þei good, þe oþir euele. All þis þing
witnesseth him-selue in his first book of his Retractaciones.

[CHAPTER XXIII.]

28 ¶ Who þei went all in fere fro Rome in-to Hostie. **cap. xxiij**.

THUS all þing sped at Rome for whech cristen men had ^{Then all his party went to}
reqwired him in defens of our feith, with all his felauchip ^{Ostia, the port of Rome.}
‖ he went forth to Hostie. Hostie is a fayr town xvj myle fro ^{Leaf 26.}
32 Rome where þat Tibir rennyth in-to þe se, for Hostium in þe
Latyn tonge is a dor, and þat is clepid so as a dor of þe se. Ther

¹ be mad *crossed through in red.*

One day he and Monica, leaning out of a window, lifted up their hearts in contemplation and fell into spiritual communion.

þei abood þe wynd and mad hem redy for to sayle. So up-on a day, as his moder and he stood lenyng out at a wyndown and lokyng in a gardeyn whech longid on-to her, in fer fro pres of puple þus a-lone, þei too talked ful sobirly of þe euyr-lestyn lif 4 whech is ordeyned for blessid soules. Thei talked so long þerof and lyft[1] up her hertis in contemplacion of þat holy place, þat þei had for-gete in maner þis world and all erdly þing, so wer þei rauyschid with[2] her holy wordis. Thei stood stille both a grete 8 while and þout swech þingis as þei coude not vttyr, and eke ageyn in[3] her holy comunicacion þei fell. Tho saide sche on-to hir son swech maner wordis: Son, as to my part, I telle I haue no delectacion in no maner þing þat is in þis world. What I schal do in þis 12 world, or why þat I am here so longe, I wote not veryly. Sumtyme I desired to abyde þat I schuld se þe a trew cristen man or I deyid. God hath graunted me þat and mech mor, for I se þe now nowt only a cristen man, but I se þe[4] a special seruaunt of God, for þou 16 hast despised all worldly felicite. This saide sche to hir son with ful sobir chere, and with-inne v. dayes aftir sche fel in a feuer, whech feuer encresed so sore up-on hir þat in mauer as for a tyme it had a-wey hir wittis. And whan sche was restored a-geyn to hir 20 wittis sche lokid on hir son, and þus sayd on-to him: Wher was I? Thei þat ‖ stood a-bout were al astoyned, and answered not. Than spak sche a-gayn in þis maner: Ley þis body whan I am ded in what place ȝe wil; haue no besynesse in no maner wher it schal be 24 byryed. O þing I pray ȝou of specialte, wher-euer ȝe be, at ony aucter wher ȝe schal ministir þe holy sacrament, in þat place haue of me sum special mynd. Sche had forgetyn, as Augustin tellith, al her cuntr and þe byrying of hir husbond whech was mad ful 28 costly and a space left for hir wher sche schuld ly. For a litil be-for her seknesse þei þat wer aboute hir, aftir grete communicacioñ of þe contempte of þe world and[5] of desire of good deth, þei inqwyrid of hir if sche was not aferd for to deye so fer fro hir 32 cuntr; sche answered to hem rith þus: No-þing is fer fro God. I am no-þing a-ferd þat God schuld not knowe fro whens he schuld

Soon afterwards a fever took her, and she lost consciousness, but recovered for a time, and gave those about her instructions as to her burial and their remembrance of her.

Leaf 26, back.

She was not afraid to die,

---

[1] MS. left *with* y *written over in red.*

[2] MS. with with, *the first crossed through in red.*

[3] MS. in heli her; heli *dotted underneath.*   [4] *inserted in red above.*

[5] MS. and and; *the first crossed through in red.*

reise me. So þe ix day aftir þe seknesse took hir̄, þat religious and her soul was released
soule, þat meke soule, was losed fro þe body, þe ȝere of hir age ĩvj, in the fifty-sixth year of
þe ȝere of Augustyn age xxxiij. And many noble men and religious her age, as we read in the
4 women ca*m* to hir exequies, as hir son tellith [in] þe ix book of his 'Confessions'. She
Confessiones. Thus was sche biried at Hostie and lay þere a m̃ ȝer̄ was buried at Ostia.
and mor̄ or sche was translate to Rome.

[CHAPTER XXIV.]

¶ The comendacio*n* & þe orison of Augusti*n* for his moder.
8 **xxiiij.**

IN þe nynth book of his Confessiones, in þe last ende, þere In his 'Confessions' he
touchith he þe deth of his modir and þe grete co*m*pleynt tells of the
mad for hir̄ both be oþir men and be him. Thus aftir oþ*er* complaint
12 þingis he seith of hir: Thi seruau*n*t, Lord, whom ‖ þou hast now Leaf 27.
take on-to þi m*er*cy, as þou knowist & as I be-leue, aftir þat made at her death.
tyme þat sche had take þi feith and þi baptem, sche defouled Augustine
neu*er* hir lippis with no v*n*clennesse whech schuld be offense says her words were
16 on-to þi lordchip; no lesingis wer̄ fou*n*de in hir tonge, no slaunder, pure,
no vice whech lo*n*gith on-to þat me*m*bir. Thou ɛaide, Lord, þat
what ma*n* with angri hert said on-to his broþir euele, or cleped
him fool, was gilty on-to þe peyne of helle. Here me, Lord, now and asks God to give
20 clepyng on-to þi grace for my moder whech stant in þi grace. her grace
Her̄ me for þe medycyne of þoo woundis whech þi son souered
in his body for þe helth of our̄ soules. Forgif hir ałł þe trespas and forgive her.
with whech sche offendid þe in þout, word, or werk. Entyr not
24 with hir i*n*-to þi dom. Lete þi mercy flete aboue þi dom.
I hope veryly þat þou hast doo now al þat I pray þe, but ȝet
alowe my gocd wil whech i offer on-to þe for hir as a deute of
hir child. Sche bond hir soule on-to þe prys of thi blod whil She was
28 ɛche lyued, for þere was no day left but ɛche wold be present pious while she lived,
where þe ɛacrifise and þe memory of þi holy blod ɛchuld be had
in mynde. Inspire, Lord, ałł þe rederes of þis book þat, in˙presens and her son asks all
of þe sacrame*n*t of þe aucter, þei may haue of þe soules of Patrik, readers to think of her
32 my fader, and Monicha, my moder, deuoute mynde, be whos at sacrament.
flesch I was brout forth on-to þis wor[l]d[1]. Many oþir holy
co*n*ceytes hath Augusti*n* her̄ if we had tyme to reherse hem.

[1] MS. word.

[Chapter XXV.]

¶ Aftir deth of his moder who he went in-to Cartage with his felauchip. cap. **xxv.**

After his
mother's
death Au-
Leaf 27,
back.
gustine
went to
Carthage,
a great port,
and lived in
the house of
Innocent,
who,
through
Augustine,
was healed
of a sore,

Whanñ his moder was ded and byried at Hostie, as we seid be-foȓ, with þe next wynd he and his felauchip sailed stȓeit 4 ‖ on-to Cartage, whech was a grete cite and strong, and mech named in þe world, specialy among*is* marchaundis. I haue mynd þat I haue red in Augustin bokes, I wot not now wheȓ, þat all marchaundise and al maneȓ makyng of schippis be-gan þeȓ. Theȓ 8 weȓ þei herborowid in a worthi mannes hous; þei cleped him Innocent. This same Innocent, swech tyme as Augustin was þere, had a greuous soȓ, whech soȓ myth not be hol, as þe lech said, with-oute*n* þat it weȓ slitte. The ma*n* was weyk and dred 12 mech þe knyf. So Augustin, meued of very compassion, prayed deuoutly to God for helth of his hoost, and sodeynly he was hool. Theȓ was gret me*r*ueyle of hem þat dwelt aboute, but þei all

as we read
in ' De Civi-
tate Dei '.
From Car-
thage, Au-
gustine and
his folk went
to Tagaste,
where all
dwelt with
their priests
under his
instruction.

with grete deuocion þankid[1] God of his werkis. Of þis same 16 myracle don at Cartage spekith Augusti*n* in þe **xxij** book of þe Cite of God, [2] so feȓ [2] as þouȝ a-noþir ma*n* had do þe same. Fro Cartage went þei hom to þe houses and[3] feldis þat longid on-to Augustin of herytage. Thus leued þei alle of þo godis whech 20 weȓ left him be his frendis, not vsyng husbondry but seld, now o part now an-oþir, for þei leued all be þat possession ny iij ȝere.[4] Augustin had take ȝet non ordres, but brout with him certeyn prestis a-mongis þoo h*e*remites whech he had of Simpliciane, and 24 þei all folowyng þe steppes of þe apostoles, dwelt to-gidir in on

hous with o soule in prayeȓ and fasting, ‖ and he him-selue, swech þingis as God had schewid to him, vttered it to oþir me*n* in writyng and techi*n*g, to her gret lerny*n*g.   28

[Chapter XXVI.]

¶ What bokes he mad whil he leued þus in his owne possession in þe town of Tagatens*es*. cap. **xxvj.**

DWELLYNG þus in his owne possession he wrot too bokes ageyn þe Manicheis, & þese cleped he De Genesi, for þere 32 tretith he mech of þe werkis of ouȓ Lord whech he wrout in þe

---

[1] o *and a stroke crossed through.*   [2–2] *in margin.*
[3] ad *in text; and in margin.*   [4] Thus *crossed through.*

begynnyng of þe world. Ther al-so mad he an ende of vj bokes of Musik whech he be-gan at Melan. The first v. bokes ar not redyly founde, þe sexte is had wher he tretith who we may ascende in owr 4 vndirstanding fro bodely and chaungable noumbres on-to goostly and permanent, whech permanent noumbres be in þat treuth whech is God. So he concludeth þat þoo inuisibil þingis whech be[1] in heuene ar vndirstand þe bettir for knowlech of bodely þingis whech' God 8 mad in erde. He seith ferþermor þat þouȝ þer be certeyn men her in erde þat haue so dul wit þat þei can-not vndirstand þis mater, ȝet if þei kepe treuly þe cristen feith, þei schul sumtyme se all þese þingis, & fele hem in swech sikirnesse þat þei may not 12 fayle. He seith eke þat summe men þat haue sotil wittis and vndirstand þis wel I-now, if it be so þat þei despise Crist, for al her[2] sotil kunnyng, þei schal be da[m]pned in hell. In þat same tyme eke, mad he a-noþir book þat is entitled þe[3] bok Of þe 16 Maistir. Þis bok is[4] ‖ in maner of a dialoge be-twix him and his son, for sone aftir þe bok was mad his son deyid. In þis book he seith þat þere is no very mayster to tech men þe treuth but God alone. That same tyme eke he mad a-noþir book whech 20 he nameth De Vera Religione, wher he tretith þat þere is no trewe ne very religion in al þe world but in þe cristen feith.

and 'De Musica', five books of which are rare; In the sixth he treats of earthly things as symbolical of heavenly,

knowledge of which cannot save despisers of Christ.

Leaf 28, back.

He wrote also 'De Vera Religione'.

[CHAPTER XXVII.]

¶ What was þe cause whi he went first to Ypone. **xxvij.**

THUS lyued our maystir in holy study and contemplacion so þat his fame be-gan to sprede, what lyf he held and 24 what doctrine he comuned to hem þat cam on-to hym,[5] so þat þe lith of his doctrine myth not be hid but raþer spred him-selue þorw þe cuntr. Of him herd a certeyn rych man þat dwelt þat tyme at Ypone[6] swech meruelous tydyngis þat þe man was gretly 28 stered to se him a[n]d[7] speke with him. For whech cause he sent messageris and letteris on-to Augustin, in whech letteris he comendid gretly his cunnyng and special his deuocion, þat he

So he lived at Tagaste,

till a rich man who had heard of his fame desired to see him,

---

[1] *inserted above.*
[2] *r afterwards inserted.*
[3] *a letter crossed through.*
[4] MS. is is.
[5] MS. hem *with* y *written above.*
[6] *part of* swech *written and crossed through.*
[7] MS. ad.

was only зoue to lernyng and good lyf, for whech exercise he had
and asked
Augustine to
go to Hippo,
for he was
ready to
follow him.
Augustine
went,
despised al þis worldly felicite. This man wrote ferþermoꝛ þat
if he wold com to Ypone he was redy to forsake al þe couetyse
of worldly possession and folow his steppes in þe wey of God. 4
For þis cause Augustyn consented on-to þe man, hauyng[1] a grete
desire to wynne swech a soule to Goddis seruyse whech was
so defouled in worldly vanyte. A-noþir cause was þere eke,
for Augustyn þoutз he schuld lyue þere in moꝛ quiete contemplacion 8
Leaf 29.
þan at hom amongis his kynrod and aqueyntauns. ‖ For he is
having the
purpose also
of building
a monastery,
and met the
man, who,
however, was
not then
converted.
in very purpos to edifie a monastery and to lyue þerin with his
brether aftir þe forme and þe ordinauns of þe aposteles. Thus.
is he come to Ypone, and þe man þat sent aftir him receyued 12
him ful worchipfully, but þe principal cause whech Augustin
supposed to spede, þat failed. For þe man herd deuoutly all
hise wordes but to þe very contempt of richesse coude he not
bring him as зet. Summe men suppose þat he cam to þat ende 16
aftirward, for, as þei sey, it myth not renne in veyn, þe labouꝛ
Of this
Augustine
speaks in
one of his
sermons,
þat ouꝛ Lord purveyid in so swete a vessel. That þese to þingis
weꝛ þe cause why þat Augustin went on-to Ypone, he witnessith
him-selue in a sermone intitled Of þe Comoñ Lif of Clerkis, wheꝛ 20
he seith þus : I, þat with þe grete mercy of God, зe se now зouꝛ
made after
he was a
bishop.
bischop, I cam зong on-to þis cite, and many of зow knowe.
I soute þat tyme a conuenient place where I schuld make a
monasterie, to lyue þere with`my bretherin. I cam eke on-to 24
þis cite for to wynne my frend on-to God, þat he schuld lyue
with us eke in þe monasterie. Me-þout at þat tyme a sikir
comyng on-to þis cite, be-cause þei had a bischop. For þat
place whech had non I refused as suspecte, þat I schuld not 28
be chose.

[CHAPTER XXVIII.]

¶ Who he edified a monastery in desert for him and certeyn
heremites. **xxviij.**

At Hippo
he made the
acquaintance
of Bishop
Valerius,
HE had not longe dwelt at Ypone or he fel in[2] aqweyntauns 32
of Valery, bischop þan of þat cite. This Valerie was
a ful goodly man, fre-hertet and namely on-to strauπgeris. So

---

[1] MS. haue, e *crossed and* yng *written over in red.*   [2] q *crossed through.*

Augustin, not fer fro þe cite þorw his fauouꝛ, edified a monasterie
in desert, ‖ and sowt all þe wodes aboute, for all þe heremites *Leaf 29,*
whech he myth fynde he gadered in-to o congregacion, as he *back.*
4 witnessith in a sermon writyn on-to þe prestes of Ypone and *whose favour he edified a*
alleggid be-fore, wheꝛ he seith þus: As ȝe know, I cam on-to *monastery in the desert*
þis cyte with my welbeloued frendis Euodio, Simplicio, Alipio, *and near the city, as he*
Nebridio & Anastasio. I cam hidir with a maner of a sikirnesse, *tells in a sermon.*
8 for I wist wel þat þe good fadeꝛ Valerius was bischop heꝛ. I cam *He went to Hippo for*
hidyr, not for to haue powere ouyr ȝou in dignite, but for to *humility and*
dwelle as an outcast in þe hous of ouꝛ Lord all þe dayes of my lyf. *not for dignity,*
I cam hidir, not for to receyue seruyse of oþer men, but for to
12 lyue¹ pesibily in desert with my breþerin. I brout no richesse
with me, but fauoured with þe grace of our Lord and with þe *and in his monastery*
good help of þe old man Valerie, I mad a monasterie here in *were*
desert with grete labouꝛ and bisinesse, whech monasterie stant *gathered the hermits from*
16 alone fer fro þe puple, and with grete þout I haue gadered þere *the woods,*
seruauntes of God whech dwelt alone, disparplied be þe wodes,
and þere begunne we for to lyue after þe maner and þe forme
of þe aposteles lif, þat all ouꝛ godis schul go in comon and no
20 man haue no maner þing propir to him-selue. Thus lyue þei²
in prayer, and wecch, and fasting, & many oþer vertues moꝛ þan *who passed their time in*
we may now expresse. That þis good old bischop gaue fauour *watching and fasting.*
and god on-to edifiyng³ of þis first monasterie witnessith Augustin
24 eke in þe forsaid sermone, Vt nobis per litteras, wheꝛ he seith *In his sermon he speaks of*
þus on-to þo same heremites: ȝe be my vyne, chosen of me, sette *the help of Valerius,*
in þe myddis of þe cherch, as þouȝ it ‖ were in þe myddis of *Leaf 30.*
paradys. This vyne haue I, in þe vertu of God, gadered to-gydyr,
28 and werkmen haue I sette⁴ þere þat þei schuld trauayle and
bryng forth frute in heꝛ tyme. To þis vyne I haue chose ȝou,
to þis heritage I haue gadered ȝou, with þe fauour of þe holy
man Valery, whech of þe cherch godis ȝaue me grete plente to *who gave him goods*
32 þe edificacion of my monastery, for my patrimonie myth not *of the church.*
suffise to þe⁵ grete expense and he had not holpe me.

---

¹ *word wrongly written and altered in red.*
² *in margin in red.*   ³ *MS. edifieng with* y *written over.*
⁴ þidir *crossed through.*   ⁵ *added in red in margin.*

[CHAPTER XXIX.]

¶ Of þe noumbyr of þo heremytes whech he gadered, and of her holy conuersacion. capi*tulum* **xxix.**

The hermits thus gathered together were the beginning of the order of the Hermits of St. Augustine.

IN þis same monastery Augusti*n*, or he were prest, gadered a grete noumbyr of heremites whech lyued, as we sayde 4 be-foꝛ, aftir þe forme and þe ordinau*n*s of þe apostoles, and he heꝛ[1] began þat ordꝛ whech we clepe at þis day, and þe cherch of Rome clepith hem þe same in aꝇ þe bullis of heꝛ preuylegis, þe ordre of þe heremites of Seynt Augustyn. First dwelt þei 8 in dyu*er*s wodes, heꝛ on and þere anoþer, and euerych of hem

From anchorites they became cenobites,

lyued as hym lyked tyl þat ouꝛ auctouꝛ gadered hem to-gidyr & mad of anachorites cenobites. He ꞩpekith him-selue[2] of hem[2] in þe ꞩermone often rehersid, þus: I cam in-to Affrik, my good 12 modyr ded, & edified, as ȝe ꞩe, a monastery in desert ferꝛ fro dwellyng of men. And blessed be God, I haue gadered þere a noumbir of breþerin whos hertis are ꞩo inspired with gostly lith þat

and followed more nearly the apostolic ideal than any of their predecessors.

not only þei be foloweri*s* of holy faderis whech lyued in solitarie 16 lif, but now þei folow þe noble steppes of þe aposteles, for al þing is como*n* on-to hem. Many faderis weꝛ be-foꝛ me whom for to folow is ful profitable, but ꞃon of hem went nyher þe

Leaf 30, back.
The habit of this order was a black cope.

apostoles lif þan I. Therfoꝛ ‖ may I ꞩey þat I aꞁ fader and hed 20 of ȝou aꝇ. The habite of þis ordꝛ was a blak cope girt with a girdil of ledir with-oute*n* ony barꝛ, as he witnessith in þe forsaid ꞩermone, hauyng þese wordes on-to þe prestis þat dwelt in þe monasterie: Go to my*n* heremites and lerne of hem to be 24 meke of hert, pore of spirit, and childyrn of obediens. Loke if ȝe be swech as þei be. Wold God ȝe were swech as I fynde

Augustine contrasted his gaudy priests with his simple hermits, for whom he made a book of rules called the 'Margarites of Paradise',

hem. ȝe be renneres a-boute þe cyte; and þei fle þe sith of men. ȝe be arayed with dyu*er*s colouri*s* and dyu*er*s furris; þei 28 are co*n*tent with a blak cloth. ȝe haue girdilis lich knytys; and þei with þongis of chamel skynnys, as Hely and Ion, go[3] girt in heꝛ lendes. To þese same heremites mad he a book of c*er*teyn reules, who þei schuld lyue, whech reules he cleped þe Margarites of 32 Paradise, and þei be comprehendid in þe first ꞩermone þat he

---

[1] *in red in margin.* [2-2] *added above in red.*
[3] *l crossed through.*

mad to hem¹ whech sermone beginnyth, Fra*tre*s mei & leticia compre-
hended in
his first
sermon to
them.
cordis mei.   Many of þo same put he aftirward in his reule whech
he called a Mero*ur as*² a man may sone p*er*seyue.

[CHAPTER XXX.]

4   ¶ Who Augustin was chose prest of þe monast*er*ie vndir Valery
þe bischop, to haue þe reule of þe cherch. **xxx.**

IN þis same tyme þe prest of þe cherch at Ypone was ded, and The priest of
the church
þis Valeri*us* gadered þe puple and þe clergie to ordeyn a at Hippo
being dead,
8 new successou*r* whech schuld be*r* al þe charge of þe cherch, for þe
bischop was old and myth not labou*r*; he was alsoo a Grek of
birth³ and coude not p*ar*fithly þe langage of þat cu*n*tre. A-mongis
all oþir Valery sent for Augusti*n*, and before all þe puple sayde it Valerius
asked the
12 was þe custom ‖ þat þei schuld haue þe chois, but neu*er*-þe-lasse⁴, Leaf 31.
þe puple knew wel be certeyn toknes þat he wold preferre Augusti*n* people to
choose a
successor,
to þis dignite.   Augusti*n* be-cause he had take ȝet non ordres stood
a-mongi*s* þe puple in a ma*n*er of a sikyrnesse, as he þout þat no
16 man schuld chese him be-cause he was not in ord*r*.   Thus as he and they all
cried out for
Augustine.
stood, sodeynly all þe puple chase him with o voys, leyd handis up-
on hym, and as þe ma*n*er was, *pre*sented him on-to þe bischop.   He
wepte, and with-drow him meruelyling sore þat þei we*r* þus set on He wept and
refused,
20 him, alleggi*n*g þe *per*el of þat dignite to haue gouernau*n*s of so
grete a puple; but þe mo*r* he refused it þe mo*r* þei desired him,
and cryed fo*r* þat Augusti*n* schuld be her prest.   Thus was he but they
insisted, and
brout on-to þe bischop, and he, with ful grete reue*re*ns and deuo- he was
invested by
24 cio*n*, gaf him his ordres.   Afftir he was þ*us* mad prest of þe cherch Valerius.
Yet when he
he dwelled stille with his h*er*emites whos felauchip he had eue*r* was priest he
dwelt still
desired, but þe bischop say wel þat it was ouyr fer*r* fro þe cite with his
hermits.
euyr for to go to and fro, a*n*d þe occupacio*n* of þe cherch was
28 grete, þe desi*r* eke of Augusti*n* eue*r* for to be with his h*er*emites, of
grete discrecio*n* ordeyned þis mene whech fulfillid⁵ both þing*is*, þat
is to seye, þat⁶ þe cherch schuld be wel s*er*uyd with þe *pre*sens of

---

¹ MS. to hem to hem, *the first crossed through in red.*
² and *crossed through and* as *written over in red.*   ³ h *added in red.* ⁽
⁴ þe-lasse *added above in red.*   ⁵ fulfill *in text*, llid *in red in margin.*
⁶ t *added in red.*

Augusti*n*, and eke he schuld not be fer fro his welbeloued heremites. The mene was þis, þat a fayͬ place schuld be mad fast be þe monast*er*ie and certeyn [1] heremites schuld be chose fro þe first place and dweͥ in þe secu*n*d with whech ouͬ Augustin myth 4 speke whan he list. This was fulfillid in-dede, and su*m*me of þe best of þis first [2] monast*er*ie [3] weͬ drawe to þis secu*n*d, and Augustin gadered to heͬ nou*m*bir mo owt of ‖ þe world, not lewid men but clerkys and lerned men, and þ*er*e sette he hem in þe same reule 8 þat þe first monastery had, þat þei schuld lyue in co*m*oͦ, and no ma*n* to haue noþing prop*ir* to him-self. This same processe writith þis docto*ur* ful pleynly in a s*er*mone De Commu*n*i Vita Clerico*rum*, allegged be-fore, and in a-noþir s*er*moͦ to þe prestis of 12 Ypone begy*n*nyng, In omn*ibus* op*er*ibus u*e*stris.

[Chapter XXXI.]

¶ Who Auguͤtin lerned þese me*n* of þe secu*n*d mon*a*sterie, & who he prechid eke in presens of his bischop. Cap*itulum* xxxj.

THESE men þus chosen to þe secu*n*d mon*a*sterye studied in 16 dyuy[ni]te [4] and in moraͥ bokes at þe comau*n*dment of her maystir, for he lerned hem so þat þei schuld come to þe cite to preche þe puple & edifye hem with Goddis word. The bischop Valery, seyng þe grete cu*n*nyng of Augustin, and eke þe grete 20 desiͬ þat he had to preche þe word of God, þankid God often sithe þat he had sent him in his age so good a vikeͬ. For, as he seid to þe puple, his prayer was herd whech he had long prayed, þat God schuld send hi*m* swech a man þat myth edifie his puple both with 24 exau*m*ple and doctryne. For he him-self was not rith redy to swech þingis, for he was not gretly letteryd, and eke born he was of þe Grek to*n*ge and coude not mech skil on Latyn bokes whech weͬ vsed most in þe prouy*n*ce of Cartage. Wherfoͬ he grau*n*ted 28 Augusti*n* leue a-geyn þe custom of þe cherchis of Affrik to prech in þe cherch in his presens. For whech þing many oþir bischoppis grucchid a-geyn þis new custom, be he rowt not, ne sette no pryse

---

[1] MS. *her crossed through.*   [2] *added in red at margin.*
[3] *wat crossed through.*
[4] MS. *dyuyte with contraction mark over first y.*

be swech grucching tong*is* þe whilis þat Augusti*n* supplied [1] swech
good ‖ werkis whech he coude not do him-selue. For be þe prechyng Leaf 32.
of Augusti*n* many soules were goten to God. He ferd lich a gret and by this means many were brought to God.
4 lith sette al̃ on hy, þat al̃ men in þe grete hous of our Lord [2] had
direccion in her werkys be his schyny*ng*. This ensaumple ran oute Throughout Africa this example was followed.
þorw þe lond of Affrik, þat þo *prestis* whech weᵽ wel-lerned men
had leue to *preche* in *presens* of her bischoppis. And as we saide
8 be-fore, Augustin gat leue of Valery þat [3] þese *heremites* whech
dwelt in þe secund monastery were admitted to preche and
schryue, not alle, but þoo whech were lerned in diuinite and
custumablely vsed in good lyf. This witnessith he in þat *sermone* Augustine speaks of the preaching of the brethren in the monastery endowed by Valerius, in one of his sermons.
12 often alleggid, Vt *bene* nostis, where he seith þus: Tho bretherin
sette in þe monasterie whech ouᵽ good fader Valery endewid, þouȝ
it be so þat þei dwelle not in þe cite, be-cause heᵽ fame was [4] mech
boᵽ a-mong*is* þe puple, þerfor haue I ordeyned þat þei [5] schul preche
16 þe word of lif on-to þe puple, and bry*ng* trew soules be heᵽ gode
ensaumples to Him þat mad al of nowt. Behold who þai deme þe
erde and by*n*de it & lose swech as þei wil eue*r* with þe fauouᵽ
of God.

[CHAPTER XXXII.]

20 ¶ Who he disputed with a grete *heretik* clepid Fortunat*us* and
*con*uicte hi*m* of heresie. **xxxij.**

I N þat same tyme þe heresie of þe Manicheis encresid in þe At that time the Manichaean heresy was advanced in Hippo by Fortunatus, and the people asked Augustine to contest him.
cite of Ypone, þorw labouᵽ and doctri*ne* of a grete capteyn
24 of hem cleped Fortunate, whech had *per*uerted many soules fro þe
trewe feith. For whech cause þe best citeceynes requyred heᵽ
prest, Augustin, to speke with þis Fortunat, & refelle, if he myth,
þe h*er*esie with whech he had deseyued many soules. Augusty*n*,
28 whech was redy ‖ to answere eue*ry* man and for to talk of þe feith, Leaf 32, back.
hope and [6] charite whech weᵽ plenteuously with-inne him, forsok
not þis conflicte, but obeied rydily heᵽ peticio*n*, inqwyri*ng* of hem
if Fortunate wold consente to þis dede. Tho went þei to Fortunate,
32 and reqwyrid him with swech instauns þat he myth not denye heᵽ

---

[1] *a character crossed through.*   [2] *in red in margin.*
[3] *þ and a stroke crossed through.*   [4] *w crossed through.*
[5] *added above in red.*   [6] *w crossed through.*

Augustine met him and had notaries to record his words. desi͞r. Thus is þe day come of þis comunicacio͞n; grete puple is gadered and notaries sette on both sides whech schuld repoɪt treuly þe wordis þat we͞r saide. For þis was euyr þe practik of Augusti*n* whan he schuld dispute with ony heretik, to write he͞r wordes, þat ɪ þei schuld not denye o tyme whech þei graunted anoþer tyme.

The contro- versy lasted two days, and was on the origin of evil. Too dayes lestid þis disceptacio͞n. The question disputed amongis hem was þis, Fro whens þat euel comth. Augustin held þis opinion, þat euel be-gynnyth in a man rith of his fre choys, for 8 þere schuld no euel be in him but he wold. Fortunate held þat euel was a natu͞r coeterne with God, þat is to sey, euene as God hath be, euyr so hath þat natu͞r euele[1] euyr be. In þis disputacio͞n

Fortunatus was van- quished by Augustine and fled. This is all recorded in a book, þis Fortunat coude not hurt Augustin with[2] non argume*n*t, ne his 12 owne opinione coude he not defende, so faylyng in his answeres & foule aschamed, he fled oute of þe cuntre, and þat heresie whech [3]he held[3] fel fro euery mannes hert. This act sette Seynt Augustin in a book, þat men aftirward schuld knowe þe conflict be-twix hem. 16

At this time, too, he made a book on In þis same tyme mad he anoþir book whech he clepith Of þe[4] Sermo͞n of Crist saide in þe hill, where he hath a notable exposicion

Leaf 33. up-on þe Pater-N*oster*, ‖ for þat same is a grete part of þat sermon whech Crist sayde in þe hill. Thus prechid þat nobil prest, Augustin, 20

the Sermon on the Mount. with grete auctorite distroyed heresie and planted new religio͞n, so þat his name[5] was spred þorw þe lond.

[CHAPTER XXXIII.]

¶ Who Augusty*n* was chose bischop Vale[r]y lyuy*n*g in þat see. cap. xxxiij.   24

All this time Valerius feared that Augustine might be appointed bishop in another city, and there- fore wrote to the bishop of Carthage, **A**Mongis all þe ioye þat þis bischop Valery had for ou͞r Lord had sent hi*m* swech a preest, he caute with þat a gret fe͞r, and in partye a gelosie, þat Augustyn schuld not go fro hym, and be chose a bischop in a-noþer cyte. For þat same had he do or 28 þis tyme had not Valery sent him owt of þe weye, weny*n*g to many men þat he schuld not sone come a-geyn. For þis cause he sent priuy letterys to þe bischop of Cartage, primate of þat lond,

[1] u *crossed through.*   [2] o *crossed through.*
[3]-[3] *in margin in red.*   [4] cr *crossed through.*
              [5] *added above in red.*

þat Augustyn schuld be promoted to þis dignite, in whech *lettres* asking for his appointment in Hippo.
he alleggid his age, his febilnesse, and eke who he was not redy in
langage to erudicioñ of þe puple and destruccion of heresie as
4 Augustin was. The bischop of Cartage þat knew Augustin wel
sent down *letter*is of confirmacion þat aH þat Valery had reqwyrid
him he held ferme and stable. This bischop of Cartage was He gathered the primates of Africa at Hippo,
primate þorw aH Affrik, þan was þere anoþir bischop *prim*ate of
8 al Numidie, and for him sent Valery, and eke for a-noþir worthi
man, þei clepid him Megasie, bischop of a cite clepid Orilamense ;
mo bischoppis sent he for and clerkys to Ypone, and whan þei were
gadered to-gidyr, be-fore þe puple sodeynly he vttir his desire þat and there asked that Augustine
12 Augustin schuld be bischop and þei both schuld lyue to-gidyr in
comoñ of þe ‖ [1] cherchis good. The puple, whañ þei herd þis, þei Leaf 33, back.
þankid God heyly and with o uoys þei cryed þat Augustyñ schuld should be appointed bishop, while he lived.
be bischop. He mad grete allegaunce ageyn þis eleccion and seide
16 it was not *conuenient* þat þei schuld chese a-new, þe old lyuyng, but Augustine demurred, for the appointment was against the statutes of the church,
for aH þat he coude say, Valerie is desir was fulfillid, and Augustyn
consecrate, and þe cure leyd only in him. And a-geyn þis maner
of eleccion wrot Seynt Augustyn aftirward to þe court of Rome, þat
20 he schuld be excused of his errour, for þere was mad a statute of
holy cherch in þe councel at Antioche, þat þere schuld no bischop
make a-noþer whil he lyued, as it is pleynly *conteyned* in þe decres[2],
capitulum viij, qua*estione* I., epi*scop*o non licet. So Seynt Augustin but the appointment was made.
24 wold not þat þing do, in him not rithfully schuld not be drawe to
oþir men in [3] ensaumple. Thus whan he was bischop with gretter
auctorite and more feruent loue, he prechid þe word of God, nowt
only in his owne diosise, but wher-euyr he was reqwyred, most
28 specialy wher heresie regned., þidir went he to defende þe feith.

[CHAPTER XXXIV.]

¶ Off þe þird monasterie whech he gadered of chanones with-
inne þe paleys. **cap. xxxiiij.**

WHanñ he was mad bischop he say weel þat for þe grete Augustine saw that, as a bishop, he must keep a household,
32 multitude of causes & þe grete prees of straungeris þat
daily cam on-to him, he must hold a houshold, and he myth not go

---

[1] cherchis *wrongly written and crossed through.*
[2] þe secunde *crossed through.*   [3] *written small above.*

and therefore he chose certain good to his refeccion euery day to nepir of þese to monasteries of whech we spoke, þerfor he chase certeyn prestis of good lyf and gret

Leaf 34. lettiruꝛ to leue with him in þat college, and ‖ þo same men bonde

priests to dwell with him aus- terely in a 'college', whence come the Canons called now Augustinian, to leue vndir obediens, chastite and fro propirte of temporal richesse, 4 as þo heremites lyued in þe to monasteries saide be-fore. And owt of þis colege cam þese chanones þat ar called at þis day of ordꝛ of Seint Augustin, þouȝ it be so þat þei be distincte in oþer habite þan[1] þei þat weꝛ with Seint Augustin, for þei went in dyuers 8 colouris a[n]d[2] furris, as chanones do now in cathedral cherchis. But be-cause þat þese chanones in blak habite kepe moꝛ streytly þe reule of Seynt Augustin, as touching þat poynt to lyue in comoñ, þerfor, I suppose, þat þei be nyher Seynt Augustin þan þe 12 othir.[3] And þerfor is þere meued a question in þe lawe wheþir

and concern- ing whom there is moved a question as to the rule. þe chanones of cathedral cherchis be bounde þorw-oute þe world for to kepe þe reule of þis doctour whech he[4] mad on-to hem, & it is cleped De Vita Clericorum, or nowt, and þei sey nay þerto, for 16 be-cause he myth bynde[5] no cherch but his owne. Wherfor me semeth þat þo chanonis whech be clepid reguleꝛ ar moꝛ ny Seint

This third monastery is mentioned in Augustine's sermon, and also the reason for its establish- ment. Augustin þan þoo þat be clepid seculeꝛ. This same glorious doctouꝛ in a famous sermone whech he mad of þe comoñ lif of 20 clerkys, and it beginnyth Propter quod nolui & rogaui, makyth mynde of þis þirde monasterie in swech maneꝛ wordes: It plesid God for to sey on-to me þat I schuld ascende to hier degre, for aftir þe tyme þat my fame was bore in þe puple, I be-gan to 24 drawe me fro euery place whech wanted a bischop. But a seruaunt may not sey nay to his lord. Wherefor, whan I was mad bischop, I aspied wel þat I must chere men þat cam on-to me with mete

Leaf 34, back. and drynk, for if I ded not, I schuld ‖ be hald on-gentil, and if I led 28 my gestis on-to þo monasteries whech I haue mad, þe custom schuld not be good, for þe most part of þo heremites desire not mech to haue grete conuersacioñ with þe puple. This was þe cause whi þat I gadered þese clerkis in o colege with-inne þe hous 32 or þe place whech longith principaly to the bischoprich. These same wordes hath he in a sermone to þe same prestis of Ypone whech be-gynnyth: In omnibus operibus vestris. Many þingis

---

[1] *written wrongly and* n *written above.*   [2] MS. ad.
[3] þer *crossed through.*   [4] *written small above.*
[5] *written small above.*

myth we plant in here, who þat he loued bettyr þe felauchip of
þe *her*emites þan of þe *pr*estis in þe cathedral cherch, and¹ what The priests were jealous of the hermits.
grucch*ing* þe same prestis made a-geyn þis affeccio*n*, but al̴t þis
4 I ley be-side and wil *pr*ocede to þe oþir part of his lif.

[CHAPTER XXXV.]

¶ Who þese *her*emites we*r* fou*n*de be þe possession of þe cherch
and what worthy men grew of his college. **XXXV.**

NOWT only þe prestis of þe colege were fou*n*de and fedde with
8 þe possession of þe cherch, but eke þe *her*emites had part,
þou3 he*r* part we*r* not so² plenteuou*s* as was þe oþir. In a In one of his sermons, 'Of prayer,' he speaks of the blessedness of hermit-life,
*s*ermone þat he mad on-to þe same heremites, entitled, Of praye*r*,
he makith my*n*de of þis mate*r*, and þus he seith: Be not wery of
12 3ou*r* praye*r*, for 3e haue bettir leyse*r* to pray þan su*m*me oþir and how he cared for the hermits.
haue. 3e be not ordeyned for to gouerne oþir men, but³ for to
leue in solitary lyf and deuoute praye*r* to God. And þat 3e
schuld pray þe more hertly, and not be lettyd with no cold whech
16 schuld withdrawe 3ou*r* deuocio*n*, for þis cause, of swech godes as
longe to þe cherch of Ypone, I haue ‖ do mad 3ou clothis & hosyn Leaf 35.
and schon þerto an hundred and xl̴, whech I wil þat þei be kept in
a como*n* vestiary, þat eu*er*y man may haue p*ar*t as him nedith.
20 Thus norchid þis noble ma*n* þese pore creatures, and on þe othir Others who dwelt with him he taught divinity.
side þoo *per*sones þat dwelt with him in þe cherch he lerned hem
dyuynyte, for at eu*er*y mel⁴ had þei notable communicacio*n* of holy
scriptu*r*, and eu*er* alle þe answeres must fynaly come fro Augusti*n*.
24 Owt of his hous, as we rede, him lyuy*ng*, were chose x bischoppes⁵, Out of his house ten bishops were chosen, and many famous men joined him,
men of gret lettiru*r* and of parfith lyf. For many famous men at
þoo dayes, seing þe grete *per*feccio*n* and holy conu*er*sacio*n* of þat
felauchip whech Augustyn had drawe on-to him, forsok all þe
28 pomp of þe world, com and lyued with him in ful gret p*er*feccio*n*,
su*m*me a-mong*is* þe *her*emites, su*m*me a-mong*is* þe prestis, eu*er*y
man aftir þat he sauored. And many of hem, wha*n* þei had be
with him 3eres and were roted in religio*n*, with his leue went fro

---

¹ *of crossed through in red.*   ² *written in red above.*
³ *written in red above.*   ⁴ *written in red in margin.*
⁵ *s added in red.*

and some of his men founded monasteries in other lands,

him in-to oþir cuntres, mad monasteries, gadered felauchip and so encresid his ordre, not only in Ypone, but þorw þe lond, him lyuyng.

[CHAPTER XXXVI.]

¶ Of þe maneres and þe habite of Seynt Augustin aftir he was 4 bischop. **xxxvj.**

In all things Augustine was sober and serious, exhorting religious people, and cheerful to secular.

Leaf 35, back.

THIS same glorious doctour, fader and norcher of clerkys, in his habite, in goyng, in sittyng, in his wordes, contenauns and maneres, was of swech sadnesse þat euery man whech cam to 8 his presens was edified be him. To religious men and women he was in his exhortaciones sad and sobir, ȝeuyng hem grete ensaumple who þei schuld do. To othir ‖ seculer men þat were occupied in þe world he was familiar, and in his talkyng had on-to hem in 12 maner of mery langage with stedfast cher of sadnesse. The o puple coumforted he with sad talking to conferme hem in her holinesse. The oþir puple gadered he on-to a perfeccion with goostly myrth

He corrected wrong-doers gently.

and deuoute iocundnesse. Transgressiones a-geyn Cristis law or 16 his holy preceptis he correctid not boystously, but fadirly and in fayre maner, þat many euele men, seing his swete correccion, wer

His clothes were neither costly nor wretched,

þe rather turned fro synne. His cloþis whech he wered dayly, & his cloþis þat serued to his bed, þei wer not ouyr costful, ne 20 ouyr wrecched [1], but in þe most mesurable maner, he ordeyned þei schuld be. In summe men we lakkyn þe grete cost of aray, and

but made in the mid-way.

with summe ar we wroth with her sluttynesse. Þerfor went þis man þe myd weye, þat he schuld ȝeue ensaumple in cloþing to hem 24 þat wer [2] his foloweris, and oþir men whech wer not of his skole schuld haue no mater of detraccion. Thus spekith he in a famous

He desired no man to give him costly clothes, which would distinguish him from his brethren.

sermon þat begynnyth: Caritati vestre. I wil þat no man ȝyue to me so precious cloþis whech þat I, as of a specialte a-boue oþir, 28 schuld wer. Ensaumple he puttith. I sette case þat sum man gyue me an amyse mor precious þan I am wone to were, þat I schuld haue swech a singuler þing passyng all my breþerin. Vphap it semeth a bischop for to were swech on, þouȝ it semeth 32 not Augustyn a pore man, born of mene men. For if I receyued

[1] d *added above.*   [2] her *crossed through.*

swech a þing and wered it, ‖ men schuld sey þat I haue founde[1] Leaf 36.
moꝛ precious garmentis in þe cherch þan I myth haue had in my
faderes hous.   Lete men gyue me swech cloþis þat in nede my

4 breþerin, be þei prestis, dekenes or subdeknes, may were þe same.
I am a-knowe be-for God and ȝou þat of a precious cloth I am
a-schamed, for it is non pertinent to ouꝛ profession, ne conuenient
to my white herys.

He required
only clothing
such as any
of his
brethren
might wear.

[CHAPTER XXXVII.]

8   ¶ Of his diete and seruyse at his table.   cap. xxxvij.

LYTIL mete for þe most partye vsed he at his table, for he
had more delectacioñ in þe heryng of holy lessones and
talkyng aftir up-on þe same þañ in bodely mete.   Flesch ete he

12 but seldom, and þat was whañ he had gestis; wortes and letuse
and swech herbis ete he most.   I trowe þat he had þe vse of Itaile
whilles he studied þere, and coude not litly out of þe same vse, for
þei ete not mech at onys.   Wyn drank he euyr ful mesurablely,

16 and þat medeled with watyr, for þe wyn of þat cuntꝛ is hoot.
Swech mete and drynk[2] as he had in vse was not warned to no
man þat wold ask it, weꝛ þei dwelleris of þe cite, weꝛ þei
straungeris.   A-mongis aĺ oþir vices he hatyd gretly detraccion,

20 specialy at mel, for a-geyn þat vis had he writyn at his table þese
too vers: Quisquis amat dictis absentem rodere vitam, Hanc mensam
vetitam nouerit esse sibi.   Þis is to sey in Englisch: What man
with wordis absent bitith his broþeris name, This bord fro him

24 forbodyn it is with blame.   Sumtyme þei þat sat þeꝛ wold speke
largely of hem þat weꝛ absent, & þañ ‖ wold Augustyn say on-to
hem þat, but þei wold leue her detraccioñ, he must rase oute þo
vers.   Eke sumtyme whan þei wold not leue lithly, he wold rise

28 and go fro hem fastyng.   Grete wast was not in his hous of sotil
metes.   For on a tyme certeyn gestis schuld dyne with him, and
a licorous felaw a-mongis hem stert in-to þe kechyn to loke what
mete was þere in araying, and fond þe hous cold.   Tho cam he

32 on-to þe bischop and inqwyrid of him what mete he had ordeyned
for his gestis, and Augustin answered him þat he knew no moꝛ
þan he.   Deuoute puple cam moꝛ to him for goostly communica-

He ate little
at table,
and lived
mostly on
roots and
lettuce.

He drank
little wine,
and that
diluted. All
were free to
his table.

He hated
detraction,
and had two
lines against
it engraved
on the
common
board.

Leaf 36,
back.

No great
delicacies
were to be
had in his
house.

---

¹ p *crossed through.*   ² *written above in red.*

Upon the poor he had compassion and gave them of the church's goods.

cioꝺ þan bodely mete. Vp-on pore men had he grete compassion, and gaf hem largely of þe cherchis good. For sumtyme made þe vesseles of syluyr whech longed on-to þe cherch to be molten, and þe weggis þerof be sold and departed to poꝛ men. And whaꝺ he 4 was in grete nede þat he myth not[1] gyue hem whech weꝛ in myschef, þaꝺ wold he openly denouns þis to þe puple, and þei[2]

He gave little to his kindred,

wold brynge him sufficiens to his entent. To his kynrod also he wold gyue part of þat same cherchis good, but in no grete plente, 8 for he wold help hem with þat good, but not make hem rich. Thus spekith he in þis mateꝛ in þat same sermon þat beginnith,

saying that the goods of the church were for the poor,

Vt nobis per *litt*eras: We bischoppis may not haue þese temporal godes of þe cherch as ouꝛ possessioꝺ, ne I þat am a bischop haue 12 not þese godes to non oþir entent but for to dispense & departe

Leaf 37.

hem on-to pore men, for þe godes of þe cherch ‖ þei be þe patri-monie of poꝛ men. And þerfor I must be ful war þat I take not ꝼe godes of my cherch fro poꝛ men and gyue it rich men, and God 16 be þankid, I haue in þis mateꝛ do wel on-to þis tyme. For I haue mech folk of my kynrod, and summe of hem rich and wel at ese, and summetyme come þai to me with þretis, sumtyme with fayꝛ

and there-fore he had never en-riched his own people. Poor men were nearer his heart than rich men.

wordis, and þus þei sey: Fader, we be þi flesch & þi blood; gyue 20 us sum of þat good þat þou hast in dispensacioꝺ. And for all heꝛ crying, þankid be God and ȝouꝛ gode prayeres, I haue no mynde þat euyr I mad with þe cherchis godes ony of my kynrod rych. Pore men be moꝛ ny myn hert þan rych men, for we[3] þat be 24 cleped in-to þe parfite lif in þe cherch, if we haue cloth and mete, we schuld be content with-al, and in tokne þerof be ouꝛ hedes schaue al baꝛ, þat euene as þe her is baꝛ þeꝛ, so schuld ouꝛ hertis be voyd fro couetise. 28

[CHAPTER XXXVIII.]

¶ Off his conuersacion and oþir blessid condiciones whech he had and vsed. Capitulum xxxviij.

He was kind to orphans, widowꝛ, and sick men.

FADERLES childyrn and widowes[4] whaꝺ þei weꝛ in ony tribulacioꝺ he wold visite, and seke men eke with his owne 32 handis wold he lefte and coumfort, and sumtyme þo whech he

---

[1] *written in red above.*   [2] *written in red above.*
[3] *written above.*   [4] þ *crossed through.*

visite weᵽ made hool and sound. Theᵽ weᵽ certeyn men whech He cast out spirits;
weᵽ vexid with wikkid spiritis and he prayed for hem, and þei
were hool. In þe xxij book of þe Cyte of God he tellith too
4 myracules of him-selue in swech maner as þow a-noþir man had
do hem. I knew, he seith, a virgine at Ypone whech virgine he healed a virgin at Hippo
receyued[1] oyle of a prest, and whech tyme[2] sche had anoynted
hir with þe same oyle and þe prest with bittir teris prayed ‖ for Leaf 37, back.
8 hir, sche was hol. A-noþir tale he tellith þere; he seyth he knew through his prayers;
a bischop þat prayed for a ȝong man in whom þe deuele had and he cast out a devil.
entered, and a-non, aftir his prayeᵽ, þe ȝong man was hool.

To elde men was þis fader a very noryce and supported hem He cared for old men, and
12 with ful grete reuerens, as men may rede in a sermon whech he in a sermon he tells his
mad a-geyn ydilnesse, and it beginnyth: Apostolus Petrus, wheᵽ young monks to nurture
he seith þus: If it be so þat þere be a-mongis ȝou in ȝouᵽ the aged and work for
monasterie eld men þat passe iiij score ȝere, whech haue lyued in them,
16 clennesse of body and soule many ȝeres, and endewred in holy
exercise, þat is to seyn, fastyng, wakyng, and oþir bodyly penauns,
These men fro þat age forward schul beᵽ non office ne no charge of
þe monastery, for þei ded whil þei myth. Grucch ȝe not þat be
20 ȝonger, þouȝ þei do not now as þei ded sumtyme, for þei[3] may not.
If þei rest whan ȝe labouᵽ, merueyle not. If þei be worchippid of me
as elde faderes schuld be, lete no heuynesse take ȝou, for þei be wel
worthi to receyue swech worchip. Therfor we wil, and in þe name
24 of Crist here we ordeyn, þat þei þat drawe to þe age of a hundred and ordains that men
ȝere, þei schal sitte stille in her beddis and sey her Pater-noster, nearing the age of 100
and ȝe with-outen grucching schul serue hem. This seruyse schul should be allowed to
ȝe do with þe bettir wil, for I wil þat ȝe knowe who þe conuersa- rest.
28 cion of hem is now in heuene, and ȝe schal þe sonneᵽ com þidir
be-cause of heᵽ prayer. A-noþir condicion had þis glorious Seynt Augustine
þat he wold neuyr occupie him-selue with non ‖ worldly occupacion, Leaf 38.
for hous ne feld wold he neuyr bye, and many heritages þat men himself never meddled with
32 wold leue on-to him he forsook hem; he seid it was moᵽ conuenient affairs, but appointed
þat her childyrn schuld haue hem þan þe cherch. The charge of yearly stewards,
his houshold, both in receyuyng and in paying, he committed
on-to þe best a-vised clerkis whech dwellid with him; on had þe
36 gouernauns o ȝere, a-noþer a-noþer ȝere, and at þe ȝeris ende he

---

[1] d *inserted above in red.*
[2] *word not distinct in text and rewritten above in red.* [3] i *added in red.*

who handed
n accounts.

þat went fro þe office ȝaue clere acountis both of þe receytis and eke of þe expenses.   He him-selue wold neu*er* beꝛ[1] keye of non office, ne no tresoꝛ, but euyr was he ȝoue to study and goostly occupacioñ.   To þese swete occupaciones inclined he his entent, 4

He com-
missioned
others to do
new works.

labourand in þe law of God day and nyth.   Newe werkis, whan þei schuld be mad, he comitted to oþir men, for he wold not haue his soule implicat with swech bysynesse, but kept it fre to holy meditacioñ and deuoute lesson.   He despised not hem þat wold 8 haue þis occupacion, ne seid not a-geyn hem, lesse þan þe werkis

He allowed
no woman
within his
house, not
even his own
relatives;

were ouyr costful, pañ wold he grucch.   Theꝛ dwelt no woma*n* with-inne his hous, nout his owne sistir ne þe douteres of his broþir, and ȝet weꝛ þei weddid to God in holy religioñ.   He wold 12 sey þus: With my sistir or my necys is þere no suspecioñ, but þere schuld come many wome*n* to hem, and eke þouȝ I be of her kyn, al my*n* houshold is not so.   He wold neu*er* speke with no woma*n*

he was never
alone with
a woman,
which is an
example to

alone, þouȝ it were rith grete counceﬂ.   If he schuld speke with 16 hem, clerkys and *seru*auntis schuld stande aboute, and þouȝ þei herd not what was sayd, þei myth se what was doo.   This cautele

Leaf 38,
back.

of so wyis ‖ a ma*n* schuld be to[2] us aﬂ a grete lernyng.   We rede þat he wold sey sumtyme to hem þat were aboute him: Leue me, 20

all, for he
knew the
power of
temptation.

in þat I wil sey as a ma*n* þat hath in þis mateꝛ gret exp*er*iens. Be-foꝛ God, þat I sey, I lye not.   The grete cedꝛ trees of Lyban, þe grete lederes of þe cristen flok, haue I-knowe þat þei haue falle be þe pestilens of lecherye, of whos fal I had no moꝛ suspecioñ 24 þan I had of Ambrose or Ierom.

[CHAPTER XXXIX.]

Of oþir m*er*uelous condicionis of þis man. **xxxix.**

He entered
no convent
of nuns
except upon
great
necessity,
and he learnt
three wise
principles
from
St. Ambrose.

THE monasteries wheꝛ nun*n*es dwelled wold he neuyr entyr with-oute a grete and a notable cause.   Thre þinggis he 28 seyde he lerned of Seynt Ambrose.   The first þat he schuld neuyr procuꝛ no wyf to no ma*n*; þe secund þat he schuld neu*er* counceﬂ ma*n* to go to werre; þe þird þat he schuld go to no feest.   The cause of þe first is þat if þe husbond and þe wyf acorde not weel, 32

---

[1] *be in text with r added in red and* ber *in margin.*
[2] a man *crossed through and* us aﬂ *written above.*

þei schuld curs hym þat mad þe mariage. And also it is not semly þat he whech is a religious man and boundyn to chastite schuld excite oþir folk to fleschly lykyng. The cause of þe secund is, if it 4 be soo þat he whech schal fytyn make ony fals chalange, þan schul men wite it on him þat ȝaue him councelt. The cause of þe þird is, if a man go often to festis he schal ete or drynk sum-tyme oute of mesuꝛ and speke sumtyme þat myth be left.

The reasons for these three wise principles.

8 Othis hated he gretly and most special in religous men, for at his bord was mad þis statute, þat what man rehersid ony oth þere, he schuld lese o disch of his seruyse ; ‖ for it was assigned of grete discrecioñ who mech mete a man schuld haue at his bord, and eke 12 who mech drynk, and alt were þei serued equaly vndir o propor-cioñ. He praised mech þoo men þat haue desire to deye, and to þis conclusiou he wold often reherse exaumples of thre bischoppis. Seynt Ambrose, whan he lay at his last ende and schuld deye, his 16 disciples þere prayed him þat he schuld ask of ouꝛ Lord lenger lyf, and he answered þus to hem : I haue not lyued so a-mongis ȝou þat I am a-schamed for to lyue lenger, ne eke I am non aferd to deye, for we haue a good Lord. This answere of Ambrose, Augustiñ 20 praised mech.

He hated oaths, and his monks Leaf 39. were punished for them.
He praised men who desired death, and often rehearsed the examples of three bishops

Anoþir bischop, he seid, lay on deying, and þei þat weꝛ aboute him desired gretly his lyf, for he was, as þei said, ful nececarie to þe cherch. He answered þus a-geyn in schort sentens : Neuyr wel, 24 but if euyr schal it be wel, why not now ? He ment as long as a man lyueth he is neuyr in parfith goodnesse, and if euyr schuld he com to rest and parfith pes it schal be at his deth, specialy if he deye weel. Of þe þird bischop seith he þat Seynt Cypriane 28 told þat[1] whan þis bischop cam to his last ende and schuld deye, at instauns of hem þat were aboute him, he prayed God to make him hool agayn. And þan, as he tellith, a fayꝛ ȝong man stood be his bed-side and loked angryly vpon him for þat desire, and rith 32 þus he saide on-to him : To suffir tribulacioñ and miseries of þis[2] world, ȝe be euyr aferd, and for to go oute of þese tribulaciones whan messageris com for ȝou, ȝe haue no wilt. What schal I ‖ do on-to ȝou ? Seldom wold he write for ony causes to lordes or 36 astates with-outen grete informacion of treuth, and whan he wrote he tempered so his wordes þat he schuld haue þe grete part of his

The words of a bishop ou dying,
and what happened to another bishop.
Leaf 39, back.
When he wrote to lords he was careful to be right.

---

[1] t *added in red.*   [2] world *commenced wrongly and crossed through.*

peticioñ.   He was moŕ redy to make acord be-twix hem þat weŕ
not gretly of his aqweyntauns þañ be-twix his frendis, for he wold
sey if he mad acord be-twix to þat weŕ not of his knowlech, he
myth perauentuŕ fauouŕ þe o partye whech had moŕ treuth, and 4
þanne schuld he wynne on of hem to his frenchip.   And be-twyx
his frendis it myth falle þe reuers, for þat man þat had not his
desiŕ wold þe rather falle fro his frenchip.

[CHAPTER XL.]

¶ Who he hatid heretikes and pursewed hem.   **Capitulum xl.**   8

HERETIKES, hated þis man with an holy angir, as þe Psalme
seith : Beth angry and synne not.   He was an hard hambyr,
euyr knokkyng up-on hem, and þei were so aferd of his argumentes
þat þei desired his deth, in so mech þat þei prechid a-mongis hem 12
to hem þat weŕ of heŕ secte, þat for to kylle Augustyn it was no
synne but an holy dede and a meritory, and what man þat durst
do þis dede, þei durst vndirtake all his synnes schuld be forȝoue of
God for þat dede doyng.   Thei layde grete wayte up-on him oftin- 16
tyme, but ouŕ Lord euyr defended his knyth whech was ful nececarie
on-to þe cherch.   For whan he was oute in þe cuntŕ sumtyme to
preche þe word of God and to lerne cristen soules þe trewe byleue,
þei leyd men of armes pryuyly in þe weye to kille him homward. 20
But ‖ by þe grace of God he was stered to take a-nothir weye, and
so was he saf fro his enmyes.   And whan he knew what perel he
was in and who meruelously God had delyuered him, him on-wetyng,
þañ þankid he God with ful deuoute hert.   But for all þese perelles 24
he cesed neuyr fro edificacion of þe puple and destruccioñ of þoo
enmyes whech berk a-geyn þe feith.   Many heresies were in his
cuntŕ at þat tyme, both of þe Donatistes and eke of þe Manicheis,
and both, with þe myty grace of God whech was plenteuously 28
with-inne him, he conuicte and ny distroyed.   The Donatistes
were þei þat be cleped Rebaptiȝatores, for þei wold admitte no
man to heŕ secte but if he weŕ baptiȝed newly with heŕ baptem.
Thei lyued in continent lif, þat is to seyn in chastite as ferŕ as 32
myth [1] be aspied [1].   þei had eke a secte with-inne hem whech þei

clepid Circumcelliones; þis meny runne a-boute on nytes with but some of them, armed, attacked men.
wepu*n* and armu*r* and compelled[1] men with strokis to her heresie.

The Manycheis had many oþer fals opiniones, for þei said þat The false opinions of the Manichaeans.
4 Crist was no very man, but lich a man, and þat he took no flesch
ne blood of þe mayde as we beleue, but he took, I wot not veryly
what þei mene, a body, þei sey, of þe eyr, in whech he ded all þoo
my*r*acles and in whech he suffered passio*n*. These folk with sly
8 termes deceyued many men.

There were also in his tyme oþir heretikes cleped Pelagianes, The Pelagian heresy.
and þei held þis opynyo*n*, þat a child be-goten of a cristen man and
a cristen woma*n* schuld[2] not be baptiȝed, ne nedith nowt, and all
12 þis secte ou*r* Augusti*n* distroyed. These be þe names of heretikes The heretics with whom he disputed.
whech wrote a-geyn hym, and to whom he gaf answe*r* ful sub-
stancial: Felix, Maximin*us*, Felician*us*, Faustus, Pasceuo*us*, Secun-
||din*us*, Petilian*us*, Permenian*us*, Fortunatus, Orestoni*us*, Gauden- Leaf 40, back.
16 cius, Julianus, and many oþir. A-geyn all þese þis souereyn maystir
of þe cherch stood as a strong geau*n*t, wrestling with argumentis
for þe clennesse of þe feith, and enforsyng of þe cherch and confirma-
cio*n* of parfite soules. Many a man eke þat was in errou*r*, þorw He brought many men
20 his preching and disputyng, was brout to þe trew wey of ou*r* Lord from error to truth.
and on-to cristen feith. Sumtyme in his prechyng wold he make Sometimes
a grete digression fro þe mate*r* þat he spak of on-to an-oþir he made digressions in
desperat mate*r*, and þa*n* wold he sey þat þis was þe dispensacio*n* his preaching,
24 of ou*r* Lord, for þe*r* was sum ma*n* in þe audiens þat had nede to
he*r* þat mate*r*. On a tyme he happid in a sermone to go fro his and thus he converted
mate*r* and speke a-geyn þe errou*r* of þese Manicheis, and a rich a rich man from
marchau*n*t þat was of þat heresie was sodeynly co*n*uerted þer-by. Manichaeism.
28 Whan*n* he was cleped to ony councelles of bischoppis or of pri*n*ces
he wold gladly[3] go to hem and euyr in þoo councelles peysed he mo*r*
þe causes þat long on-to God þan þoo þat long on-to men.

[CHAPTER XLI.]

¶ Of many bokes þat he mad aftir he was bischop. cap. xlj.

32 AL þat tyme whil he was bischop he was gretly occupied in He wrote many books
studying and wryting and makyng of bokis. On of þe when a bishop, and
first booke he mad is entitled to Symplian. This Simplician, aftir one to Simplician,

---

[1] MS. compelled, *first* l *dotted beneath.*   [2] be *crossed through.*
[3] gadly *in text*, gladly *in margin.*

who was
chosen
Archbishop
of Milan,
Seynt Ambrose was ded, was [1] chose archbischop of Melan.   For
whan Ambrose lay in deying, þe clerkis of þe cherch comound
a-mongis hem who schuld be bischop aftir, and he assigned hem
þat þei schuld chese Simpliane.   This same was þe man, as we 4

Leaf 41.
and who
brought
Augustine to
the faith.
‖ saide befor, þat with holy lif and deuoute exhortaciones brout
Augustin to þe feith.   And whanne he herd sey þat Augustin was
bischop at Ypone and famed þorw þe world as for þe grettest
labourer in study and þe grettest enmye to heretikes, eke þe grettest 8

Simplician
sent
Augustine
questions
dissoluer of qwestiones þat was leuand,—heryng al þis he sent to
him certeyn questiones, praying him to dissolue hem and declare
on-to him þe doutis þat þei conteyned.   And Augustyn wrote on-to

and was
answered
in two books.
him a-geyn with ful grete reuerens to notable bokes in whech 12
he declareth his questiones with swech wordes þat þei be ful
delectable to studious men.   [2] This book beginnyth Gratissimam [3]

At this time
Augustine
wrote his
'Confessions'
plane.   In þis same tyme wrote he xiij bokes of his Confessiones,
in whech bokes he schryuyth him ful deuoutly of his euel dedis 16
and of his good dedis; he praysith our Lord both mercyful and
rithful.   Be þese bokes he his-selve was excited to ful holy lif & þe
makyng of hem inflawmed his hert to gret loue of our Lord.   I dar

—books
which will
move the
hardest
hearts.
sauely sey þere is not so hard-hertid man in þe world þat redith 20
þese bokes and vndirstand hem, but þei wil ster his hert to swech
deuocion þat, perauentur, he hath not had experiens of swech deuocion be-for.   For all þe processe of þese bokes and all þe wordes
are steryng on-to þe loue of God, and þo ar spoken with so swete 24

He wrote also
'De Opere
Mona-
chorum'.
langage þat þei [4] sounde no-þing but deuocion.   He mad þat tyme
eke a book whech he clepith Of þe Werkis of Munkis, for in his
cuntr at þoo dayes were encresed many monasteries of munkis and
mech noumbir of religious men, for all þoo heremites whech lyued 28
in desert, to whom he was first fader and norcher, wer cleped at
þat tyme munkis, for *monnos* in þe opir tonge is as mech to sey as

Leaf 41,
back.
The institu-
tion of
St. Benet.
solitari, ‖ and so *monachus*, þat is [5] to sey, [6] a munk, is swech a man
þat lyueth in solitary lyf.   But whan Seint Benet cam, þan mad be 32
þe ordr of þo men whech be clepid now munkys propirly, for [7] oþer
orderes ar now distincte in her propir names, and at þat tyme þat

---

[1] *chop crossed through.*   [2] *In þis same tyme crossed through.*
[3] *sane crossed through.*   [4] *i added in red.*
[5] *MS. it.*   [6] *y added afterwards.*
[7] *a character crossed through.*

Augustin was, þis *monachus* was a comoun name to all religious.
For not only Seint Benet mad þese Cenobites, whech is as mech to
sey as many men lyuyng to-gidir in on hous and vndir o reule, but
4 Seynt Augustin mad swech eke, for his *principall* labour, as we
rede, was þis whanD he cam first to Affrik, to gadere[1] swech solitari
men and bryng hem to o lyf and o reule.　For Augustyn was be-
foꝛ Benet, as ferforth as I haue red, vp-on a hundred ȝeꝛ and fifty.
8 So þis book, De Op*ere* Monachoꝛ*um*, of munkys werkys, mad he to
þis entent.　Summe of þese religious men saide þat it was not
nedful[2] on-to hem[3] to praye[3], but þei weꝛ bounde[4] to labouꝛ with
heꝛ handes.　Thei weꝛ meuyd to þis opynyoñ be a texte of Seint
12 Poule, whech seith þat he whech wil not labouꝛ schal not ete.　And
in a-noþir place he seith þus : Be nyth and eke be day haue we
laboured þat we schuld greue non of ȝou all.　Summe held þe
reuers opynyoñ and enforsed hem with þe gospell wheꝛ he seith :
16 Take hed at þe birdis of þe eyr, þei sowe neythir ne repe, and ȝet
ȝouꝛ Fadeꝛ of heuene fedith hem.　And in þat same place he seith :
Take hed at þe lylyis of þe feld, þei spynne not ne carde, and ȝet
Salamon was not clad so freschly in al his ioye.　This *contencioñ*
20 roos on-to so grete *partye* þat all þe cherch was set o rore with þis
mat*er*, so ferforth þat þe bischop of Cartage, whech hith Aurelius
at þat tyme, wrote down on-to ‖ Augustyn letteris in whech he
prayed him and reqwyrid him, in Cristis name, þat he schuld
24 ordeyn sum remedye in þis mateꝛ.　And for þis cause ouꝛ fadeꝛ
Augustin wrot þis book in whech he schewith þat certeyn houres
it is[5] most *conuenient* to religious men to synge, rede or pray.
And whan þo orisones aꝛ do whech aꝛ ordeyned be *constituciones*
28 of þe cherch, þañ is it ful nececarie to do sum labouꝛ with hand,
þat ydilnesse, whech is[6] step-modiꝛ of all vertu, schul non entꝛ
haue in hem.

(marginal notes:)
‘De Opere Monacho-rum’ was written to settle the question of the labour of monks, who were at dissension over two texts.

Through Aurelius,

Leaf 42.

bishop of Carthage,

Augustine wrote this book.

---

[1] MS. gadered, *final d dotted.*
[2] MS. not only leful ; only le- *crossed through and* ned *written above.*
[3]—[3] *written in margin twice and once crossed through.*
[4] þerto *crossed through.*　　　　　[5] *written above in red.*
[6] stp. *crossed through.*

[CHAPTER XLII.]

¶ Of oþir bokes whech he wrote at þat same tyme. **cap. xlij.**

IN þo same dayes he wrote eke þe bokys Of þe Trynyte, xv,
of grete and hy sentens, oute of whech bokes aH þe dyuynes
þat haue writyn sithe, specialy in skole mateȓ, haue þe reulys 4
of aH dyuynyte.   For Hugo de Sacramentis, and þe maister of
sentens, Seynt Thomas Alqwyn, and aH oþir, haue heȓ special
groundes þeȓ.

He made eke a-noþir solempne werk clepid Of þe Cyte, and þe 8
cause why he mad þis book is þis: Whech tyme þat Rome was
take of hethen men, þe same hethen men scorned cristen men and
blasphemed Crist in þis maner : Thei saide as long as Rome seruyd
his goddis Iubiter, Iuno, Appollo, Minerue and swech othir, so long 12
was it kept be permision of þoo immortal goddis, þat þere myth
non of her enmyes ouer-com hem.   But aftyr þat tyme þat Petir
and Paule had brout in þe feith of Crist, a-non aH her enmyes
had þe bettyr of hem, of whech ymaginacioñ[1] þei added to her 16
blaspheme þat Crist had neuyr so mech poweȓ to defende his
puple as had Iubiter whech stood in heȓ capitoH.   A-geyn þese
grete blasphemes Seynt Augustin answered in þese xxij bokes.
In þe first v. bokes he repreuyth þe errour of hem ‖ þat seyde alle 20
þe richesse of þis world and aH þe prosperite is ȝouen on-to men be
þoo immortaH goddis, for he schewith heȓ pleynly þat þoo ydoles
whech þei clepe goddis ar dampned spirites, and þoo[2] men þat ded
worchip on-to hem regned in as gret myschef as euyr ded ony 24
men.   In þe oþir v. bokes he laboureth a-geyn þe errour of hem
þat seide good and euel in þis world haue her variauns aftir place
& tyme and persones, þat sum place & sum tyme and sum persone
schal haue ioye euer and sum noñ.   In þe oþir xij bokes he spekith 28
of too citees, Ierusalem and Babilome ; Ierusalem, as he seith, longith
to God, Babilome to the deuele.   These too citees spryngin of too
loues. The loue of ouȓ-selue, þat causeth þe cite of þe deuel, whech
growith in heith tyl he comth on þat abusion þat he despiseth God. 32
The loue of God, he makith þe oþir cite, and he may growe so hy to

---

[1] *þai crossed through.*
[2] *þat crossed through and* þoo *written over in red.*

Goddis plesauns þat he schal, for Goddis loue, despise alł worldly
felicite.   Be-side þese werkys he mad many a book, tretys, epistoles, *He also wrote many other*
sermones, omelies, þat a man schal not fynde a clerk at þese dayes *works, all of which no man*
4 þat may sey he haue red alł, for þe noumbir of hem ar gessid on-to *has read.*
a þousand.   Of his werkis spekith a gret clerk in a vers rith þus.
Mentit*ur* q*u*em se¹ te totu*m* legisse fatet*ur*.   Thus it meneth in
Englisch : He lyeth þat seith he hath red al þi bokes.

[Chapter XLIII.]

8   ¶ Who Augustyn red ouyr alł his bokes a litil be-foř his deth
& corrected he*m*. ‖ **Cap. xliij.**   **Leaf 43.**

A FTIR tyme he had mad alł þese bokes he ouyr-lokid hem *After he had written all*
    a-geyn, þat þeř schul no-þing be þerin but trewe.   This *these books,*
12 þing ded he for many causes, on was for he mad many bokes or þe *he re-read them,*
tyme þat he was gretly vsed or ex*er*cised in holy scriptuř.   A-noþir
cause was for certeyn materis whech ² he had wrytin, þei weř dirkly
seid, wherfor he declared þoo materis in þis secu*n*d writyng.   The *and having reasons for changes,*
16 þird cause was þat he was not a-schamed ³ to be a-knowe þat he
had wrytyn mech þing whech myth a be bettir, and for þis cause
he mad þat book whech he clepith his Retractaciones.   And þat *he wrote his 'Retracta-*
he schuld haue þe moř leyseř to study and write, specialy for in *tions'.*
20 too cou*n*cellis alł þe bischoppis of þe lond had reqwyrid him þat
he schuld entend on-to exposicio*n* of holy scriptuř, for þis cause
certeyn ȝeres be-foř his deth he prayed ful mekely þe clergy and þe
puple þat fyue dayes in þe weke he myth haue pesibily to his *He gave five days a week*
24 study i*n* scriptuř, and þe oþir too dayes wold he ȝeue attendau*n*s *to study and two days to*
on-to heř causes, to sette rest and pes be-twix hem⁴.   But for al *his people,*
þis grau*n*t oft-tyme was his studie inter*r*upt for heř causes, to his *but his work was*
grete vexacio*n*, but special coumfort of his puple.   For þis skil⁵ *interrupted;*
28 he ordeyned a-noþir remedye : he say wel þat he fełł fast in age,
and deth, þat no ma*n* may escape, was ful ny, be-cause he felt him- *and therefore, feeling also*
selue so febil ; he dred eke þat aftir his deth sum ambicious ma*n* *that he was getting*
schuld be mad bischop, whech schuld distroye al þat euyr he had *feebler,*

---

¹ *in margin.*   ² ch *added in red above.*
³ d *added above in red.*   ⁴ I *crossed through.*
       ⁵ cause *crossed through and* skil *written over in red.*

he asked the
Leaf 43,
back.
people to
choose some
man to attend
to them and
afterwards
take his see.
edified; þerfor laboured he on-to þe puple þat þei schuld chese
sum good man and iuste þat ‖ myth occupie þat se aftir his deth,
whech man schuld determyn þe causes of þe puple, lest þat þei
were grete causes, þo wold he kepe to him-self.   To his desir 4
þei consented aɫɫ and mad compromisse on-to his persone þat
whom he wold name þei schul consent on-to him.   Vp-on þis

Thus he and
they chose
Heraclius one
of his clerks.
Augustin named on of his clerkis, þei clepid him Eraclius, a man
wel-named in þe puple whom Augustin had enformed in þe weye 8
of Crist in þe best maner.   And to þis man comitted Augustin aɫɫ
þe charge of þat diosise, lest þan þere com ony grete causes, þat he
schuld haue þe mor leisir to study and wrytyng.   Thus er he deyid

After his
' Retracta-
tions' he
wrote other
books.
he ouer-say aɫɫ his bokes and mad þese Retractaciones.   But aftir 12
making of þat werk he mad many oþir bokes whech be not touchid
þerin, as a man may se in þe redyng.

[CHAPTER XLIV.]

¶ Who his cyte was be-segid of dyuers naciones.   xliiij.   16

At this time
Hippo was
besieged by
the Alans,
Goths, and
Vandals.
The home of
the Alans.
IN þis same tyme iij sundry naciones beseged þe cite of
Ypone; þei ar[1] cleped[2] þus, Alani, Gothi and Wandali.
These Alani dwelle in a gret cuntr her in þis part of þe world
cleped Europe, whech cuntr þei calle Sithia; it is hens northest 20
toward Constantinople.

The home o.
the Goths.
Gothi dwelled[3] fast by hem, for þese cuntres occupied ny fro þe
grete flod cleped Danubius[3] un-to þat cuntr whech we clepe
Denmark, for of þese Gothis cam þese Danes.   24

The home of
the Vandals.
After scourg-
ing Europe,
these people
invaded
Wandaly dwelled sumtyme in þe same place wher Lumbardes
dwelle now a-boute Melan and Pauye.   Aɫɫ þese puple þus gadered
to-gidyr ded mech harm her in Europe a-boute Rome and in Ytale,
and þan went þei ouer þe se in-to Affrik, and þere distroyed þe 28

Leaf 44.
Africa and
besieged
Hippo.
cuntr, and ‖ at þe last ende of Augustin lyf, þei beseged þe cite of
Ypone.   Vnder þis tribulacion Augustin had ful heuy dayes and
wept both day & nyth for þe myschef þat he say whech þese men

They spared
nobody.
ded, for þei spared no cherchis, ne prestis, ne nunnes, ne non ordr. 32
And whan Augustin say sum deye in captiuite, sum in prison,

---

[1] *inserted above.*   [2] d *written above.*
[3] us *crossed through.*

summe of þe swerd, and þat þe seruyse, þe messis, þe ympnis of þe · and the services of the church ceased.
cherch cesed, and many cherchis weᵽ brent in þe cuntᵽ, and þe
clerkis fled, so þat sacramentis weᵽ not ȝouen, and þouȝ a man
4 wold haue hem, þere was no man to gyue hem, he seing [1] al þis,
had ful grete sorow, so þat he fell in-to greuous seknesse. But
ȝet, amongis al þis sorow he had þat consolacioñ of þe wise man
whech saide þus : He hath no grete wisdam þat sorowith whan
8 stones falle, and whan þei deye þat must nedis deye. In þis · Augustine prayed to God
tribulacioñ he cleped his breþerin to-gidyr and þus he saide on-to
hem : Behold now, in what mischef we stand in, and I se no
remedye ; God wil punisch us in þis wyse for ouᵽ synnes. Wherfor,
12 I haue prayed my Lord þat he schuld delyueᵽ us of þese perelles, · for one of three things,
or elles send us paciens þat we may suffyr hem mekely, or elles, if
he se þat we be worþi for to haue hem lenger, I haue prayed God
þat he schal take me oute of þis lyf. This same prayeᵽ þat he
16 prayed, þei prayed all, and so on of þese iij peticiones was graunted · and in the third month of the siege he fell ill.
him, for in þe þird month aftir þei had be-segid þe cyte, þe feuerys
took him so soᵽ þat [2] he was fayn to kepe his bed.

[CHAPTER XLV.]

¶ In what maner ‖ Augustyn deyid, and what occupacioñ he · Leaf 44, back.
20 had in his last sekenesse. **Capitulum xlv.**

IN þis same seknesse of whech he deyid þere cam on-to hym · Before he died a man came asking to be made whole ;
a certeyn man, praying him in þe name of ouᵽ Lord þat he
wold touche him with his hand, for he seide if he wold ley hand
24 up-on him, he schuld make him hool of þat seknesse whech he had
longe boᵽ. Augustyn answered to hym a-geyn and seide he was · Augustine demurred,
not wys in his desire, for if he had swech poweᵽ to make men hool
he wold rather exercise it on him-self þan on oþir men. The man
28 replied on-to Augustyn in þis maner : He saide þat he had in · but the man insisted, and
maner of a goostly consolacioñ, in whech he was warned þat he
schuld go to Augustyn þe bischop, and with touching of his hand
he schuld be mad hool. Augustyn, seing þe grete feith of þis man,
32 leyd his hand up-on him & blessed him in þe name of God, and · Augustine cured him.
þus was he mad hool. Thus encresid þe seknesse up-on him þat

---

[1] seying *crossed through*; seing *in margin*.   [2] *part of* w *crossed through*.

Augustine
knew he was
dying,
he vndirstood wel he schuld sone deye, and be-cause he had prechid
ofte sithe þat þere schuld no cristen man passe owt of þe world
with-outen mornyng and compleint for defautes in whech he hath

and made his
notary write
the seven
Psalms of the
Litany for
him to read.
falle, þerfor he mad his notari for to write him þe vij Psalmes, þoo 4
same whech we rede with þe Letanye, in a fayr parchemyn skyn,
and þis was sette on þe wal a-geyn his beddis hed.   Þese red he
with ful gret deuocion and grete wepyng be-for his deth.   And
þat þere schuld no man interrupte him of þis deuocion, ten dayes 8
be-for his deth he ordeyned þat þer schuld no man com with [1]-inne

Leaf 45.
þe chaumbyr wher he ‖ lay but his leche and þei þat brout him
mete and drynk, and all þis tyme with ful grete deuocicn and

On the fifth
kalend of
September,
he passed
away,
mech wepyng he comended his soule to God.   And þus þe v. kalende 12
of September, with hool mynde and all þe membris of his body not
hurt but hool, standyng his breþerin a-boute him, and comendyng
hys soule to God, he ȝald þe goost on-to þe Fader of heuene.   Thus
hath he left in erde his holy foot-steppis, many men & women 16
of his religion taute be his doctrine.   He hath left eke grete

leaving the
church the
treasure of
his books, in
which he is
immortal.
instruccion to þe cherch in tresour of his bokes, þat þouȝ his body
be drawe from vs, ȝet his spirit abideth with us, as þe poete wrot
ful wel of all hem whech leue emolliment of wrytyng be-hinde hem ; 20
rith þus he wrot in Latin: Viuere post obitum vatem vis nosce
viator, Quod legis ecce loquor vox tua nempe mea est.   Thus mene
þei in Englisch: Thou man þat passist by, if þou wilt knowe þat
a clerk lyueth after his deth, That þou redist I speke, þi voys eke 24

He lived
seventy-six
years,
is myn.   Augustyn lyued clerk and bischop ny xl. ȝere, alle þe
dayes of his lyf, or seuenety and sex.   Thus endith þe lyf of þis
glorious doctour whom all cristen men ar bounde to do worchip,
most specialy clerkys and lerned men þat haue grete stuf oute of 28

The Author
hopes the
gentle woman
for whom he
wrote will do
the Saint
honour.
his bokes to her lernyng.   And as I hope, ȝe gentyl woman, ȝe
schuld plese wel þis Seint if ȝe wold se his place onys in a ȝer,
and þouȝ ȝe left a day in heruest of ȝour labour, he coude make
retribucion in oþer party.   Thus I comende ȝou to God and me to 32
ȝour prayeris, þat we both may com sumtyme wher our Fader is,
we schal prey both   Amen.

---

[1] inne *wrongly written and crossed through.*

LIFE OF ST. GILBERT

[Capgrave's Prolog.]

TO my wel-beloued in our Lord God maystir[1] of þe order of Sempyngham[2], whech ordre is entytled on-to þe name of Seynt Gilbert, I, ffrer I. C.[3], amongis doctouris lest, send 4 reuerens as to swech dignyte, desiring clennesse to your soule and helth to your body. Now with-inne fewe dayes was notyfied on-to me þat þe lyf of our fader Seynt Augustyn, whech þat I translat[4] in-to our tunge at instauns of a certeyn woman, 8 was browt to your presens, whech lykyd ȝow wel, as it is told, saue ȝe wold I schul adde þerto alle þoo relygyous þat lyue vndyr his reule. But to þis I answer þat it was not my charge, but if men like for to knowe þis mater diffusely þei may lerne it in a sermon 12 þat I[5] seid at Cambrig þe ȝer be-for myn opposicion, whech sermon vnphap I wil sette in Englisch in þe last ende of þis werk. Than aftir ȝe had red þis lyf of Seynt Augustyn ȝe sayde to on of my frendes þat ȝe desired gretly þe lyf of Seynt Gilbert 16 schuld be translat in þe same forme. Thus mad he instaunce to me, and I graunted both ȝour petycion, this[6] for I wold not frustrate him of his mediacion. To þe honour of God and of all seyntis þan, wil we begynne þis tretys, namelych for the 20 solitarye women of ȝour religion whech vn‖neth can vndyrstande Latyn, þat þei may at vacaunt tymes red in þis book þe grete vertues of her maystyr. For her may þei loke as in a glasse, who þei schal transfigure her soules lych on-to þat exemplary in whech 24 þei schul loke. Of þe interpretacion of his name, what it schuld mene in Englisch, for we haue it not redily in our bokes of

Leaf 46.

For the master of Sempring-ham,

who had seen and liked his 'Life of St. Augus-tine'.

Capgrave writes this work.

His sermon preached at Cambridge.

This book is for the Leaf 46, back. maidens who know little Latin.

The meaning of the name 'Gilbertus'

---

[1] In the margin, M. Nicholas Reysby.
[2] simpyngham with e written over.
[3] In margin, in a later hand, John Capgrave.
[4] MS. transalat, a dotted underneath.   [5] inserted above.
[6] in margin.

interpretaciones, we wil speke in swech maner as auctouris whech dyuyde names in partes. Gyla, þei sey, is a word of Hebrew, as mech to sey as he þat passeth fro o cuntꝛ to a-nothir. And ber is a welle, or a pitte, eke deruyed fro þe Ebrewe tunge. Tus[1] is a Lateyn word, in Englisch a swete gumme, whech we þrowe in ouꝛ encenseris whan we schal doo a special honouꝛ to God. Thanɴ soundith his name þus on-to ouꝛ heryng: This holy man was a walkeꝛ heꝛ in erde þat passed fro þe welle on-to[2] þe swete sauouꝛ.

The welle clepe I þe holy baptem in whech he was wasch fro Adam his synne. The swete sauour name I þe holy opynyoɴ of this man whech sauoured so swetely in þis land þat it mad many men to selle al þat þei[3] had and folow þe steppes of pouerte. Of this sauour spak þe blissed apostel[4] whan he saide: We be þe good odour of ouꝛ Lord Crist in euery place,

both to hem þat schul be saued ‖ and eke to hem þat schul perisch. To summe be we sauouꝛ of lyf and to summe sauouꝛ of deth. So semyth it þat þe clene lyf of Seynt Poule, and þe deuoute preching of hym, was on-to hem whech weꝛ chose to be saued a sauouꝛ of euyr-lastyng lyf, & to hem þat weꝛ reprobat a sauour of euerlastyng peyne. Aͬ þis is seid to acording of Seynt Gilbertis name þat al his lyf from his baptem on-to his deth ran in swech a swete sauouꝛ þat ȝet-at þese dayes þe deuoute virgines of his ordre beren witnesse þat of þe rote of his doctrine

sprange aͬ þese fayre flouris of virginite. This is þe preamble or elles þe prologe of Seynt Gilbertis lif, whech lyf I haue take on hand to translate out of Latyn rith as I fynde be-fore me, saue sum addicionis wil I put þertoo whech men of þat ordre haue told me, and eke othir þingis þat schul falle to my mynde in þe writyng whech be pertinent to þe mateꝛ.

[CHAPTER I.]

capitulum pᵐ.

THIS man was bore in þat same place cleped Sempingham. His fader was bore in Normandye, his modyr lady of þis place be-foꝛ seide. His fadeꝛ, as þei sey, was a knyte of Normannye

---

[1] Thus *in text; tus in red in margin.*   [2] *added above in red.*
[3] i *added above.*   [4] *In margin in red,* 2 Cor. 2.

whech cam in-to þis lond with Kyng William at ‖ þe Conqwest and Leaf 47, back.
weddyd þe lady of þis place, so þat he heritage Seint Gilbert
was very eyer of þis possession & of many othir.   That þis is
4 likly to be soth, I a-legge a testimonie whech I haue be informacion As the Lords Beaumont
of my Lord Beamound, Ion, þat now lyuyth.   He seide þat his came of two bloods,
kynrod cam first out of Frauns with þis same Kyng William, Norman and English,
and on of hem, a notable knyte, weddid þe lady of Folkingham
8 at þat tyme, and so of her issewe cam all þe Beamoundis þat haue
be sithe.   Swech many othir myth we reherse & make þe boke
ouer longe and tedious to þe reder.   Than was þis man medeled so did Gilbert.
with too blodis, Norman of þe fader side, Englisch of þe moderis
12 side.   What auctoris write of þese too naciones & what comendacion
þei reherse of hem is pertinent to sette her in magnyfying of þis
man.   The Normannes, þei sey, þei cam fro Norweye &[1] conqwered Character-istics of the Normans.
þe lond wher þei dwelle, a puple gentyl of condicion, wise and
16 redy in batayle & grete tilleres of corn.   The descripcion eke of
þis nacion must mech a-corde her-to, be-cause þei conqwered us
and at þis day her succession dwellith with us.   So semeth it
þat þis man was not bore of[2] no wrecchid nacion, ne of no seruage,
20 but of puple gentil & fremanly & large, both on þe fadir side
and ‖ þe moder.   He was in his ȝong age, and in his simpilnesse Leaf 48.
ful gracious lich on-to Iacob, whom for his clennesse & innocens In his youth Gilbert was gentle,
þe modir Rebecca, þorw inspiracion of God, preferred to be lord
24 of all his breþerin, lich as þis man is preferred to be maystir
of al þis religion.   And also, as it is seid in þe bok of Iob[3]:
The lampe whech was despised in þe þoutes of rich men was destined to lead men.
arayed agayn a-noþir tyme; in whech ȝe schal vndirstond þat
28 þoo vertues whech grew with þis child in ȝong age, þan despised
of þe world, were ordeyned for to be hald in mor reuerens in
tyme comand.   He was at þat age set to skole and lerned groundly When young he went to school and learned the sciences.
in þoo scienses whech þei clepe liberal, as gramer, retorik, logik
32 and swech oþir.   But his corage at þat tyme was mor enclyned
to lerne good maneris þan sotil conclusiones, eke be-cause aftirward
þat he was ordeyned to be a techer of vertuous lyuyng, it was
conuenient þat he schuld first be a disciple in þat in scole of

---

[1] *written above.*   [2] *part of* w *crossed through.*
[3] *In the margin in red,* Iob 12.

He was free
from the
common vices
of children.
honestie.   In al his ȝong age was he clene fro swech vices as
childyrn vse, as lying, wauntown ragyn, and oþir stynkyng
condiciones.   Euene þanñ be-gan he to be lich a religiou*s* man,
to whech lyf he was applied be God.   For in alł his lyf, as þei 4
bere witnesse þat sey his *conuer*sacioñ, touched he neu*er* woma*n*.

Leaf 48,
back.
Touchyng ∥ clepe I vicious handelyng in þe selue or ellis swech
man*er* circu*m*stauns of bodely a*p*roximacioñ be whech ony man
myth deme euele.   8

[CHAPTER II.]

cap. ij.

In his young
age he
followed the
rules of
religious life.
IN þat same seculeꝛ lyf and in þat tendyr age, he folowyd,
as he coude and myth, þe reules of religious lyf, and to
hem alł of whech he had ony poweꝛ he ful benyngly gaf exau*m*ple 12

He taught
children
spelling, &c.,
þe same reules to folow.   For first was he a maystir of lernyng
to þe smale petites, swech as lerne to rede, spelle and synge.
Tho childyrn þat were vndyr his disciplyne he taute not only
heꝛ lessones on þe book, but be-side þis, he tawt for to pley[1] 16

and playing.
in dew tyme, and here playes taute he þat þei schuld be honest
and mery with-oute*n* clamou*r* or grete noyse.   For þouȝ he had
not at þat tyme exp*er*iens of þe good customes whech be vsed
a-mong*is* religious men i*n* monasteriis, ȝet had ouꝛ Lord God 20
at þat age put in his brest þese holy ex*er*cises, for he taute[2] þoo
disciples þat he had to kepe silens in þe cherch[3]; alł an on ouꝛ to
go to bedde & eke to ryse[4] to heꝛ[5] lessones; alł wente þei to-gidyr
to heꝛ pley or ony oþir þing.   His moost labouꝛ and grettest 24
desiꝛ[6] was to wynne soules to God with word and eke ensau*m*ple,

He was like
Leaf 49.
Athanasius,
who, in his
childhood,
for þe best sacrifise on-to God is þe gelous loue of soules.   Lich
on-to þis ma*n* was þe holy Athanas in his ȝong dayes,[7] ∥ þat same
Athanas whech mad Quicu*n*q*ue* Vult.   We rede of him þat in his 28
childhod he wold gader to-gydyr many childyr of his aqweyntauns,
and lede hem to þe watirside, and þis was at grete Alisaundꝛ.
Than wolde he enqwyre of hem wheythir þei were cristen or

baptized
heathen
children.
nowt, and if þei weꝛ not *cr*isten, he made his felawis, as in game, 32
to make þe child naked & so dippe him þries in þe cold watyr,

---

[1] C. 29 play.   [2] C. tawht.   [3] C. chirch.   [4] C. rysse.
        [5] C. there.   [6] C. desyere.   [7] *þat crossed through.*

he standing sadly and saying þe very sacramental wordis of baptem. This noyse cam to þe bischoppis ere, whech at þat tyme hite Petyr; he sent aftir þe childyrn and enqwyred of hem what
4 Athanas saide on-to hem, what þei answered, vnder what forme he wasched hem, and ¹whan he sei þat¹ all þing was doo rith as þe cherch vseth, he determyned þat þo childyrn weʀ baptiȝed, notwithstanding þat it was doo in pley, comaundyng his prestes
8 to take þe childyrn and sey ouyr hem² þe oþir orisones whech þe cherch vseth. Al þis is seid for ouʀ Gilberd, þat in so ȝong age had so sad condiciones and so grete ȝel to lede soules to heuene. Whan he was promoted to þe ordre of presthod and had *When he became priest,*
12 soules in gouernauns³ and eke had receyued poweʀ to make *priest,* ministracion of þe goostly giftis whech be vertue of oure Lordes ‖ blod ar left in þe cherch, þan, as a trewe steward of his Lordes *Leaf 49, back.* tresouʀ, he departed his Lordes whete to hem þat dwelle in þe *he was a true*
16 housold of ouʀ feith, to ech of hem as it neded. Þat is to seyn, *steward of his Lord's wealth.* þe word of good exhortacion was not hid in him, but he delt it oute frely to hem þat wold lerne. For his auditorye was so endewyd with lernyng þat it sempt in all heʀ gouernauns þei had
20 be norchid in monasterye amongis þe seruauntis of God. Thei vsed non insolent drynkyngis⁴, ne no longe sitting þere, ne⁵ vsed *His people went to no* not to renne to wrastillingis, beʀ-baytingis and swech oþir onthrifty *vain wrest-* occupaciones, whech summe men now on dayes preferʀ be-for dyuyne *lings and bear-baitings,*
24 seruyse; this used þei nout, but þei used to pray deuoutly in þe cherch, to pay treuly heʀ tythes, to walk a-boute and visite *but paid their tithes,* pore men, to spend heʀ good in swech weye as is plesauns of God and coumfort to pore. Who-so had seyn hem⁶ with-inne þe cherch
28 he myth sone discerne wheþir þei weʀ Gilberd parischones or *and behaved* nowt, he had tawt hem so wel to bowe heʀ bakkes and heʀ knes to *devoutly.* God and so deuoutly to bid heʀ bedes.

[CHAPTER III.]

cap. tercium. *Gilbert was first in the*
32 IN his first promocion he was in housold of þe bischop of *household of* Lincoln, cleped Robert Bloet. Thidir was he ‖ drawe first *the Bishop Leaf 50.* *of Lincoln,*

¹⁻¹ C. 29 b. what he sayde þat þus : *in our MS. a* d *has been erased after* sei.
² *added above in red.* ³ C. governans.
⁴ MS. drynkyns, *with* gis *written over last syllable.* ⁵ *inserted above.*
⁶ C. 30. them.

& mad a chapeleyn half ageyn his wil, for he was special with þe
lord, & to him was comitted to ransake all þe greuous crimes or
synnes þorw-oute þe diosise, he to correcte aftir his discreciõ.

For he was a general iuge, as it semeth, to make his remissiones 4
and *comminaciones* rith as he list. In all þis astate he was not
prowd of beryng, ne founde in no costly aray, but þe heyer he was
in dignite þe lower was his soule [1], for in all his mevyngis no-þing
seculer, but lych a chanoñ reguler or a cloystirer, semed he euyr. 8

In so mech þat whil he was in þis seruyse in court he fastid gretly,
he wook [2] as to oþir mennys wakyng *importably*, prayed euyr, and
eke oþir goostly [3] exercises wer neuyr left behynde. He was so
wel occupied in þat *administracion* þat he wold compleyne of him- 12
selue aftirward [4] whan he had begunne þis religiõ, þat he was

mor parfit in lyf be-for þat *conuer*cion to religiõ þañ he was aftyr,
notwithstanding þat aftir tyme he had take þis holy habite he was
enmye grete I-now on-to his owne body. But þat he dyde lesse 16
penauns to his body aftyr he had take þe religiõ, it is not to

aretten to slauth and necligense, but rather on-to charyte, whech

entendith mor to oþir mennys profith þan his owne. ‖ So rede

we þat Seynt Martyn had lesse vertue ȝoue on-to him after his 20
promociõ to þe bischoprych þañ he had be-fore. This man whech
we talk of now, be-for all vertues loued poueite, for a grete and

a good archideconry profered to hym be þe same bischop Robert,
he fully refused. For he wold sey sum-tyme þat þese benefices of 24
grete expense be often-tyme a redy wey to losse of a mannes soule.
For whech cause all þe goodes whech left of his benefises be-side
his neccessarie lyuyng, he gaue it frely on-to þe profite of pore men.
Whañ he was oute of his owne possessiõ he receyued euyr Crist 28

as his gest in faderles childyrn, in widowis, in elde folk, in seke
and feble, whom he susteyned with his propir goodis, and eke with
þe cherchis prouentis, clad hem & fed hem. And þat he schuld
go [5] on-to þe grettest summe of perfecciõ, all þat he had he gaf 32
to pore men swech as he, þorw þe inspiraciõ of our Lord, had
chose and made to lyue in wilful pouerte, whech [6] her-aftir for his
temporal goodys þat he spent in worchip of our Lord, schuld

---

[1] sole *in text*; soule *in margin*.   [2] C. 30 *b.* woke.
[3] exercise, *dotted beneath.*   [4] he *crossed through.*
[5] *added above in red.*   [6] schuld *crossed through in red.*

receyue him[1] in-to euyr-lastyng tabernacles, as þe gospel berith
witnesse.   Thus, of trewe dispensyng of worldly goodes and grete
loue whech he had to soules, he was worthi ‖ of our̃ Lord to receyue Leaf 51.
4 a dobyl reward.

[CHAPTER IV.]

cap. quartum.

THO he þoutȝ a-mong oþir þingis þat virginite was a grete
astate, on of þe grettest vertu þat may plese God,
8 whech frute bor̃ be hem is most alowed in heuene, for þis cause
he ordeyned first seuene maydenes whech, be his techi*ng*, wer̃ He took seven
inflaumed[2] with þe loue of God, þat þei schuld be sperd up fro maidens and shut them up
þe vanytes of þe world and serue our̃ Lord in qwyete contem- from the world,
12 placyon̄.   So vndyr þe wal of þe cherch of Seynt Andrew he mad giving them cells by
hem celles wher̃ þei myte prey and haue parte eke of all dyuyne St. Andrew's church, and
seruyse, both in seying and in eryng.   Aftir þat he ioyned on-to appointing women and
her̃ seruyse oþir certeyn women þat wer̃ not letteryd, and men religious men to tender
16 eke þat wer̃ conuerted to religion̄, but no clerkys ; þese alle wer̃ them.
ordeyned to þe seruyse of þe forsaid virgines.   Aftir þis don he Then he appointed
ordeyned certeyn clerkis, letterid men and boundyn to streyt clerks to govern them.
reules, þat þei schuld haue þe gouernaunce of all þis puple forseyd.
20 On-to þese alle ordeyned he mete, drynk, cloth, and oþir neccessaries
of his rentys and of oþir good lefully goten.   To her̃ soules eke
ordeyned he goostly mete, on-to þe nu*n*nes þe reule of Seynt The nuns were under
Benedict, on-to þe clerkys þe reule of Seynt Augustyn, be-side St. Benedict's
24 þese certeyn institucio*n*es he ordeyned, as þe holy a‖noyntyng Leaf 51,
taut him, whech be þe Holy Gost is sent fro heuene.   Thus he back.
sette hem lawes medeled with swech attemp*er*auns þat a-mo*ng*is rule ; the monks under
dyuers kyndes, dyuers habites, dyuers degrees, he exorted hem in St. Augus-tine's.
28 our̃ Lord þei all schuld haue but o soule and on hert fixid in God.
What schal we sey mor̃ of his co*n*gregaciones ?   Be-side þo elmesse- He made alms-houses,
houses whech he mad for pore men, for seke me*n* and women in
lang17or̃, for misellis, for wydowes, for faderles & modirles, whech
32 houses he sette i*n* dyuers degres and i*n* dyuers disposicio*n̄*, be-side
all þese, he edyfied i*n* his lyue þirtene co*n*uentual cherchis with all and built thirteen
oþir houses p*er*tinent, four̃ of chanons dwellyng be hem-selfe, nyne conventual churches.
of nu*n*nes with her̃ breþerin and clerkys, & *persones þat wer̃*

---

[1] *added above in red.*   [2] MS. infalaumed ; a *dotted beneath.*

onlerned ordeyned to seruyse of þe nunnes, as we seid be-foꝛ.

At his death he left nearly 2,200 religious folk, and might have made more monasteries had his conscience let him. And verily, as we suppose, he left at his deth swech persones dedicate to God vp-on too þousand too hundred, be-side hem þat· weꝛ dede er þat tyme he passed from vs.   And many moo monas- 4 teries myth he a mad, ne had be þe streyt consciens whech he had in receyuyng of worldly good, for with ful gret dreed and mech heuynesse receyued he worldly rychesse whech was proffered him;

Leaf 52. sum-tyme was he compelled ‖ for to take þo ȝiftis; summe-tyme he 8 refused hem, so was honest pouert roted in his hert and so wel beloued. Thus semeth it þat he was sette in þe mene weye, as was Salamon þat sayd on-to God [1]: Gyue me, Lord, neythir rychesse ne pouerte, but graunt me swech þing whech is nedful on-to me.   So 12 þis man had desire to þe mene, neþir to be rich, ne for to want, but to haue swech þing as was neccessarie to þe [2] grete noumbyr newly gadered be him, þat þei schuld not fayle of heꝛ dayly prouysion.

God exalted him for his meekness. His purpos was euyr to dwelle a-mongis hem þat weꝛ meke, þerfor 16 it plesed ouꝛ Lord for to heyne him þat him-self so lowed.

[CHAPTER V.]

His fatherliness is known throughout England. WHO þat he be-had in his prelacye and who faderly he was at al tymes on-to his subiectis, I suppose, veryly, þat it is 20 now not onknowe on-to al þe kyngdom of Ynglond, in so mech þat his childyrn be so encresed and growen to swech a noumbyr as we may se at [3] eye, þat rithfully we may applie þoo wordis of scriptuꝛ His seed has increased, by reason of his virtuous life. to him whech weꝛ said to Iob [4]: Thi seed, he said, schal be 24 multiplied and þi kynred encresed as herbes on þe erde.   This multiplying of his religion, þe wise men þat lyue now suppose Leaf 52, back.[6] veryly it be [5] þe myracle of his good lyf. ‖ The man stood in a maneꝛ of merveile to all þat knew hym for þe grete prerogatif 28 of good dedys with whech he was endewed, eke for þe new plantes of mercy and charite whech he had griffid in þe gardeyn of Cristis

---

[1] *In margin in red,* Prouer. 30.   [2] *inserted above.*
[3] þe *crossed through.*   [4] *In margin in red,* Iob 5.
[5] be veryly *crossed through in red.*
[6] *The embellishment of capitals in red is omitted from this and the following page.*

cherch, more-ouyr for þe grete multiplying and wise gouernauns
of þe same. For He þat pored wisdam in his breest for to þinke
and to begynne swech þingis, He gaf him vertue in þe administra-
4 cion & conseruacion of þe same. It is open at þis day what ^{His holiness is known openly;}
cunnyng Seynt Gilbert hadde & what holynesse, for and þese
giftes had not com fro God, þer schuld neuyr a risen on-to so
parfite an ende, for þe man tawt no-þing but þat he ded, for in al ^{he did all that he taught.}
8 his lyf his doctrine was accordyng to his werkys ; his holy doctrine
expressid his clene lyf and his holy lyf brout his doctrine on-to
effecte, þat is to se, a parfith ende. Aftir tyme þat he was
preferred to haue gouernauns in dispensyng of Goddis giftes, he
12 ded þe part þat longed on-to his office, he left rith nowt þat
longid on-to his goostly helth or elles to þe charge þat longed
to gouernauns of his breþerin. The man was plesaunt and mery, ^{He was a pleasant man,}
wys in wordis and of vsed eloquens fulfillid, hauyng no-þing in his
16 wordes þat was likly to be lakkid, wherfor ‖ with grete reuerens ^{Leaf 53.}
was he be-loued both of his owne familiar puple and eke of
straungeres. In all his behauyng owtward he was conformed
on-to his breþerin ; he was, if I schuld not lye, þe forme & þe
20 exaumple in whech þei myth loke for to transfigur her lyf to þat ^{the perfect example for his followers,}
exemplarye. Meke he was a-mongis hem as on of hem, as it is
seyd in Salamon : A prince haue þei mad þe be with hem as on of
hem ;[1] for al þat euer he comaunded his subiectis to do he fulfillid
24 him-self ; his clopis wer not whiter þan oþir of his felawes ; his ^{not different from them in clothes or food.}
mete was not dite mor deliciously þan[2] it was for couent ; he had
no special chambir for to slepe in, but in þe dormytori he took his
rest ; his bord was not owt of þe refectory, lest þat gestis caused
28 it. In his riding had he no costful hors, no wastful aray, not
many hors, ne many seruantis, but on of þe on-lerned of his ordre
and too of þe clerkis whech schuld be pryuy and se al his conuer-
sacion, at all tyme þei went with him. In his rydyng he spent ^{When he rode he told no vain tales by the way.}
32 not[3] þe tyme with veyn tales or flying tydyngis, but with Psalmis
and orisones sewe he al þe weye, euyr hauyng a purs redy to gyue
elmes to pore men whech þat he mette. His In to whech he
schuld come was stuffid with ‖ habundauns of vitaile ful discretly[4], ^{Leaf 53, back.}

---

[1] a crossed through.   [2] MS. þat.   [3] inserted above.
[4] 1 written above.

His inn was free to all. nowt only for him-selue but for hem þat wold ask it and had nede þerof. At mete was he myri; he talked moꝛ þan ete, and with solacious countenauns wold he glade his gestis.

[CHAPTER VI.]

Cap. vj.   4

He accused himself of over-eating, when he had eaten little. HE wold compleyne sumtyme whan he roos fro þe bord þat he had synned in vnmesurable etyng or drinkkyng, whan þei þat weꝛ *conuersaunt* with him ¹had *meruei*l¹ who þat a man myth lyue with soo litil mete or drink; whaꞝ he schuld sitte to ete 8 often-tyme he wold wepe for be-cause, he seyde, þat oure nature eu*er*y day is compelled of very nede to receyue mete and drynk þat He abstained from meat, but ate fish, except in Lent and Advent. he fayle not. Fro flesch and aꝇ þat longith to flesch abstined he euyr, lest þat he weꝛ sek, þanꞝ þorw counceꝇ of his frendis he 12 wold ete su*m*. Fysch ete he þorw þe ȝere, saue in Lentoꞝ and in Aduent, þan wold he non ete; his mete was þaꞝ wortys, letuse and oþ*er* herbes, whech he ete as þei had be delicasises; whan he was febil þei weꝛ fayn to dite him fisch in swech man*er* þat he 16 knew it nowt. This did his *ser*uauntis for pite of his febilnesse He gave the first part of his food to the poor. and whan his mete cam be-fore him þe first part wold he gyue to God, whech was boꝛ to sum poꝛ man; ny al þe oþir del departed he on-to hem whech soten a-boute him. In his refeccioꞝ he took 20 Leaf 54. moꝛ ‖ heed þat his soule schuld be fed with holy scriptuꝛ þaꞝ his He worked after eating, and read. body with delicat metis. Aftir mel wold he haue sum bodely labouꝛ, and þaꞝ rede and pray, and so occupie his tyme. Thorw-oute þe He wore the same clothes, Winter and Summer. ȝere was he clad equally; he wered no mo clothis in Wyntir þanꞝ 24 in Somyr; with o cote ²he went² and no more, for furres wered he It was wonderful how his old body lived. neuyr. Thou schuld had merueyle if þou had seyn þe membres of þat eld body, who þe bones and þe skyn myth vnneth hange to-gidir, his schulderis croked, his teth oute of þe mouth, who þat swech an 28 eld body myth lyue whan alle hete was drawe fro him, both natural and accidental, þat for discoumfort sumtyme his body was ny *contract*. Be-twix þe lynand and þe hayir he chase þe mydwey, and al for he wold haue a conformi̧te be-twix his subiectis and him, 32 and eke for he wold fle þe veynglorie of þe world whech make me*n*

---

¹⁻¹ *in margin.*   ²⁻² *written above in red.*

ofte to lose heꝛ mede. This myd wey clepe we, þat he vsed, wollen [*] *He wore woollen cloth next his body.*
cloth next his body, for hayir wered he non, ne lynand wold he
non were. When he was compelled¹ be þe prouocacioñ of natuꝛ
4 to go to bed and² to rest he wold sey first certeyn Psalmes whech *He said Psalms before resting.*
he knew of³ vse, first for him-self and for his breþerin, þañ for
kyngis and bischoppis, and aꝺ⁴ cristen folk. This was his ‖ vsage, *Leaf 54, back.*
at seuene of clok he wold go to rest; seldom wold he ly on his bed,
8 but he sat⁵ þeron comounly. His clobis whech he wered on day *He wore his day-clothes at night, and had no pillow.*
he put hem not fro hym at eue, but lay with hem al nyth; ne
vndir his hed wold he no pilow haue, so þat whan he slept his hed
hing down with-outen sustentacle and touchid sumtyme his brest.
12 We rede in þe elde faderes lyues of Egipt þat þei cleped slep heꝛ
enmy be-cause at þat tyme, as þei þoute, þei sesed fro þe seruyse
of God. So ded ouꝛ Gilbert, as I suppose; he wold not ly soft
þat he schuld not slepe longe, for þei þat haue mech mete must
16 haue mech slep. And þerfor þat on-mesurable diete & þat diuturne
slepe was forbodyn be Crist whan he saide to his aposteles⁶: Be-waꝛ, *Christ forbade much sleep.*
he said, þat 3ouꝛ hertes be not greued with ouer mech mete, or
drynk, or slep. On his bed had ouꝛ maystir Gilbert no clobis but
20 of wolle and no bolstering but strawe. Whan he was sette þere
onys schuld⁷ no man heꝛ him speke a word tyl in þe morownyng.

[CHAPTER VII.]

cap. vij.

A FTYR þat laudes weꝛ said in the cherch þan wold he reherse *After Lauds Gilbert*
24   certeyn seyntis lyues; þan wold he sey certeyn orisones⁸ *rehearsed saints' lives,*
for hem þat aꝛ ded and assoyle hem; after þis wold he mak a *and made his*
meke and ‖ a long confessioñ, not only for him-self but for aꝺ his, *Leaf 55.*
asking of his breþerin of aꝺ his defautes forgyuenesse, and he *confession.*
28 assoiling hem aꝺ and gyuyng hem aꝺ his blessing lich as Seynt Iob
ded þat euery day offered on-to God for helth of his childyrn.⁹

¹ *d written above.*   ² *not clear in text and re-written above.*
³ *a character crossed through.*   ⁴ *his breþerin crossed through.*
⁵ *sad in text; sat in red in margin.*   ⁶ *In margin in red, Luc 21.*
⁷ *d added in red.*   ⁸ *s added in red.*
⁹ *In margin in red, Iob i.*

He was never
idle. This maystir Gilbert was neuyr ydil, but al þe day occupied, eythir
in redyng, or in orison, or in lesson, or in contemplacioñ, or in oþir
holy werkys, now and now chaungyng fro on to a-noþir, aftir tyme
and leyser þat he had.   And þouȝ he had mech to do ȝet went he 4
fro no mateᵖ til it hadde a parfith ende, ne he letted neuyr no
circumstauns of his perfeccioñ for ony straunge mateᵖ, þat is to
sey, for no temporal profith he putte not Goddis seruyse behinde [1],
ne þe holy obseruaunces whech longed to þe cloyster weᵖ not lettid 8
with besinesse whech was oute-ward.   In compassioñ he was [2] a
fadyr to aH men, in contemplacioñ moᵖ suspense þan oþir men.

He wept in
the singing
of Psalms. Offten wold he wepe in ympnis & Psalmys redyng, and in þe swete
songis of þe cherch whan he herd þe melodye, so was his soule 12
repleschid with swetnesse, but ȝet had he moᵖ delectacioñ in þe
wordis þañ in þe notes.   And a-geyn þese veyn þoutes þat come
sodeynly on us, avoyding þe swete deuocion þat we wold haue,

Leaf 55,
back. a ‖ meruelous vsage had he.   For in-as-mech he knew wel þeᵖ 16
myth no man want hem, he sette certeyn merkys of his fingeris and
his ioyntis in what place of þe Psalme he was, þat sone aftyr þe
temptacion was voyded he myth retorne a-geyn on-to þe same place

He chose one
of his people
to succeed
him. of his orison.   And ȝet moᵖ-ouyr, þat he schuld fulfiH al rith- 20
wysnesse, he chase on [3] of his subiectis whom he knewe be þe
Holy Goost þat he schuld succede in his office aftir his deth.
This man chase he specialy, and to him he mad his profession and
permitted his stabilnesse on-to þe hous of Sempingham, and so 24
of [4] þis same mannes handes took Gilbert þe habite of professioñ.
What constans and manhod was in þis mannes hert is ful manifest
in too maueᵖ þingis.   On is þat þe grete causes he went a-boute he
sped hem wyth-outen ony vexacioñ or perturbyng of soule.   A-noþir 28

He forgave
all wrongs. is þat alle þe wrongis whech were [5] do to him or his at þat tyme,
he bare hem so paciently þat he was neuyr mevid for hem.   Be-side
aH þis vexacion þat he had owtward, þere was a-noþer þing whech
stood nyher his hert, þe grete besinesse in spirith, for þo houses 32
whech he had rered, for þe soules whech he had gadered, for þe

Leaf 56. grete fere þat he hadde þat he schuld heᵖ ‖ no euel tytandis of
hem.   And whan it happed þat ony euel report was mad he wold

---

[1] *written above.*   [2] MS. a a fadyr; *perhaps* as a fadyr.
[3] MS. of his of his, *the first two words crossed through in red.*
[4] MS. þis þis, *the first crossed through.*   [5] *written above.*

blisse God, and speke sum mery wordis and turne all in-to solace. He brushed aside evil report,
He loued treuth and rithwisnesse so wel þat whan he was vexed
with ony materis, eythir with-oute þe religion or with-Inne, he
4 wold sey sumtyme he had leuer chese to be exiled, or elles his
þrote to be cutte, þan he schuld suffir in his tyme þe lawes of þe and insisted ever on the lawe of the Church.
cherch & þe good customes of religion schuld fayle.

[CHAPTER VIII.]

cap. viij.

8 IN þe last ende of his age, not-with-stande þat he was blynd, Though he was blind in his old age,
ȝet þe grete strength of his soule was not apeyred, for as
grete ȝel and as grete bysynesse had he at þis age to encrese of
religion and snybbyng of vices as euyr had he in his ȝong dayes.
12 His witte as fresch, his vndirstandyng as redy, his mynde as tow, yet he possessed all his other faculties.
his reson as clene were at þat our, and all oþir þingis þat longe to
þe soule as euyr þei were, whech was merueyle to se[1], specialy in
a man þat hadde a hundred wyntyr in age[2]. He myth her with þe
16 best. His tonge fayled not of his office. His hand qwaked not
with no palesye. His feet wer stabil to ber his body, and his[3] oþir
membris. Non of hem denyed his seruyse ‖ to þe body; lych Leaf 56, back.
he was on-to Caleph or Moyses, whech too at grete age had þe vse
20 of all her membris, saue þis differens is þere, þat þis man had lost
his sith. It is worthi[4], as summe men þink, þat þei whech serue
God with dew obediens schuld haue her membres obedient to hem[5].
For in þe mynde of þis man of whech we speke now was ful grete
24 hete[6] of charite, both on-to God and to all men, for in his hert Crist
wanted neuyr, men myth know be his mouth whech was euyr
spekyng of Crist. Eke his tonge and his handis wer euer redy to He was ever ready to help his neighbours.
help of his neybouris. This was þe cours of his lyf; þis was þe
28 maner of his lyuyng; þese be þe experiment of his vertues; þese
be þe good aray of his tecches with whech he was magnified with
grete men; for in vertu he was gretter þan þei, and nowt only was
he folower of þe blissed lyf of religious men, but he had a lif in He was a paradigm to his followers.
32 him-self whech religious men may folow: let se what man at þoo
dayes was so commendable of good[7] werkis þat he myth be set as

---

[1] C. 32. for to se.   [2] C. wynteyr of age.
[3] C. for to bere his body and all his.   [4] C. wordy.   [5] C. them.
[6] C. hete *omitted, and* grete *appears* greme.   [7] we *crossed through.*

He was
better than
other men,
equal to þis man; what man coude now gader so grete richesse with
swech [1] pouerte, ȝet [2] most meruayl of all, a seculer man, dwellyng
in court, seruyng in court, and newly drawe oute of þe world, whech

Leaf 57.
|| lerned neuyr of no man þe reules swech as [3] longe to þe monasterie, 4
þat he schuld [4] be parfite so sone and so sone knowe þoo reules [5].
Mor-ouyr þat he schuld [6] make reules in whech so many persones [7]
schuld [8] rise to parfitnesse, of þis had men wondyr. Wherfor þis
man for his holynesse was beloued [9], and for his magnificens stood 8

and he was
honoured
by all.
in meruayl [10] to men, but both to God and man he stood in grete
worchip. Kyngis and princes þei honoured him, bischoppes and
prelates þei receyued him ful deuoutly.

Þei þat wer ny him and eke þat dwelt fer fro him, þei loued 12
him, and schortly to sey, al þe puple held him in grete reuerens.
Eke þe vertu of our Lord whech gaue him al þis grace added
þertoo ful grete ioye, for he þat sette all þese good werkis in him
mad þe same werkys to schyne with vertues.   16

[CHAPTER IX.]

cap. ix.

Though these
are not the
days of
miracles,
AND þouȝ [11] it be so þat þese dayes be not vsed with myracles as
þe former dayes were, in [12] whech wer doo many myracles,
for as þe [13] Psalme saith, we se now no toknes, now is þere no 20
profete for to telle us what schal befall; and þouȝ it be so þat
Seynt Gilbert be mor worthi to be in worchep for his merytory [14]
dedes þan for doyng of myracles, ȝet on-to þe wytnesse of his good

Leaf 57,
back.
|| werkys, be-side þe grete bysynesse he had in wynnyng of soules, 24
whech is of mor vertu þan curyng of bodies, ȝet were þere, þorw þe

yet many
deeds were
done through
his holy life,
grete merit of his holy lyf, doo many toknes þorw whech his doctrine
was commended and his holynesse confermed. And euene as þorw
his wordis and his dedes þe rudenesse of many a soule was reformed, 28

and by his
vestments.
rith soo be þe touchyng of his cloþis, his hosen, or his girdyl, or
swech oþir [15] þingis whech [16] he touched his lyue, many a body was

---

[1] C 32 b. such.   [2] C. ȝet þe.   [3] C. as *omitted*.   [4] C. chulte.
[5] C. reules þer-of.   [6] C. chulte.   [7] *final* s *added above*.   [8] C. schulde.
[9] C. belowed.   [10] C. grett [mer]uell.
[11] MS. þow *dotted under and* þouȝ *written above*.   [12] *inserted above*.
[13] spl *crossed through in red.*   [14] *first* y *inserted above.*
[15] MS. oþis, s *crossed through and* r *written over in red.*   [16] *in margin.*

restored to helth aftir þe feith whech þei put in him.   Theʀ Some of his bread was kept sixteen years, and many were healed by it.
was bred kept sextene ȝere aftir his deth, on-corupte, on-mouled,
whech he blessed and sent to a[1] deuoute woman whech asked þat
4 in Goddis name, of whech bred many men haue ete and be holed
of dyueris seknesse.   Thus aftir he had fulfillid þe grete merites
of his perfeccio� and[2] sette in a parfite stabilnesse aꝶ his congregaciones, eke whaꝶ ouʀ Lord had disposed to rewarde his laboures
8 with euerlastyng ioye and þe tyme of his clepyng was ny, he
be-gan to wax more feble þanꝶ he was wone to be and sayde on-to
his bretherin he schuld not long lyue with hem, for þat þe membris
of his body be-gan to fayle, and nature, whech is propicius to helth,
12 had withdrawe sum-what[3] ‖ bir fauouʀ.   Thus, seknes growyng, and Leaf 58.
age of an hundred ȝere touching, he was in party compelled for to Finding himself growing feeble,
passe fro þis lif in whech he was gretly broken for penauns whech
he had þolyd in Goddis seruyse, but ȝet were aꝶ his[4] membris
16 hool as we saide be-fore, saue his sith.   Tho sent he letteris on-to he sent letters to the Churches of his order, saying that he was near death,
aꝶ þe cherchis of his order, in whech he notyfied on-to hem þat his
day was come in whech he schul leue his body here and goo to
Goddis mercy, praying hem deuoutly in þoo same letteris þat þei
20 schuld recomende his soule[5] with heʀ prayeris to God, most specialy
at þat tyme whan it schuld forsake þe body.   Eke in þoo same letteris
he gaue Goddis blessing and his[6] to alle[6] þat aftir his decese[7] schuld
loue þe ordre and kepe þoo congregacionis in parfith loue and
24 charite, and defende þe same ordre fro heʀ enmyes.   More-ouyr to
alle þat þis[8] comaundment fulfillid he sent pleneʀ absolucioꝶ of aꝶ and giving absolution.
þoo defautes in whech þei had trespased eythir a-geyn þe reule or
his instituciones.   And in þoo same letteris he wrot on-to aꝶ þoo
28 þat in þe order schuld make ony discord or ony scisme þat þis
present absolucioꝶ schul neuyr fauouʀ hem, but þat þei schuld
knowe hem-self, but if þei ded penauns þat þei weʀ reprobat of
God. ‖

---

[1] *written above in red.*   [2] St sent *crossed through.*   [3] *what in margin.*
[4] *þoo crossed through in red and his written above.*
[5] *inserted above in red.*   [6-6] *inserted above in red.*
[7] MS. dicese, e *written over in red.*   [8] *inserted above in red.*

cap. x.

THUS whan þe tyme was come in whech þat holy soule schuld leue þe In of his body[1]; in þe nyth in whech our Lord[2] Iheſu

When near death he was at Cadney, was born, it happed him to be at a hous of his in a ylde, whech 4 hous þei clepe Cadney, for in þat same hous at þe begin*n*ing of his seknesse he receyued þe sacra*m*entis of penau*n*s and of hosiłł, and þus many dayes aftir þat abode þe tyme assigned be ouꝝ Lord in whech his soule schuld passe fro his body with gre[te] auyſement 8

and was removed secretly to Sempring-ham, lest his body were arrested. and ful ryp deuocioꝛ. Thoo þei þat weꝝ with him, his chapeleynes and breþer*in*, þout3 þei wold remeve him fro þat place, for if it so happed þat he had dyed þeꝝ, þei weꝝ a-ferd þat su*m* man of gret myth wold a-reste þe body be þe weye in his caryage and take here 12 tresouꝝ from hem. Therfor þei caried him whil he was on lyue be othir weyes þan þe comown weye, and browt him to Sempyngham, for it was *conuenient*, as he*m* þout3, þat his body schuld ly þeꝝ whech he had sette a place, hed of ałł his monasteries. And in 16

All the leaders of his order went to him, þis space fro C*r*istmasse tyl þat day whech he dyed[3] ouꝝ Lord grau*n*ted him swech a space þat ałł þe soue*r*eyni*s* of his ordꝝ and ałł þe prouostis of his cherchis myth come and visite him, for so

Leaf 59. þei dede come on-to him and eke many a ‖ disciple of his, for þere 20

and were blessed. had þei his blessing and noble exhortaciones of pes & vnite of þe rigouꝝ eke and þe hardnesse of þe ordir, who it schuld be kept aftir his daies, and þus instruct þei went hom fro hi*m*. The last day of his temp*or*al lyf, whan ałł were owt of þe hous, he sat be his 24

His successor was with him. beddes side, he þat was successouꝝ in his office, takyng heed at him what he wold comau*n*de. And aftyr he had long be stille in silens as ma*n* þat schuld sone passe, he, no man seand, no man herand, but with þe Holy Gost replet, þus spak in þe goost. For 28 þou3 his bodyly[4] sith were rest fro him, 3et vndirstood he in his soule þat his successouꝝ was ny him, wherfoꝝ þese wordes of þe[5] Psalme, distinctly, openly, and wyth sad auyſement he sayde in þis

What he said. wise: He departed, he gaf to pore men. And þanne he rehersed: 32 He departed to many men. He gaf, and not seld, to pore men, not

---

[1] MS. soule, *with* body *written over in red.*   [2] *inserted above in red.*
[3] h *crossed through.*   [4] ly *in margin.*   [5] s *crossed through.*

to rich men.   And þan last he seid þus: To þe schal þis longe
heꝛ-aftirward.   Thoo spak he oþer þingis to þat same man whech
we can-not reherse.   These wordes, as I suppose, weꝛ ful *conuenient* His words were
4 on-to ouꝛ maystir, whech departed alt his goodis to many folk whech appropriate
he had called to þe seruyse of ouꝛ Lord, & gaf alt þese goodes
for pure charite, for he seld hem nowt, hopyng to haue of hem ony in him who gave his goods
worldly profith. ‖ To pore men gaf he þese goodys, non to rych, for Leaf 59,
8 þoo giftis ȝoue to pore men,[1] þei þat lyue in wilfult pouert for þe back. to the poor.
loue of God, schuld receyue him in-to euyrlastyng tabernacles.
To rich men he gaf it nowt, for þei nede not, and eke for it is ful
hard on-to hem to enter in-to þe kyngdam of heuene.   For þese For his deeds he is in
12 þingis þat he ded heꝛ, now is he in ioye and þis þat schuld be his heaven.
successour, he lerned for to do lich as he saide.

[CHAPTER XI.]

Cap. xj.

THE last day of Seynt Gilbert lif was a Sattirday; we schuld He died on Saturday, the
16 clepe it a Sabat-day be þe moꝛ congrue name.   Sabat is as Sabbath-day,
mech to sey þat day whan men rest of heꝛ werkys.   This day was
conuenient to his deth, for þann rested he of alt his labouꝛ whech
he had in þis mortal body.   He myth sey at his deth: Nite is
20 I-goo and day schal come; þe dirknes schal not take me ne trede
me.   The ouꝛ of his deth was whil þe couent was [2] at laudes [2], at when Lauds were being
mateyns, for at þat tyme as Iob sayth: Praisen God, ye morow said, on the
sterres.   That same Sabatday, þat is to say, þe fourt day of 4th of February, 1189,
24 Februarij, þe ȝere of þe Incarnacion of ouꝛ Lord, a þousand,
a hundred, eyty and nyne, swech tyme as nyte chaunged in-to
day, whilys þat þe laudes were sayde in þe couent, þis man passid
fro þe þirknesse of þis lyf, fro þe ‖ laboures of þis world, ful of age Leaf 60.
28 moꝛ þan a hundred ȝere.   Whidir þat he went ȝe schal here, for to over100 years old.
dwelle in þe hous of God, for to prayse God þere for euer, wheꝛ he
is sette in his ordre, þat is to say, a-mongis þe sercle and þe dauns
of virgines, as we hope, and as [3] reuelacion was mad to sum folk He is now with the
32 aftirward, þer hath ouꝛ Lord graunted him his sete.   Aftir his virgins of heaven.

---

[1] MS. to pore men or elt; or elt *crossed through and* pore men *again
written over it.*
[2-2] *inserted above.*   [3] *in margin.*

Distant
people knew
of his death
by visions,
and knew he
had joined
the heavenly
virgins.

deth weʳ certeyn visiones & reuelaciones mad to *persones* of grete
credens, þorw whech visiones þei þat weʳ dwellin*g* fer fro him had
very knowlech of þat oure and very certificacioñ þat he was ioyned
on-to þe felauchip of au*n*gell*es* in heuene. For þou3 it be so, as we
beleue, þat euery man receyueth mede aftir his werkys, and as
treuth sayth, þoo frendis þat be þe god of richesse, receyue þe
makeris i*n*-to euyr-lastyng tab*er*nacles, of grete rith-wisnesse þis
man is for to beleued þat he is ioyned to virgynes, for as mech as
he mayde both body & soule & mayde i*n* feith *per*seuered euyr, and
eke aʎ his erdly goodes 3aue on-to virgines, and for þe virginite of
many folk laboured aʎ his lyf.   For euene as he þat receyueth a

In that he
had his
reward.

rith-ful[1] man in þe name of a rithful ma*n* schal take þe mede of
a rithful ma*n*, euene so he þat[2] receyueth many virgines in þe

Leaf 60,
back.

name ‖ of virgines schal receyue þe mede of virgines.   Eke for as
mech as þis ma*n* was *pr*elate and begyn*n*er of mech nou*m*byr, both
of me*n* and women whech schuld avowe chastite, and be-cause þe

He has a
centenary.

nou*m*bir centenarie is applied as for a speci*a*l reward both to
prelates and to maydenes, þerfor hath þis man for þoo too þis
special reward.

[CHAPTER XII.]

capit*ulum* xij.

His body was
kept four
days, and all
his priors
came to the
burying.

THUS was þe soule of this blessed man translate on-to heuene
and þe ded body kept up-on þe ground fouʳ dayes with
exequiis and missis after þe good customes of þe cherch.   In þat
same tyme aʎ þe priour*is* and souereynes of þe ordre weʳ sent
aftir to be at þe byrying of her maystir.   Whan þei weʳ gadered

His progeny
numbered
2,200.

to-gidir and anou*m*bered, þe su*m*me of his progenie cam on-to[3]
too þousand and too hundred.   The fourt day aftir his deth, þat

On Tuesday

is to sey on þe Tewysday, were gadered to-gidir many prelatis,
both of his ordre and eke of oþir religio*us*, with mech folk of
þe cuntʳ[4] þat came þedir for reue*r*ens of þe man, and aftir tyme

they washed
the body,

þe masse was sayde, þei wasched þe body with watir, whech watir

Leaf 61.

was kept, for þei þat drank þerof weʳ restored to bodely ‖ helth.

arrayed it,
and buried it,

Aftir his wasching þei arayed him lych a prest, and þoo þei byried
him betwix too auteres, on of ouʳ Lady, Seyn Mary, þe oþir of

---

[1] C. 31 ryghtfull.

[2] h *crossed through.*

[3] MS. on-to a þou, *with* þou *crossed through.*

[4] C. contre.

Seynt Andrew þe apostel. He was so layd at þat tyme þat þe between two altars,
women myth com to þe graue on þe o side and men on þe oþir
side. The ston a-boue was not layd on-to þe tyme þat all men where, as it lay, all might
4 whech weᵽ present, as for heᵽ last leue, myth come an touche touch it.
þe body with what þing þei wold, and kisse it for reuerens of his
holynesse. Childyrn, maydenes, ne no degre, had no feᵽ, no horrouᵽ
in cyssyng of þat ded body, for feith gaf hem boldnesse to touch
8 it and loue sent hem boldnes to kisse it. What mornyng þeᵽ was There was great mourning.
of all folk, what lamentation of clerkis, what wepyng of maydenes,
for as mech as þei haue lost[1] heᵽ hed and heᵽ principal, heᵽ fader
and her schippard, and for þei schuld no moᵽ haue him to her
12 consolacion, weᵽ long to telle. But ouᵽ Lord God þat wrout all
þese werkys in his seruaunt, be whom þis same seruaunt Gilbert
had grete prosperite in all his werkis, this same Lord wold neythir
defraude his werkman of his mede ne þe good werkys of heᵽ
16 parfith ende, as it schal be schewid in þis next declaracioñ. Many miracles
Be-side þoo myracles whech weᵽ do þe day of his byryng, and
be-side þe myracle ‖ do in substitucioñ of his successouᵽ, þer fell Leaf 61, back.
many oþir grete, of blynde men, def men, bedred, dropesie, ffevyrues, were done through him.
20 wodnesse, and oþir grete seknesse, whech weᵽ cured, summe be þe
watyr in whech he was waschid, summe be oþir relikes of him,
sum be dremes and visiones, summe in þe same place of his
byryng, summe in oþir places. It is no doute þat his werkes weᵽ
24 ful plesaunt on-to ouᵽ Lord, wherfor þat he schuld stand in þe
moᵽ worchip a-mongis men, ouᵽ Lord mad his werkis to be
magnified aftyr his deces, in so mech þat, be þe comaundment of
Innocent Pope þe þird, Hubert bischop of Cauntirbyry and[2] Hubert of Canterbury,
28 a-noþer bischop of Hely, eke þe abbot of Borow, with many oþir, the bishop of Ely, and the abbot of Borow inquired into these miracles.
mad diligent inquisioñ and redact all þis in a forme and sent it
vp to þe court.

[CHAPTER XIII.]

cap. xiij.

32 AND when ouᵽ holy fader þe Pope had receyued þis infor- Pope Innocent III canonized Gilbert,
macioñ with[3] councel of his breþerin, þe cardinales, he
mad þis man, þis Seynt Gilbert, to be a-noumbred and ascribed

---

[1] he *crossed through.*

[2] bi *crossed through.*   [3] his *dotted underneath.*

in þe cathaloge of seyntes. A cathaloge is a schort writyng of
seyntes, in whech wrytyng is *conteyned* of what cuntꝛ þe seynt

and com-
manded his
feast to be
held
was & eke his holy lif. The Pope comau*n*ded eke þat same tyme
his feest to be solempnyȝed in þe cherch and made collectes to 4

Leaf 62.
be seyd in his *commemoracion*. He co‖mau*n*ded eke his body

and his body
to be trans-
lated.
to be translat, as it was fulfillid aftirward. For þese causes
þis faderis day schuld be solempniȝed with þe moꝛ deuocioꞥ and
with more besinesse, because his lyf was holyer, his doct*r*ine 8
moꝛ holsom, his labouꝛ moꝛ feru*e*nt, his frute moꝛ plenteuo*us*,
his deth moꝛ prouable, his *m*yracles moꝛ euydent þaꞥ su*m*me
oþir, and þ*er*for he, be liklynesse, hath be-for God moꝛ ioye and

Let the
Church Joy in
the Joy of her
son !
be-foꝛ men moꝛ worchip. Ioye be mad be ouꝛ moder þe cherch 12
of þe ioye to whech hir son is now newly browt, and to hir worchip
and profith of hir childyrn synge sche [1] þe praysyng of God and
hir owne, þat þorw þe prayeꝛ of hir meritis sche myth make pes
with vices, put awey adu*er*sities, brynge in þe strength of vertues, 16
þe profite and encres of very religioꞥ, owre londes and cuntres,
God ouꝛ makeꝛ grau*n*tyng, dispose in euyrlastyng pes, confermyng
þat ouꝛ Lord Ihe*s*u Crist, to whom with þe Fadeꝛ and Holy Gost
eu*er* be worchip and ioye &c.   Amen.   20

[CHAPTER XIV.]

Heꝛ is þe secund p*art* of Sei*n*t Gilbert lyf, þe capitule 14.

B E-cause þat a gret part of iustise is for to do non euel and
þe profite of þe same iustise is for to do good, and eke 24
for it is not i-now to ouꝛ helth þat we take not oþ*er* me*n*nes

Leaf 62,
back.
good wrong‖fully or desire it wrongfully, but we be bou*n*de
for to ȝeue owne goodes for þe loue of God frely. For þis cause

Gilbert
worked for
the increasing
of religion.
þis very prest Gilbert stodied euery day to bere schidis to þe 28
holy fyꝛ whech brent in þe tabernacle, both nyth a*n*d day, for
þe fire of charite þat was in the tabernacle of his breest brent
him-selue, a ful deiectable offeri*n*g to ouꝛ Lord. And þat he
schuld not renne in blynd pr*e*sumpcioꞥ, ne vse maneres with-oute 32
consid*er*acion, but þat he schuld renne and take þe summe of his

---

[1] *l crossed through.*

merites, the best maner of perfeccioñ and þe trewest way to
perfeccioñ with grete bysynesse, he both soute and took. The
first grouɲd of his werk he sette in heith of mekeɲesse, whech
4 vertu dispisith in euery man his owne excellens, for þe veri place
of meknesse is in heuene. Therfor he put a-wey þe mater of ⟶He despised worldly
al erdly goodes fro him-self, for þoo same goodis sette a man worth,
in fals excellens and þrowe a man al vndir-fote. He þrew fro
8 him all pride whech schuld ryse[1] of vertues þat weɼ with-inne
him. He took ful gret heed to þe voys of ouɼ Lord þat seith: If
þou wilt be parfiþt, go selle all þat euyr þou hast and folow me.
This man ded þus. He gaf his goodes to pore men, not for ⟶and gave all to the poor,
12 vanyte but for charite, and for þat gift þe mynde of his rith-
wisnesse schal dwelle with-outen ende. Whañ ‖ he had determyned ⟶Leaf 63.
in his hert þat all his goodes schuld be departed on-to poɼ men,
þañ chase he swech pore whos pouerte was honest, knyt[2] with ⟶who were honest.
16 þe dred and eke þe loue of God, for his desire was to sowe his
sedes in þe blessingis of God, þat he myth repe in þoo same
blessingis. In þat same tyme, þat is to seye, in þe regne of ⟶In the reign of Henry II,
King Herry þe secunde, as he writith in þe book mad of the as is said in his book on
20 construccioñ of monasteriis, in þat same time[3] were in þe town monasteries,
of Sempyngham certeyn maydenes seculeɼ, whos soules þe seed
of Goddis word, sowyn be þis same Gilbert, had so touchid þat
þei were rype on-to religioñ lich as corn is white to heruest.
24 These same maydenes, desyring to be victouɼis of heɼ kynde & eke ⟶certain maidens at Sempringham had been led
of þe world, euery day entendyd to no[4] oþir þing but to plese and by him to forsake the
to be kynt to þat[5] spouse whech is in heuene. This, aspied be world.
Seynt Gilbert, specialy whañ he had in his avow mad a promisse
28 þat his possession of Sempyngham and of Tyrington schuld be ⟶He gave his possessions
ȝoue to God, ferþermoɼ þat he wold ȝeue þis to pore, and eke to God.
he fonde no men at þat tyme wold lyne so strey[t]ly as þese
women were disposed, for þis cause, he determyned to gyue þese
32 goodes to swech pore whech were poɼ in spirit & myth ‖ chalange ⟶Leaf 63,
þe kyngdam of Heuene[6] for hem & for oþir. This man Gilbert back.
mad him frendes with swech rychesse as he had, whech frendis
schuld receyue him in-to euerlasting tabernacles. The first frendes

---

[1] rise *crossed through in red.*   [2] Ɉe *crossed through.*
[3] *inserted above in red.*   [4] MS. no no, *the first crossed through in red.*
[5] MS. þat þat.   [6] w *crossed through.*

þat he made weꝛ not of men but of wommen. Wommen chase
he first for þe similitude whech ouꝛ Lord rehersed in þe gospeƚƚ [1]
of a womman þat had lost a dramme and found it, who sche
cleped hir frendes to ioye with hir [2] for hir dramme þat was 4
found. So þese maydenes first chosen were cause þat many oþer
schuld be cleped aftirward. A dramme is a certeyn mony of
gold weying þe viij part of an vnce. Oure Gilbert be-gan his
perfeccioꝺ at þe febiller kende, for to þe febiller kynde nature 8
techeth þat we schuld do ouꝛ benefetes. þe councel of God is
swech also [3] to help þat þing whech is moost febil, eke þe mede
for þis help is þe gretteꝛ, ferþermoꝛ [4] oure Lord in þe gospel to
þe febelest kynde applied þe grettest reward, þe hundredfold frute 12
to virginite. Gilbert norchid þis astate, and þerfor hath he part
of her reward. Be-side al þis, ouꝛ Gilbert, aftir þe rith ordre
in elmesse-ȝeuyng, gaf his goodes to hem þat were rithful, aftir
þe councel of Salamon wheꝛ he saith: Gyue þi goodes on-to good 16
men and receyue not ‖ þese synneres to þin elmesse.

His first friends in religion were women,

for it is noble to benefit the feebler kind.

Gilbert has the reward of virginity.

Leaf 64.

[CHAPTER XV.]

Capi*tul*um xv.

Seven maidens were the beginning of the Gilbertine order.

SEUENE maydenes, as we saide be-fore, fulfillid with heuenely
desires in worchip of þat noumbir of seuene giftis longing 20
on-to þe Holy Goost, þese were beginneres of þis holy religioꝺ
vnder ouꝛ fadir Gilbert. These seuene bodily virgines, offered to þe
noumbyr of þese seuene giftis, mad her virginite the moꝛ merytorye
be-cause þei weꝛ arayed with vertues. [5] What profitith a laumpe 24
þat hath non oyle? What profitith cleue flesch whan þe soule is
corrupt? What profitith a body clene and a hert defouled? Be
þis weye schuld þese hethen men be vertuous whos lyf is al synne.

They were clean in body and in mind.

Therefor, þat þese maydenes schuld be clene in soule & body, to heꝛ 28
soules he ordeyned clene instrumentis, heꝛ bodies with whech þei
schuld werk heꝛ owne helth [6]. And be-cause þat no man whech
seruyth God may serue wel God and be occupied with temporal

---

[1] *In margin in red,* Luc. xv.
[2] *inserted above in red.*
[3] *inserted above in red.*
[4] *in black and red in margin.*
[5] *O crossed through.*
[6] *E crossed through.*

besinesse,[1] eke be-cause v*i*rginite is a tendir þing & may sone be
tempted of þe sotil deceytes of þe serpent, þe Deuele, whech is ful
eld of tyme and ful sotil of kynde & sone deceyueth virginite,

4 namely, whann̄ it is sette so open þat it is schewid to þe world,—
for tresour̄ openly bore is put in gret *perel*, ‖ —for þis cause he sperd Leaf 64,
þese virgines fro þe noyse of þe world, fro þe sith of men, þat þei baok.
whech schuld[2] entyr in-to þe p*r*iuy chau*m*byr of þe spouse þei They were
shut in from
the world,

8 schuld only entende on-to þe swete halsyng of þe same spouse.
He wold not þat þei schuld walk to se vanytes, as ded Dina, but
þat þei schuld hide hem in her̄ tabernac̃e, as dede Sarra, or in
her̄ *conclaue*, as ded Our̄ Lady.   And for it is not I-now for to[3] and they lived
according to

12 absteyno fro euel but if we doo good, þerfor he mad to hem a lawe the law which
Gilbert made
of holynesse & tawte hem þat same with whech þei schuld plese to for them.
þe heuenely spouse & cleue euyr to his chast halsyngis in alĺ maner
clennesse.   Thus gaf he hem a lawe of lyf and of loue,[4] of chastite,

16 of meknesse, of obediens, a[n]d charite, and all oþir vertues whech
lede to euyrlasti*n*g lif, he comau*n*ded hem to kepe.   Thei, as good
disciples, ioyfully receyued hem & deuoutly fulfillid hem.   Ther̄
schone, or ellis schyned, in þe soule of þese women, a fayr̄ beute of

20 *p*recious *p*erles, of swech goostly richesse as our̄ Lord tellith in þe
gospelĺ, þat a man schuld selle alĺ þat he hath for to welde þis.
And þouȝ þei lyued in flesch and not aftyr þe flesch, ȝet wost he wel They were
supplied with
as longe as þei were in flesch, be-side swech neccessaries as longe to all things

24 þe flesch, þei myth not lyue, ‖ þerfor al þing þat is nedful to our̄ Leaf 65.
fleschly febilnesse, as mete, or drynk, or cloþi*n*g, or houses, alĺ þese necessary to
life,
ordeyned he to þese maydenes and her̄ seruauntis in best maner̄,
in mesur̄ and discrecion̄, þat is to seyn, swech houses as long to

28 religion̄, with a cloystir, or a clauser̄, wallid abowte, and in þoo and dwelt in
a cloister by
houses he sperd þe handmaydenes of our̄ Lord, euyr for to dwelle the church,
built with the
þer̄ in solitarie lyf; and þis werk was undyr þe wal of þe cherch help of
Alexander,
of Seynt Andrew, in þe strete or town of Sempyngha*m*, on þe north bishop of
Lincoln.

32 side, first axid and had þe counsel and þe help of Alexau*n*der, þan
bischop of Lincoln̄.   Dore was þere non mad in þe wal [5] but on, &
þat was not open but swech tyme as schal be touchid afterward;

---

[1] *In margin in red,* 2 Thi 2.   [2] *et crossed through.*
[3] do good *crossed through.*   [4] MS. lore.
[5]-[5] *added in margin ; the added passage continues on the next page.*

In the wall
was a window
through
which they
received
necessaries;

þere mad he⁵ ¹a wyndowñ þorw whech þei myth receyue swech neccessaries as longe to her lif, for þouȝ þei weᵽ in the world he wold put hem oute of þe world, fro her lond, from heᵽ kynrod, from heᵽ fadir hous, þat þus exiled fro aħ þese, lich a cherch, and 4 þei a cherch, þat is to seye, a congregacioñ in o feith and o charite,

for the rest,
they were cut
off from the
world.

forgeting heᵽ puple and heᵽ fader hous, fro aħ curiosite and aħ couetyse, or *concupiscence*, fro aħ pride, þus clene I-schake to þe hy kyng, schuld make a complacens in desiryng of her beute.² 8 Thus bonde he heᵽ bodies with-inne þoo walles at þat same place

Leaf 65,
back.

Sempingham. ǁ

[CHAPTER XVI.]

caᵐ. xvj.³

BVT he wold not, þouȝ he *prisoned* heᵽ bodyes, bynde heᵽ soules 12 fro God, but þis was his entent to close hem, be-cause þat *conuersacion* in þe world is wone to⁴ departe many men fro þat familiarite whech þei schuld haue with God. Eke be-cause þat

Gilbert
appointed
maids to wait
upon them.

þei myth no-where go oute, þerfor he ordeyned on-to heᵽ seruyse 16 *certeyn* maydenes not lerned, in a pore seculeᵽ habite, whech schuld brynge on-to þat wyndowne mad in þe wal aħ þing þat was neccessary for hem, and receyue of hem at þat same hole swech

The hole in
the wall, or
window, was
not always
open;

þingis as was *conuenient* to bere out. That same hole left he ope, 20 but not euyr ope, for it was opened but at certeyn tymes whech weᵽ assigned, for he wold a sperd it for euyr if it had be so þat men or wommen myth a leued with-oute mete or drynk or oþer neccessaries. For a dore was mad beside, but neuyr open 24

and the door
was only for
Gilbert to
enter by.

with-oute⁵ his special comaundment, not for þe maydenes to go owt, but for him to entyr on-to hem for goostly coumfort, or techyng of religioñ,⁶ or visiting of þe seke, or swech oþir

He alone kept
the key of it.

neccessarie causes; eke of þat dore was he gayleᵽ him-self; no 28 man bare þat keye but he. Whidir þat he went, wher-euyr he dwelt, þe key of þat dore was with hym, so was he gelous loueᵽ

Leaf 66.

of here clennesse. Aftir þis he stodyed soᵽ þat þere schuld ǁ no þing owtward breke þat pes whech þese solitarye folk had in heᵽ 32

---

¹ but *crossed through.*   ² *In margin in red,* Ps. 4 4 (Psalm 4 v. 4 ?)
³ *In margin,* 16.   ⁴ p *crossed through.*
⁵ oute *in red above.*   ⁶ o *and a stroke crossed through.*

clauseꝛ.   He lerned eke of religio*us* men and wise me*n* þat it was *It was not safe that*
not *conuen*ient, ne sykir, þat seculeꝛ maydenes renny*ng* a-boute þe *secular maids*
world schuld serue swech solitarye p*er*sones, for euel speche often *should wait upon the*
4 tyme appeyreth ful good maneres, and eke þei þat ru*n*ne so a-boute *nuns,*
schuld bryng clateri*ng* tydi*n*gis, whech myth apeyre þe soules of
þe nu*n*nes, for þis cause þoo same seculeꝛ maydenes, with þe good
counsel of heꝛ fadeꝛ Gilbert and p*ar*ty with heꝛ owne deuocio*n*, *so these, too, took a habit;*
8 desired [1] to haue a religio*us* habite and so dwell with þe nu*n*nes ;
and, as þei desired, so had þei.   For þeꝛ, wha*n* þei weꝛ clad in a ful
pore lyf, þei serued þe nu*n*nes and lyued in ful honest *conuer*sacio*n*.
Thus of o kyrnel whech ouꝛ fou*n*douꝛ [2] þrew in þe erde grewe now
12 a-noþer ere be-side þe first spryng whech was þe nu*n*nes.   Þan
wha*n* Sei*n*t Gilbert say þe good ȝel of þese seculeꝛ maydenes þus *but being simple and*
chaunged on-to God, he was ful mery for deuocio*n* of heꝛ feith, but *unused to hard life,*
be-cause þei weꝛ inexp*er*t, not vsed in swech, and simpil and lewed *they were just as*
16 as touchi*ng* lettirure, for swech ydiotes al day be-hest moꝛ þing *incapable of*
þa*n* þei may fulfill, þerfor wold not he, ouꝛ fadir Gilbert, gyue hem *fulfilling the difficult*
no hard p*re*ceptis ne ley no greuo*us* birden on heꝛ schulderis whech *precepts of religion*
þei schuld þrowe awey aftirward and repent, ‖ to grete schame of *Leaf 66,*
20 hem-self and grete vylony to religio*n*.   Therfor þese neophites ar *back.*
for to proue, þat Sathanas transfiguꝛ not him-self in-to an aungell *as Satan is of*
of lith ; þat þe wolf do not on his bak a schepis wolle ; þat þe ostrich *transfiguring himself into*
tak not þe wengis of an hauke ; þat þe asse haue not þe leones *an angel, &c.*
24 membris.   All þis is seid be þe auctouꝛ of þis lif whech is of þis
Seynt, þat he calleth hem neophites þat he newly *conu*erted to
religio*n* ; for neophites weꝛ cleped i*n* eld tyme folk newly *conu*erted
to þe feith, and all þese transumpciones folowing reher*s*ith ouꝛ
28 aucto*ur* to þis ent*ent*, þat me*n* of religio*n* schuld not haue faiꝛ *Examples*
*con*diciones owtward and euel inward, as malys i*n* soule lich a wolf *for men of religious life.*
and *inn*oce*n*s in wordis lich schepis wolle, and soo may men
expou*n*ne all þe othir *tra*nsumpciones.   For þis same cause þat
32 þese folk schuld [3] vndirstand what þei ded, and eke þat þei schuld
proue, as heꝛ age grew, what þei schuld answeꝛ, þis noble mayst*er*
told hem be-foꝛ all þese perell*es* and lerned hem all þe scharpnesse
of religio*n*, all þat eu*er* þei had lerned be experie*n*s or be tellyng of

---

[1] *final* d *above in red.*
[2] MS. fou*n*der, *with* er *crossed through and* ouꝛ *in red in margin.*
[3] vnd *crossed through.*

Gilbert taught his sisters to follow the ascetic life.

oþer men. To his sisteres he prechid þat þei schuld despiſe þe world & cast fro heꝛ hertis aꝟ maneꝛ of *propirte*, þat is to seyne, þei schuld þink no-þing was heꝛ, but al comoun, as religious folk must doo: he taute hem þe man*er* who þai schuld chastise[1] heꝛ[2]

Leaf 67.

flesch to trauayle ‖ and to occupye hem fro ydilnesse, and neuyr to sitte qwiete fro labouꝛ in prayeꝛ or occupacioꝝ. He taute hem for to wake & not to slepe mech, to fast longe & not to vse metes oute

Their living was harsh and they were enclosed as in a prison.

of tyme. Wrecchid mete, scharp cloth, þis wold he[3] þei schuld haue; no gay aray, but sperd in cloystir as in prison, þat þei schuld do no euele; to kepe silens, þat þei schuld no euele speke, but be occupied with orisones and meditaciones to avoyde euel þoutes. Thei answered on-to him at þat tyme þat aꝟ þese preceptis plesed hem weel, to take hardnesse for softnesse, labouꝛ for ese, heuynesse for swetnesse, aꝟ þese þingis wold þei gladly suffer, so þei myth

Their poverty drove them to holiness;

come wher þei desired. The nede of pouerte *con*streyned hem, and labouꝛ in beg*ing*, for to desire to beꝛ hy þingis, to þat entent þat þei myth be sykir of euyrlastyng reward. The loue of God, eke, þat drowe hem to þis same ent*ent*, and helth of her soules þorw

and making a virtue of necessity, they came to good.

whech þei myth deserue euyrlastyng rest. So of nede þei mad vertue, and þouӡ in summe of hem weꝛ not þe very entent of perfeccioꝝ, ӡet it lettid not but it gat hem þe ende of good werk. But þis holy man wold not bynde hem sodeynly to þis perfeccioꝝ,

Gilbert gave all one year's consideration.

but lete hem haue a ӡere of a-visement, þat of þat grete dilacioꝝ schuld growe þe desire of religioꝝ.

4

8

12

16

20

24

[CHAPTER XVII.]

Leaf 67, back.

cap. **xvij.** ‖

But seeing that woman's business profits little without men, Gilbert chose certain men to govern his women.

THAN say ouꝛ fadeꝛ in his inwardly consideꝛacioꝝ þat, with-outen mennys solace and puruyaunce, womennes besinesse profitith but lytyl; þerfor chase he certeyn men whech schuld ouyr-se heꝛ possessiones and haue gouernauns of aꝟ þo grete materes whech longed on-to hem. Summe of þese chase he of his plowmen and of his seruauntes, summe of pore mennes childyrn and beggeres whech he had norched fro her childhod. He was lich

28

32

---

[1] MS. chastite, *with se over in red.*   [2] flech *crossed through.*
[3] MS. hei, i *dotted beneath.*

þe seruaunt of whech þe gospel[1] spekith, þat at þe comaundment
of our Lord went in-to þe lanes & stretes of þe cite, & swech as he
fonde pore or febil, brout &[2] compelled hem to enter þat his lordis
4 hous schuld be ful. To þese men, þus newly gadered, whech he
say wer inflawmed with þe [loue][3] of euerlastyng lyf, to þese same,
at her peticion, he ordeyned a tokne of meknesse, an habite whech
signified to hem þat þei schuld despise þis world and for-gete þe
8 vanite þat longith þerto. And þoo same *preceptis*, ful hard and
not esy, of whech we spoke be-fore, he wrote on-to hem, and taute
hem þat þei schuld not fall fro mynde. He taute hem ferþermor
oþir vertues þat longe propirly to þe soule, as meknesse, obediens,
12 paciens, and swech oþer, whos exercise is hard and mede gret,
& þei, as deuoute disciples, took þese *preceptis* glad‖ly and mad
her avow to fulfill hem for euyr. Thus is þe tresour, or elles þe
talent, doblid, þat our Lord took him[4], for our Lord put first in
16 his mynde to make a congregacion of women, and now newly he
hath dobiled þis ȝift whan he gadered þese men. Thus is þe
iunctur of women and men ioyned as broches for þe crowne of
þe spouse, þus mad be þe handis of þe hye werkman. Now is
20 þe tyme come þat þe welbeloued masculyne with þe welbeloued
feminine schuld go oute in-to þe feld of þis world, for to dwelle in
þe villages and in þe cytees of puple. Now was þe day come þat
þe vyne whech our Lord planted[5] schuld fulfill þe erde with his
24 rotes, and sprede his palmes to þe se, and his braunches to þe oþir
flodes ; þat is to say, þat þe membris of þis ordre schuld sprede þe
braunchis of good exaumple, þat it schuld be know wyde. Thus
be *processe* of tyme, be þe wil of our Lord God, þe seed whech he
28 had sowen be þe first faderes of þis weye, many rich men, noblemen of Ynglond, þat is to seye, Erles, Barones, and oþir, seyng
and approuyng þis werk whech God had be-gunne, and seyng
be-for what goodnesse was disposed aftir[6], þei offered many
32 possessiones to our fader Gilbert, & monasteries, in many prouynces,
vndyr his reule and gouernauns, þei be-gunne ‖ to edifie, of whech
helpes Alisaundr bischop of Lincoln was first, and Kyng Herry

Marginal notes:
To these men he ordained a habit which taught them to despise the world,

and he taught them virtue and hard exercises.

Leaf 68

So is his treasure doubled,

for unto the women of his order are joined men.

Many noblemen of England, seeing his good work, helped him, and founded monasteries under his rule.

Leaf 68, back.

---

[1] *In margin in red, Luc 14.*   [2] *added in red.*
[3] *MS. with þe of everlastyng, etc., of commencing a new line.*
[4] *In margin in red, M[t] 25. (Matthew xxv.)*
[5] *with his rotes crossed through in red.*   [6] *added in margin.*

Some gifts
Gilbert
received, and
some he
refused, for he
wanted his
people to live
poor.

þe secunde, he confermed aĺ. Ouꝛ fadir Gilbert receyued þese possessiones with ful gret dred; and summe was he in maner coact to receyue; summe refused he and wold not haue hem, be-cause his desiꝛ was fro þe begynnyng of his ordre þat his progenie schuld 4 lyue in honest pouerte. Honest pouerte clepe we þat a man is not in myschef for his dayly nede, ne he hath neythir no gret superfluite of good. This was þe cause þat he wold not haue ouyr mech whan it was ȝoue him, for often-tyme it is seyn þat a-mong gret multitude 8 of puple and gret plente of richesse rise ful gret spottis of pride, as it is said be þe wise man¹: In þe multitude of þe puple² ioye of þe

His first
intention was
to keep only
his seven
maidens, but
when great
gifts were
given him

kyng. For his first purpos at his begynnyng was for to a kept no moo but þoo seuene whech he had sperd up, þat as long as þei 12 lyued þere schuld be no moo. But he sey be þe wil of ouꝛ Lord þat rich men had multiplied many monasteries to encres of þis ordre; he wold not be contrarie to Goddis wil, ne lette þe deuocion of þe ȝeueres, ne be rekles of þe sustentacioñ to þe seruauntis of 16 God, knowing wel þat þis was Goddis uertu, and not his; wherfor,

Leaf 69.

he acceded
in allowing
the order to
grow.

he comitted al þis disposicioñ ‖ to þe profund counceĺ of ouꝛ Lord whech vsetȝ þe seruyse both of good & euel after his plesauns.

[CHAPTER XVIII.]

cap^m. xviij.³   20

On the
growth of his
people, how-
ever, Gilbert
thought him-
self unworthy
to rule so
many;

W̶HAN ouꝛ maystir Gilbert say þus þe childyrn of God grow sco vndir his tuycioñ and say hem profiten day be day in þe weye of God on-to þe tyme in whech þei were gretly magnified, he demed of him-self, as it longith to good soules to haue hem-self in 24 litil reputacioñ, so demeth he him-self on-worþi for to be in swech heith þat he schuld haue gouernauns ouyr so many parfit persones.

and decided
to give his
order to abler
governors.

He þoutȝ, þerfor, þat he wold put þis byrden and þis honouꝛ fro him, and comitte his flok to on or elles many whech weꝛ abiler and 28 mytier þan he, þat þei schuld haue it in gouernauns. He was in þis cas a foloweꝛ of Moyses whech seid on-to ouꝛ Lord: I pray þe Lord sende him þat þou schal sende⁴, menyng herby that he was not able to be sent. And in a-noþir place Moyses saide to God: 32

---

¹ *In margin in red, Prouer 14.*   ² *added in margin.*
³ *In margin, 18.*   ⁴ *In margin in red and black,* Exo. 3.

Whom schal þou gyue, Lord, for to be Gouernouꝛ and principal
ouyr þis multitude, whech multitude þou hast mad growe in-to
a grete puple? Thou knowist þat fro þat tyme þat þou spak to
4 me, þi seruaunt, þat I schuld take up-on me to be president ouyr
þis puple, sith þat tyme I am a man of lower lyf, þat is to seye
a man of seculeꝛ ‖ conuersacioñ, whech schuld be holier þan othir,
and am not. I knowe ful [1] wel þat þe dom schal be ful greuous to
8 hem whech ar prelates, for þei must answeꝛ for hem-self and eke
for heꝛ subiectis, and I am ful euel aferd þat if I be not bettir þan
my flok, I schal be turned fro þe first to þe last. Swech maneꝛ
wordes had he often and swech desires to leue his prelacye. In al
12 þis besinesse he herd telle þat þere schuld be a gret congregacioñ
of þe ordre of Cystewys, whech was neuly be-gunne þat tyme be
Seynt Bernard. Wheꝛ it was hold, i rede not, but þe Pope Eugenie
was þere, whech was sumtyme disciple to Seynt Bernard. To þis
16 congregacioñ went ouꝛ Gilbert,[2] purposing for to comitte þe cure
of his childyrn to þe kepyng of þese monkis. For þese mennes
conuersacion knewe he best be grete familiarite whech he had with
hem, for often þei come and weꝛ loggid with him, and to þese only
20 told he his counsell, for þei weꝛ neweꝛ and of harder reule þañ þe
blake munkis be. Wherfor he [3] supposid þat his ordꝛ schul be in
most sikirnesse if it weꝛ committed to hem, for heꝛ new fundacioñ
and heꝛ streytnesse was moꝛ accordyng to his conceyt. His answeꝛ
24 had he of þe Pope and of þe abbotis whech weꝛ present: ‖ þei
saide it was not conuenient þat prelatis of her order schuld be
preferred to þe gouernauns of an-oþir ordre, specialy wheꝛ wommen
were. Thus frustrat of his purpos, he took his leue, and, be þe
28 comaundment of þe Pope and counsel of þe prelates þere present,
he was mad maystir and principall ouyr þat congregacioñ whech
he had begunne. Ouꝛ Lord wold not þat þe congregacioñ at
Sempingham schuld wante heꝛ owne kepeꝛ whech was bettyr on-to
32 hem þan ten oþir, as Helchana sayd to Anna.[4] For ouꝛ Lord had
disposed þat same congregacioñ to rise to þe moost parfith noumbyr
whech was at þat tyme of an-othir condicion. This religion, whech
we clepe ouꝛ sistir, was but ȝong at þis tyme, for sche had no tetes
36 as ȝet, of prelates and souereynes, to gyue soke on-to þe tendyr age

Gilbert said he was of lower life since he became governor of his people.

Leaf 69, back.

He heard of a Cistercian congress,

which the Pope attended;

and to this he went, proposing to give these monks charge of his people.

The Pope and the

Leaf 70.

abbots, however, would not agree,

and made him principal of his order,

which was young then.

---

[1] þa crossed through.
[2] pp. crossed through.
[3] s and a stroke crossed through.
[4] In margin in red, 1 Reg. 1.

of heẜ subiectis, ne for to gyue mete of substauns to hem whech were growe in-to more perfeccioⁿ, whech eke schuld dispose aⁿ þe flok with¹ proteccioⁿ owtward and inwardly² *conferment*.

<h2>[CHAPTER XIX.]</h2>

Gilbert was given authority because there was none

THUS, be ouẜ holy fader Eugeny was comitted aⁿ auctorite to our maystir Gilbert in³ þe kepyng of þis holy flok, for þere was not founde a bettir ne more sewireẜ kepeẜ þa�65 þat same man

Leaf 70, back.

whech was gaderer of þat puple, & eke ‖ so gelous a loueẜ of hem 8

more fit to have it.

and þe first laboureẜ in þat holy vyne. Neuyɼþelasse, he held him-self onworþi to þe birden of swech a wyte; he alegged þe importunyte of his age, þe onworthþinesse of him-self to swech dignyte, þe simpilnesse to þat maystirhod, his lownesse eke to so 12 hye a prelacye. Aⁿ þis drede⁴ had he in his soule þat he was not

He thought himself unworthy,

worþi to be *preferred* to swech dignite; he dred eke to lese þe solitarie rest of his *contemplacioⁿ*, for weel he wist þat þoo secret councellis whech he was used too, and þe bysy swetenesse of *contem-* 16

and knew his contempla- tion would be interrupted;

placion, schuld often be interrupt with worldly occupacion and bysy oure whech longeth on-to *prelates*. Alle þese excusaciones of meknesse were not amitted of þe Pope, but þe ʒok of aⁿ þis birden

but the Pope gave him the charge.

was leid in his nek, for þe Pope comitted aⁿ þis cure on-to him, 20 be-cause he say þat he had no grete appetite ne desiẜ þertoo. The purpos of ouẜ fader Gilbert was euyr to dwelle a-*mongis* hem þat be meke, and þe wil of ouẜ Lord God is euyr of custom to exalte

When Gilbert knew God's will he no

hem þat moost meke hem-self. Thus, whan þis Goddis owne man 24 knew wel þat þe dome of God had ordeyned he schuld take þis

Leaf 71.

charge, he was no moẜ hardy to ma‖ke ony resistens a-geyn þe

longer resisted,

disposicion of God whech had chosen him to þat werk. Thus wold he not lese þe grete habundauns of vertues whech were 28 with-inne him with obstinacye, wherfor he mekly receyued þis obediens of God and þe comaundment of Goddis vykeẜ, þe Pope, trostand for þis obediens to receyue sumtyme þe moẜ mede, be-cause he had no grete delectacion to be preferred to swech an office. He 32

---

¹ *profi crossed through.*   ² *ly added in margin.*
³ *inserted above.*   ⁴ *final e added in red.*

put his owne wil, his owne profit be-hinde, only for þe welfare and
helth of many othir.   He was ful weel lerned be-fore in þe stody
of *contemplacioñ*, and now be-gan he to lerne who he schuld profith ^{and tried to get the profit}
4 in *ministracioñ* of actiue lyf, for he wold haue þe frute of both lyues, ^{of both lives, the active}
þat is to sey, both *nctyf* & *contemplatif*.   He myth ek moꝛ lefully ^{and contemplative.}
be a dispenser of þoo worldly *goodis* rather þan a-noþir man,
be-cause þe same goodis weꝛ his sumtyme.   For he gaf hem to poꝛ
8 men with whech he dwelled as a poꝛ man, nowt as a gouernouꝛ of
his owne, but as a procura*tour* and a seruaunt of oþer mennes
ricchesse.   For þis cause and many oþer holy toknes & many good ^{Pope Eugenius}
reportes whech weꝛ said of him, þe Pope Eugenie had in maneꝛ of ^{sorrowed that}
12 an heuynesse[1] þat he knewe neuyr ouꝛ ‖ fader Gilbert or þat ^{Leaf 71, back.}
tyme, for if he had knowe him, as he seyde, he wold a promoted ^{he had not}
him to þe archibischoprych[2] of ȝork, whech stood voyd at þat ^{known Gilbert}
tyme.   Thus cam oure fader hom in felauchip long tyme with ^{sooner.}
16 Seynt Malachie, archibischop of Yrland, and Seynt Bernard, abbot ^{Gilbert returned to}
of Clareualle, to whech too men he was so familiar in þat viage ^{England with St. Malachy}
þat in her presens, þorw his deuoute prayeꝛ, a certeyn man was ^{and St. Bernard,}
mad hool of seknesse whech he had.   He receyued eke toknes of
20 loue both of þe bischop and þe abbot, þe staues of heꝛ croses with ^{who gave him presents.}
whech aftirward weꝛ doo many myracles; and in *special* Seynt
Bernard gaue him a kerchy, and þerin a *certeyn* relik, as summe
sey; but I vndirstand þat þis kerchy was goodly bordred on þe
24 endes, for *orarium* soundith soo in gramer.   Thus is he com hom
a-geyn to Sempyngham, frustrat, as we saide, of his purpos, in
whech, of very meknesse, he had þout to a leyde a-wey þe ȝok fro his
nek, and a put þis office on sum notable man of þe religion of þese
28 Cistewys; but ouꝛ Lord þus with heuenly warnyng, as we suppose,
kept him in þis office as moost parfith & abillest.

[CHAPTER XX.]

cap. xx.[3]

32 WHAN he was þus *constreyned* þat he must kepe þis offise ^{He chose men}
     him-self, ‖ þan chase he owt of his owne religion certeyn ^{Leaf 72.}
me[n] to beꝛ þe birden of *gouernauns* with him lich as Moyses ^{to govern his order,}

---

[1] ssc *inserted above*.   [2] archi *added in margin*.   [3] *In margin*, 20.

ded as we rede be þe councell of Iethro, prest of þe hethen lawe,[1]
he assigned certeyn men to haue gouernauns vndyr him and alle

but attended to important matters himself.

þe grete causes he wold redresse him-self. Thus ded our maystir;
he chase men of sufficient lettirrur, of holy *conuersacion*, ordered 4
aftir þe custom of þe cherch, whech schuld haue vndyr him þis
gouernauns. Men wer chose for þis cause, for it is mor *conuenient*
þat men be preferred in gouernauns þann women. Letteryd men

These men were learned.

wer chose and no lewed men, þat þei schuld haue cunnyng to 8
tech oþir. Ordred were þei for þis skil, for þei myth not elles
haue cure of soules[2] lest þan þei wer in holy ordre.[3] Than chase
he men for to gouerne women; letteryd men for to teche þe weye
of Heuene both to men and wommen; clerkis eke, þat þei myth 12
be þe bettyr keperes of þoo scheep whech Crist bowt with his
blood. All þis ded þis man be holy inspiracion of our Lord
God, and be good councell of holy men and wise men; for, as

Maidens must have succour of monks.

þe decres of our form-faderes ber witnesse, þe monasteries of 16
maydenes may not stand with-outen help and socour of munkys,

Leaf 72, back.

or clerkys, ‖ whech must be spiritual faderes to swech tendyr
soules, to gouerne hem in þe swete ȝok of our Lord. But for

But as no monk may dwell with women,

as mech as þe lawes of holy cherch defenden þat no monkys 20
ne clerkys schul dwell with women, but þei schul be fer remevyd,
ech of hem fro oþir, so ferforth þat women schuld not come
nyher þe monasterye þan to þe porche of þe same, þis same
prohibicion folowyd þis man in þe moost streytest wise, in so 24

Gilbert set the men's dwelling far from the nuns, and the canons only entered the nunnery to administer the sacrament.

mech þat he sette þe dwelling of þe clerkis ferr fro þe dwelling
of þe nunnes, as a man schuld sette in o cyte or in o town too
dyuers places of dyuers religion. So wer þese chanones fer sette
fro þe nunnes, þat þei schuld not come with-inne þe nunnes in 28
no maner but only for ministracion of þe sacramentis. In þis
mater may be seyd þat habitacion of men and wommen in o
place was forfended in eld tyme for grete perell þat fell, moost
specialy for feyned folk þat used her synne vndyr colour of 32
holynesse, as a man may rede in dyuerse places of Seynt Ierom
Epistoles. Thus our Lord ful mercyablely and meruelously can
make his seyntes to schyne with grete ioye of consciens in þis

---

[1] *In margin in red*, Exod.   [2] ules *added at margin.*
[3] *added in margin.*

erde, for þem þat he iustifieth he maketh ful gret; for he is God sets His lights on high,
not wone to lyte a lanterne and hide it vndyr a buscheli, but
to sette it vp in heith on a [1] chaundeleȝ, þat aii men whech
4 schul ‖ entre in-to þe hous of ouȝ Lord may se lith. Our Lord [2] Leaf 73.
wil schew often to þe world what þo men be whech he louyth;
for þe grete dignyte whech þei schal reioyse aftirward, ouȝ Lord [2]
schewith be-fore be grace of myracles, þat þei whech se aii þis and shows by miracles who
8 þing may knowe þe bettyr be very weye of trewth and with shall after-wards be
sikyrnesse of hope come to þe lif þat euyr schal lest. Swech blessed.
pite on his seruaunt, Gilbert, hath þe grace of God vsed, first
gyuyng him good werkys with whech he schuld schyne, and
12 aftirward grauntyng vertue of myracles to make his werkes
open.

[CHAPTER XXI.]

HYS paciens a-mong aii oþir vertues was to hym a very Gilbert's patience was
16   crowne, for þat was grauntet him of God þat he schuld crown of his
want no vertu but þat he schuld be kepeȝ of aii vertues. God virtue.
wold þat þe onyment of vertue whech was with-inne him schuld
be stered & rolled with many tribulaciones, þat aftyr þat rollyng
20 it schuld haue [4] þe moȝ odouȝ. He wold [5] eke þat þe smal seed
of mustard schuld be al to-broken whech schuld be þe moȝ
poynaunt aftir þat giindyng. Al þis is seyd for ouȝ fader Gilbert, He was accused of aiding
whech was accused to þe kyng Herry þe secunde þat he gaf à Becket in
24 fauouȝ to Seynt Thomas of Cauntirbyry in his exile and sent France, and
him in-to ‖ Frauns grete plente of mony. For whech cause Leaf 73, back.
Gilbert was endyted and many of his felauchip for fauouryng
of þe kyngis traytouȝ, and writtes weȝ sent oute þat Gilbert and writs were issued for his
28 aii þe prioures of his ordȝ schuld be exiled. And in þis cause exile, though he had only
ouȝ fadeȝ was not gilty, þat is to sey, to send mony ouyr þe aided the Saint in
see; but be-foȝ Seynt Thomas exile, whil þat he was hid in priuyte England.
in Ynglond, Gilbert gaf him good and sent him to his sustenauns.
32 For, as we rede in þe lyf of Seynt Thomas, a chanon of Sempyngham A canon of his order

---

[1] candel *crossed through.*   [2] *in margin.*
[3] *In margin,* 21.   [4] *inserted above.*
        [5] wold *twice, the first crossed through.*

ordᵽ led Seynt Thomas fro Northampton to þe se, þorw many
priuy weyis and fennys onknowe to many men.   In þis same
mateᵽ, be-cause S.[1] Gilbert was of swech reputacioñ as touching
holynesse, he was reqwyred to come be-fore þe iuges & make 4
þeᵽ a bodely oth wheythir he was gilty in þis mateᵽ or nowt.

But þis refused he, for he saide he had leueᵽ be exiled þan swere,
for he wold not leue a bad exaumple to hem þat schuld come
aftir him.   Lich on-to þis mateᵽ rede we in þe book of Machabees 8
of þe good old man cleped Eleaȝarus whech wold not ete swynys
flesch forboden be þe lawe of Moyses.   He saide he wold rather
dye, and whan he was counceled of his frendes þat he schuld
feyne him to ete it he wold not, neythir for feᵽ of lesyng of 12

his lyf, ne for counceﬅ of his ‖ frendes; he seide þat ȝong men
schuld not take exaumple of elde Eleazar to breke þe lawe of
Moyses for feᵽ of deth.   So was ouᵽ old man eke disposed þat

he wold not leue þe chirch on-defensed whil he myth leue it, 16
ne he wold not feyne for to leue it; for if he had do soo, he schuld
a be holde a-mongis men hertles; he schuld ha be causeeke þat
oþir men schuld a be moᵽ feynt, and moᵽ-ouyr, be-fore God he had
runne in grete offens.   20

[CHAPTER XXII.]

cap. xxij.

IN þis same tyme whiﬅ ouᵽ fader stood in þis perplexite, ouᵽ
Lord chaunged þe kingis hert whech was þan in Normannye,
and letteris weᵽ sent fro him ouyr þe se to þe iuges of þis lond, 24

þat þis cause whech touched Gilbert & his bretherin schuld be
differred fro hem to þe kyngis audiens.   Mery & glad was ouᵽ

fader in aﬅ þis abydyng, and whañ þei alle tremuled for feᵽ, as
no wondyr was whañ þei had mad hem redy to forsake kynrod 28
and cuntre and neuyr to come a-geyn.   His hert in al þis tyme
was trosting in God, for he þout as Seint Iame seith, a ful grete
ioye was com to him whan he was assayed with dyuers temptaciones.[2]   A-noþir vexacioñ had ouᵽ mayster whech was not lytyl. 32
Certeyn bretheren of his whech he had conuerted fro þe world ‖

---

¹ *inserted above.*   ² *In margin in red,* Iacob 1.

and norchid fro her childhod turned in-to malice, were wery of
her order and of her profession, turnyng aīl heꝛ goostly *conuersa*-
ciō to lust of etyng and drynkyng and leccherye, so ferforth
4 þat þei diffamed ouꝛ maystir & his felauchip of grete vigo*ur*,
and moꝛ-ouyr wrytyn and sent on-to þe Pope, *compleynyng* and
allegg*ing* many þing*is* whech weꝛ not soth. Vp-on þis come *certeyn*
bullis fro Rome þat þis mateꝛ be indifferent per*sones* schuld haue
8 his examinac*ion*. Thus was ouꝛ Gilbe*rt* cleped to appeꝛ in-to
þe ferþest parties of þis[1] londe, and to answeꝛ to þese accusac*iones*,
not-withstand his grete age and febilnesse. But þis ma*n*, ful of
constau*ns*, was not aferd of peyne, ne labo*ur*, ne cost, ne þretyng
12 of þe iug*es*, ne fayre suas*iones* of oþir; aīl þese myth not make
him to consent for to goo oute of þe parfith weye whech he had
be-gu*n*ne, for he wold sey often he had leuer his þrote weꝛ cut
þan ony þing schuld be left of þe first *profession* and þe first
16 institucion whech he had mad. But wha*n* þis mater was discussed,
it was founde þat his accuseres weꝛ fals, and þus was þe blessid
man proued as metal in þe fornays, and pes sent fro heuene
on-to þe cherch and his religion. For wha*n* his ‖ adu*er*saries
20 fayled of heꝛ proues & coude with no craft haue þat þei desired,
þei were compelled be God and schame i*n* her consciens to pray
him of forgifnesse, in whech prayer þei desired þat he schuld
sumwhat tempir þe gret hardnesse of religiō and suffir hem
24 not to be kept so streith as þei weꝛ be-foꝛ. The good old man
with-oute*n* ony difficulte receyued hem to grace, and in tokne
of enteꝛ loue, he kis*s*ed hem aīl; eke, in þat temp*er*auns whech
þei desired of aīl scharpnesse[2] of religiō, partye with auctorite
28 of þe Pope, partye with wise councéll of religio*us* men, he
*promi*sed hem to fulfiīl mech of heꝛ desiꝛ. In þe last ende of
his age, lich a-noþir Iob whech was smet in his flesch with ful
greuous wou*n*des, he was smet with blyndnesse, for he lost þe
32 site of his body. But þis strok was not smet of God as an
enmye, but as a frend prouokyng a ma*n* to batayle a[n]d[3]
behestyng victorie to him. For of þat defaute of blyndnesse in
his body grewe on-to him a grete perfeccion of vnderstanding

---

[1] *Inserted above in red.*   [2] MS. schrapnesse, *with* as *over in red.*
[3] MS. ad.

His blindness brought greater holiness. in his soule, and he was aftir þat tyme replet with grace of the Holy Goost moꝛ habundauntly. For now wex he absent to seculer þingis and more present to euerlasting desires, as a man þat aftir grete laboures had grete delices of contempla- 4 cion ‖.

[CHAPTER XXIII.]

Leaf 75, back. cap. xxiij.[1]

His daily occupation was prayer and virtuous talk; HIS occupacion be þe day was[2] in prayeꝛ, or in heryng of good lessones, or in goostly coumfort of his breþerin, euyr talkyng 8 of uertu; of swech occupacion sesed he neuyr, saue swech tymes as nature requyreth his inclinacion; for, saue þo tymes, euyr his mouth or his mynde was not ydil. If ony man had interfered wordes whech weꝛ not plesauns to God, ne soundyng to uertuous lif, þei 12

but he spoke seldom schuld gretly displese him. He him-self spak but fewe wordes; he had moꝛ delite to heꝛ þan to speke, for all þat he spak was soundyng on-to grete profit of vertuous gouernauns. He þoute

remembering the words of David; often of þat verse of þe prophete Dauid, wheꝛ he seith[3]: Obmutui, 16 et humiliatus sum et silui a bonis. He was down, he seyth, and meked him-self, and kept silens, þat he schuld not speke good. It was þe condicion of Dauid, and soo hath be of many holy men, to speke but fewe wordes and but seldom, for þei were euyr aferd of 20

for, as Solomon said, in much speech sin wanteth not. þat Salamon seith,[4] þat in mech speche synne wanteth nowt. This caused ouꝛ maystir to sey but fewe wordes þat he schuld vse hem wel. Euyr was his mynde on-to heuene and euyr bidding soft bedes, often wold he a-mong his orisones say, Who long Lord schalt 24

Leaf 76. þou[5] ‖ for-gete me? And woo is me þat my good dwellyngplace

Gilbert lamented the distance of death. is kept so long fro me! Sum-tyme, whan we supposed he had be a-slepe, his handis weꝛ cured with his mantel, but his eyne sey we lift up to heuene, and euyr softe wordes herd we of his mouth. 28

When he had talked long he burst out into his confession. Sumtyme eke whan he sat in talkyng with othir men, if þe talking were long, he, as in partye aferd þat þeꝛ was do sum excesse of speche, sodeynly wold brest oute and say his confession, mekly askyng absolucion, and þan aftir wold he asoile deuoutly þem 32

[1] In margin, 23. [2] was twice, the first crossed through.
[3] In margin in red, Ps. 38. [4] In margin in red, Prouer 10.
[5] in margin.

whech were a-boute him þat tyme.   Be nyte tyme he was ocupied
moost with orisones and ful pryuyly wold he goo to his rest, first
knelyng longe be-for his bed.   And whaɴ his cubiculeres wold
4 loke if he[1] lay wel, þaɴ wold he blame hem þat þei mad his bed no
bettir ouyr-nyth.   Þese wordes were in maner of excusacioɴ, for He desired only God and the saints for his night-companions.
he was loth þat ony man schuld se in what maner he rested ; for to
þat pryuyte he desyred[2] no moo secretaries but God and seyntis
8 with whom he wold talk þe moost part of þe nyth.   What schuld
we speke of his diete, with what scarsnesse of mete & drynk he
was fed ?   He loued so wel þe comoɴ refeccioɴ þat whaɴ he was in He would
grel‖te languor, as it kendly folowith age, he wold not, for no prayer Leaf 76, back.
12 of his breþerin, ete in þe dortour ; he wold neuyr be absent fro þe never eat in private,
same hous wher þei[3] alle had her refeccioɴ, not-withstand þat
þe refectorie was fer and many greces þer-too, whech was grete
difficulte to an old man for to clyme.   Whaɴ he was prayed of his
16 disciples þat he schuld spare his grete age and his seknesse, he
wold in a maner of a holy ire answer & sey : Gilbert schal not be
exaumple to his successoures for to ete delicacies in his chambyr.
For þis cause were þei fayn for to bere him, on on þe o side, but was led to the
20 a-noþer on þe othir ; and with grete labour þus cam he to þe common refectory.
bord, to whech, whaɴ he was come, he pyned his body with hungir
rather þan filt it, euyr þinkyng of þe vesselis longing to our Lord
and euyr hauyng mynde of his congregacioɴ.   Whan he was bore He spent his
24 fro þe bord a-geyn to his couch, alle þe othir part of þe day he days in prayer.
spent in þe same vse, þat is to say, prayed or herd holy[4] lessones,
or comowned in deuocion.   And þat he schuld haue þe uery ende
of all perfeccioɴ, be-cause he had ascended fro o uertue to a-noþir,
28 and eke be-cause he was gretter in uertue þan he supposed ‖ him- Leaf 77.
self, for he knew weel þat a vertu is neuyr þe lasse þouȝ it defende
not him-self, for þis cause he purueyed pees a-geyns all perelles
whech myth falle to þoo congregaciones mad be him ; eke þat He settled the debate
32 debate whech was a-mong þe lay puple of his ordre for dyuersite among his lay-people on
of metis, þis same debate with consent of al his chapetr and in diversity of foods and had
presens of Hewe, þan biscop of Lyncolɴ, he sette in rest and pes, it written in his 'Congre-
and oþir menes of pes ordeyned he,[5] and mad hem to be write and gations'.
36 kept in his Congregaciones,[6] with-oute ende to endewre.

¹ in margin.   ² MS. desered, y over in red.   ³ i added in red.
⁴ s crossed through.   ⁵ above in red.   ⁶ in margin in red.

[CHAPTER XXIV.]

capi*tu*lum **xxiiij.** [1]

THese be þe myracles whech oure Lord wrout be his seruaunt
Gilbert whil he leued in þis bodely lyff.   A chanon of his
þat had be & was euyr *in* his felauchip whan he went fro o place 4
to a-noþir, whech ma*n*nes name was cleped Albyne, aftir a grete
febilnesse þat he had take of labou*r* in his iornay, fel in a greuo*us*
fevou*r*, in so greuo*us* þat he myte not goo with his maystir as he
was wone to doo, so þat ou*r* maystir was fayn to abyde at a place 8
whech þei clepe þe ylde; þere abode he, abydy*n*g þis ma*n*nes
recury*n*g, and went no ferther.   And whan ou*r* good fader had loy
þere longe and wex wery, desiri*n*g to fulfille ‖ his iornay, he sent
a messanger on-to þis man,[2] comau*n*dyng him in vertue of obediens 12
þat he schuld no mo*r* suffir þe fevyr to come on-to him, but þat he
schuld with-oute ony letty*n*g[3] come on-to his maystir in a*ll* hast.
Be þe same messa*n*g*er*, eke, he commau*n*ded on-to þe feueres þat
þei schuld no[4] mo*r* be bold to vexe his seruau*n*t.   Wha*ñ* þis 16
message was doo, þis same Albyne inclyned his hed to þat pr*e*cept,
as religious ma*n* schuld do, saying þat he was redy to obeye his
maystir in a*ll* þing.   The next day cam, and eke[5] þe ou*r* in whech
þe fevyrues were wont to take him, and all þe toknes we*r* come, as 20
schakyng, aky*n*g of þe hed and swech oþir; þan spak þis Albyne
on-to þis seknesse as to a lyuysch creatu*r*, in swech mane*r*: What
menest þou þat þou wilt now vexe me a-geyn?   Hast þou no
mynde who þat my maystir forbad þe þat þou schuld no mo*r* vexe 24
me?   But now I commau*n*de þe in my maysteris name þat þou
obeye to his precept and besy þe no mo*r* to my vexacio*ñ*.   A-non,
as he had said þese wordes, he blessed him with þe signe of þe holy
crosse, and sone aftir he felle in a swete slep, and aftir he wook he 28
was delyuered of þat sekenesse, ne many ʒeres aft*er* was not he
vexed with þe feu*er*ys.

---

[1] *In margin,* 24.   [2] *in red in margin.*
[3] *MS.* letty, *corrected in red.*   [4] *in margin.*
                [5] whech *crossed through.*

[CHAPTER XXV.]

cap. xxv.[1] ‖   Leaf 78.

A N-oþir chanon was þere of þe place cleped Sixelens*es* whech had in his feet a violent and intollerable peyne. This man, 4 trostyng in þe grete veitue whech ouȝ Lord had put in his maystir, made menes to þe mynist*er* of ouȝ maystir þat he schuld kepe him þe watyr in whech oure maystir schuld wasche his feet at eue. For þat was his custom, as þei sey, to wasch his feet eue*ry* nyth.

A canon of Sixhills(?) was cured of pain in his feet by washing them in water so used by Gilbert.

8 As þe man desired, þe wat*er* was kept, and he, with grete deuocioñ, wasched þerin his feet and þerby was mad hool. The grete feith of þe o man and þe clene lyuy*n*g of þe oþir, þorw þe myth of God, browt þis myracle to ende.

12   ¶ Ther was eke a knyt dwellyng a-boute Oxenford, þat, for helth[2] of his soule, was mad a chanon in þe place at Osneye. This man sone aftyr his profession was mad celereȝ of þat hous, and not long duryng in þat same office, he fèlle in þat seknesse whech þei clepe 16 podagra, whech is a seknesse, as þei sei, of hem þat haue led heȝ lyf in grete delicacye; and it causeth swech peyne in þe feet þat it priuyth a man of his walkyng. This ma*n* þus hurt, herd telle of þe grete myracles wrout be ouȝ fader Gilbert, an who many places 20 and what noumbir of p*er*sones weȝ edified ‖ be his doctrine. Of þis fame he *con*iected in his soule þe veri soth, þat swech þingis myte not be do witȝ-outen vertuo*us* lyuyng. Wherfor, with grete trost of his soule, he *con*uerted him to God and to þis Seynt, and 24 mad menes on-to hem þat were dwellyng with Gilbert, þat he myte haue a peyre of old sokkys, or pinsones, whech ouȝ maystir had ofte*n* wered. He had swech as he desired, and a-non, as he had vsed hem a-while, his feet were hole. A long tyme aftir þis þe 28 same peyne þat was in his feet fel to his handis, and more peyne it was to him þere þan it was in his feet. Thoo took he þe same sokkys and wered he*m* on his handes, and fro þat day forth both his handis & his feet weȝ hool.

A cellarer of Osney suffered from gout in his feet.

Leaf 78, back.

He was cured by wearing Gilbert's socks.

His hands were likewise cured.

---

[1] *In margin, 25.*   [2] fo *crossed through.*

[CHAPTER XXVI.]

Cap. xxvj.[1]

A goldsmith
in burning
fever was
cured by
drinking from
Gilbert's cup.

Owre maystir had a cuppe of whech he drank often, and, as it semeth, it was of tre bounden with siluyr, lich as religious in þis lond vse mech. This cuppe was broke with sum fal and 4 sent on-to Beuyrle, on-to a goldsmyth, for to repayr it. This goldsmyth, whan þe cuppe cam, lay in þe brennyng fevyr, for so happed it þat þat same tyme was þe hour of his seknesse. And

Leaf 79.

whan he herd þat þis was ‖ our maysteris cuppe, and þat of custom 8 he drank often in þe same, he desired gretly to drynk of þis cuppe. So was þe cuppe filt with drynk, and of þat same drynk this man had his helth.[2]

Another man
was cured of
fistula by
Gilbert
washing his
feet on
Maundy
Thursday.

¶ A-noþir man, of þe noumbyr of hem þat were no clerkis in þe 12 same ordre, had in his foot a soor whech þei clepe þe fistula. And so happed on Maunde Þursday whan all þe breþerin schuld be waschid, he desired gretly þat our mayster schuld wasch him. So was it ordeyned þat he was sette where our deuoute fader schuld 16 in his cours wasch all þe rowe, þat, be his touching, as he be-leued, verly þe man myth be hool. The good old man in his cours of waschyng cam to þis sek man, and with both his handys con-streyned his sore foot, be-cause he þout it was not clene. [3]Thus he[3] 20 constreyned it[4] with waschyng, but in þat same handelyng, corrupt blood ran oute of þe woundys and oþir mater swech as sores haue, and all þis waschid oure fader ful clene with þat same watir of þat holy mynystery. What schal we telle long tale? Be þan he had 24 waschid a-wey þis blood and þis oþir onclene mater, all þe foot was hool.

A prioress
was saved
from death
through

Leaf 79,
back.

Gilbert's
mediation.

¶ There was eke a prioresse of his nunnes þat lay so seek þat euery man loked[4] whan sche schuld deye. He herd telle of hir ‖ 28 þat sche was so ny þe deth, and be a messager comaunded deth þat he schuld not take hir at þis tyme, for sche was ful necessarie on-to þe relygion. Sone aftyr þis he visite þis woman him-self, and his bak was but turned fro hir in his goyng þat sche was coumforted 32 a-non, for all þe noyhous humoures went oute fro hir sodeynly be a swet, and eke þe grete constriccion of hir wombe was resolued meruelously.

---

[1] *In margin*, 26.　　　　[2] *in margin.*　　　[3-3] *in margin.*
[4] *inserted above.*

[CHAPTER XXVII.]

ca^m **xxvij.**[1]

IN þat same tyme was a grete debate be-twyx Steuene, kyng of The land was desolate in
Ynglond, and Herry, duk of Normannye, aftirward kyng. King Stephen's
4 This debate was so grete and þe parties so strong þat al þis lond days,
at þat tyme was ny lost.   For þe feldes lay with-oute tilth, þe
smale townes had no dwelleres, þe wallis weᵽ falle down and stretes
distroyed.   Grete townes weᵽ ny desolat; þere wat not elles[2] but and the people at
8 pray and[3] þeft and brennyng, euery man a-geyn oþir.   This mad discord.
oure mastiris hert gretly affrayed be-cause he say þe lond ny
distroyed, and in special for þe newe religioñ whech he had be-
gunne was ful likly to renne in desolacioñ.   Vp-on þis sorow and Gilbert sorrowed,
12 heuynesse þe good man prayed nyte and day þat ouᵽ Lord schuld
haue mercy on his puple ‖ and sende an ende of þis desolacioñ. Leaf 80.
Sodeynly, as he lay and prayed, was schewid on-to him a book in
whech book was writyn þe noumbyr of þoo ȝeres in whech þis but he was shown a book
16 desolacion schuld lest.   Whan he had red þis scripture he fel down telling the
plat and mad grete sorow, for he supposed veryly þat alł þese ȝeres duration of the trouble,
were for to come.   For if it so were þat þis persecucion schuld last
so longe, alł þis lond schuld, be possibilite, be distroyed.   Tho he
20 þat schewid him þis book gaf him coumfort and notified on-to him
þat þese were þe ȝeres whech he say of þat hool persecucioñ; of
whech, summe were passed and summe for to come.   There he lete
him haue knowlech who many were passed and who many to come;
24 and as þis vision schewid, so folowid þe dede, for þat same ȝere
merked in þe book cesed þat debate and þat desolacioñ.   This which comforted him.
reuelacion was a grete coumfort[4] on-to ouᵽ fader and on-to oþir
men to whech he opened his councełł.

28   ¶ We knew also in þat same tyme a noble woman[5] of grete A woman bore still-born
ricchesse, whech, as often as sche conceyued, þe childyr þat sche children,
baᵽ weᵽ bore ded.   A-noþir woman dwellyng be-side had a[6] girdyl Leaf 80,
with whech oure fadeᵽ ‖ Gilbert had often be girt next his flesch. back.
32 This girdil was take be þis woman to þe oþir woman whech myth and was helped by
not bryng forth childern o-lyue, and sche used it continuely next Gilbert's girdle.

---

[1] *In margin*, 27.	[2] *a stroke crossed through.*
[3] d *added above.*	[4] t *added in red.*
[5] *in margin.*	[6] gil *crossed through.*

hir flesch.   Sone aftyr sche *conceyued* a child, and þaꝼ a-noþir,
whech childyrn leued on-to mannes age and weꝼ worþi men both
in honouꝼ and rychesse.

[CHAPTER XXVIII.]

Cap*itulum* **xxviij.**[1]   4

THer was a man, eke, of Staunford, at þat tyme had a wyf þat
baꝼ no childyrn.   So happed ouꝼ maystir in a iornay to chese
his hostel at þis mannes hous.   Whan he was com þidir, þe woma*n*
herd gret report of his holynesse, and þout[2] þat be his merites sche 8

A woman caused Gilbert to sleep in her bed that she might have children.

myth *conceyue*, lych as þe woman Sunamite *conceyued* be þe *presens*
of Helise.   Trostyng þus on þis mannes goodnesse, sche mad ouꝼ
fader Gilbert bed in þat same place wheꝼ hir husband[3] and sche[3]
were wone to ly.   Gilbert went forth on his iornay; þe goodma*n* 12
of þe hin cam hom, and in[4] þat same bed, as þe woman be-leued,
be meritis of ouꝼ fadeꝼ Gilbert, sche *conceyued*[5] a son, and cleped
hym, whaꝼ he was boꝼ, aftir þe name of þe good old man Gilbert.

Her son was
Leaf 81.

And whan ouꝼ fadeꝼ herd sey of þis || chaunce, with grete merthe 16
he sent a cow to þe woman, praying hir to norche wel his child.

called after the Saint, who sent her a cow.

¶ It happed on a tyme, eke, ouꝼ maystir to ly at London; happed

A place next Gilbert's inn in London caught fire.

soo, þat a place next þe In wheꝼ he lay was sodeynly on fyre.   So
whan it cam ny his chambir, þei þat were a-boute him cryed up-on 20
him to go þenne and fle swech grete pereł.   He wold not him-self
remeve ne suffir no þing in þe hous to be caried oute, but comaunded
hem þat þei schuld lede him and sette him at þe wyndowꝼ whech
he myth best se þe fiꝼ.   Whan he was sette þere he[6] be-gan to 24
pray, sumtyme loud, sumtyme soft, sumtyme saying, sumtyme

Gilbert refused to leave the inn, and the flames spared it.

singing.   So þe fiꝼ cam so ny þat ałł oþir fled, but he sat stille
and meued not, and sodeynly þe flaume of þe fiꝼ, as þouȝ he had
dred þe *presens* of ouꝼ maystir, left þat coost and went to oþir 28
place, sparing þat hous wheꝼ he sat and alle þe houses whech
longed to þat In.   He þat was lord of þat In and keper þankid
God ofte sithe, saying with grete feith þat þorw þe me*r*ytes of
Gilbert his place was saued.   32

---

[1] *In margin,* 28.   [2] þout *twice, the second crossed through.*
[3-3] *in margin.*   [4] *inserted above.*   [5] d *added above.*
[6] *in margin.*

[CHAPTER XXIX.]

cap. **xxix.**

Euene as be þe inobediens of þe first man, Adam, mankynd
lost þe dew *dominacion* ‖ of hym-self and of oþir þingis
4 þat be vndyr him, rith so be þe meknesse of þe secunde man Crist,
þei þat folow his steppis recure swech rite þat þei may haue al
þing in subieccion. Treuth saith þus to us in þe gospell: If ʒe
haue feith as grete as a mustard seed, or ellis, If ʒour feith be as
8 a mustard seed, ʒe schal sei on-to þis hill, go fro þis place and falle
in-to þe se, and it schal be soo. And in a-noþir place he saith:
I say ʒou treuly, what-so-euy[r] [1] ʒe aske in ʒour prayer, be-leue,
for ʒe schal take it. In our fader Gilbert haue we þe exibicion of
12 þis *precept*. Be-cause he was obedient to Him þat mad him, whom
wynde and water obeyen, *þerfor* our Lord graunted to him for to
werk many *þingis*, and to haue comaundment ouyr þese elementis.
For to his *preceptis* were þese elementis buxum, wynde, se and
16 fire, and alle þei bowed to þe strength of his uertue. O special
cronycle wil we allegge in þis mater. Our fader schuld ones saile
ouyr þe watir of Humbir for visitacion of his flok þat was in þe
prouince of [2] ʒork, [3] or elles he cam fro ʒork in-to þis cuntre,
20 & þat is [4] moost likly.[3] The wynd blew oute of the south with
swech impetuosnesse and mad þe wawe so for to rise, þere durst
no man goo. He was compelled to a-byde at a grange whech þei
cle‖pe [5] Heseleschop, a-bidyng þe ende of þe storm and coumfort
24 of fayr wedyr. He lay þere long and was wery of þat lyf, and
mech mor wery for he had grete hast to see þoo *persones* whech he
went to visite. He asked of hem þat schuld lede him what wynde
was best to lede him ouyr þe watyr. Thei saide þe north wynd
28 wast best, if it wold blowe. He answered þat he supposed þe
northest schuld be mor *gracious*, but he comaunded hem in our
Lordis name, in whom was all his trost, þat þei alle schuld with
a good deuocion sei a Pater-*noster* to our Lord. This made he
32 hem to do þat no man schuld deme þat he trosted on his owne
merites, and þat he schuld fle þe praysing of men, whech was euyr
his appetite. Aftyr þei had sayde þis orison he comaunded his

---

[1] MS. euy. [2] *god crossed through.* [3-3] *or elles … likly, in margin.*
[4] MS. it. [5] hel *crossed through.*

set out for
the shore.
hors to be sadeled and aH his meny to make hem redy.   Thus þei

The sailors
put to sea;
hast to-ward þe brynk of þe watyr, and þe tempest be-gan sumwhat
to cese.   The schipmen sayde ech to oþir, lete us take þe watyr in
Mary name; we aᷓ likly to haue a good freyte.   This saide þei of 4
grete sikyrnesse, for þei trostid mech vp-on þis mannes vertue.

the storm
ceased, and
Thus make þei redy heᷓ schippis, and þe same wynde whech ouᷓ

Leaf 82,
back.
maystir desired, þei had; þei goo in-to ‖ þe vesseles, drawe up her

they had the
wind they
desired.
sailes, and with a fauourable wynde þei londe wheᷓ þei desire. 8
The most merueile in þis mateᷓ was as þei told þat[1] wheᷓ present,

When they
arrived at
their port the
tempest rose
again.
þat whaᷓ ouᷓ maystir was londyd þe same tempest roos a-geyn
& þat same wynd in þat place where he took his schip, þat aH
men myth knowe þat þe face of heuene was noth chaunged at þat 12
tyme but be his merytes.

[CHAPTER XXX.]

capitulum xxx.[2]

Aftyr þat tyme þat ouᷓ maystir was passed oute of this
world,[1] certeyn dremes were schewid to certeyn vertuous 16
persones, in whech dremes þe tyme and þe houᷓ of his deth was
notified and oppenly declared þat þis man was ioyned on-to þo

The night
Gilbert died,
a prioress of
York saw
a vision,
seyntis in heuene.   For þat nyte in whech he passed fro þe world
swech a vision was schewid on-to a prioresse of nunnes, not of his 20
ordre, but of a-noþir, in þe prouynce of Ʒork.   The woman say in
hir vision a grete cherch standyng in a fayᷓ place, and on þe west
side of þe cherch a gret hous, in whech hous many men weᷓ bysi

of prepara-
tion for the
burial of
a man.
to aray aH swech þingis as longe to byryng of a man, þat is to sey, 24
a bere arayed with cloþis of silk, with candeles and a crosse and

Leaf 83.
mech oþir þing, as longith to þat solempnyte.   And in þis ‖ drem
þis same persone, þis prioresse, had gret merueyle, for sche had
neuyr in aH hir lyf seyn no swech solempnyte[3] a-boute no ded 28

It seemed to
her that she
asked what
man was
dead, and
was told that
it was Gilbert.
man.   A-mongis þe puple, whech was gret, as sche þoute,[4] sche
spak on-to on and prayed him to telle hir what maner man þis
was þeᷓ ded for whom aH þis aray was mad.   That same persone
Ʒaue hir þis answere, þat maystir Gilbert of Sempingham was 32

---

[1] *inserted in red above.*   [2] *In margin, 30.*
[3] *part of the word over in red.*   [4] l *crossed through.*

passed fro þe world, and ouᵽ Lord wold þat he schuld be byried
with swech solempnyte. Aftyr þis answere he þat lay on þe bere
rose up, as sche þoute, and took a crose in his hand and be-gan to
4 synge a song in Latyn with a note of swech melodye þat sche had
neuyr herd no swech. The letter to þat same note was þis: Pure
mentis gaudia ostendam*us* eia in vocis melodia. The Englisch is
þis, as I suppose: The ioye of ouᵽ clene mynde lete us schewe now
8 all in fere with voys ful of melodye. Whaᵫ he had songe þis vers
all þe puple folowyng sang þe same, and soo went þei forth on
processioᵫ in-to þat same cherch. Whan þis womaᵫ say þis
bischop þus syngyng and on lyue, sche saide on-to him whech told
12 hir þat Gilbert was ded: Wenest þou þat I knowe ‖ not maystir
Gilbert? I knowe hi*m* ful weel, and he is not ded, for þou saide
he was ded, and he is ȝondir in þe processioᵫ. Than þe ma*n*
saide to hir agayn: Knowist þou nowt what fell to Seint Ion þe
16 Euangelist? Euene as he had þe moder of ouᵽ Lord in kepyng,
so had þis ma*n* in gouernau*n*s many p*er*sones whech folowid hir
virginite. Tho spak þe nu*n*ne to him a-geyn: I knowe wel what
fell¹ to Seyn Ion, for he is þe aduocat of ouᵽ place, and I can his
20 lyf ny be hert. And þaᵫ said þe man to hir²: Rith as ouᵽ Lord
hath do with Seynt Ion, rith so wil He do with þis man. In þis
mene-while þe procession went fro þe hou*s*, and sche inqwired of
him whidir it schuld goo. He saide þat all þe processiones of þe
24 world schuld mete with þat processioᵫ. Thus talkyng, þei³ entred
þe cherch, and þat processioᵫ stood stille be-fore þe grete crosse.
A-non sche say many processiones entre in-to þe cherch, mo þan
sche coude noumbyr, of whech sche knew many, and þan sche dred
28 hir for þe grete noumbyr þat sche schuld be trode vndir fote. In
þis dred sche wok, and felt so swete a sauouᵽ in hir⁴ nase þat sche
had neuyr felt non swech, for al þat day ‖ and many dayes aftir
þat swetnesse a-bood, with whech swetnesse sche was gretly
32 refrecchid. In þis tyme of her wakyng hir sistir rang to mateyns
& sche roos, gadered all heᵽ sisteres, and told hem pleynly þat sche
wist be hir drem þat maystir Gilbert was ded. Not long aftir be
a messageᵽ þat was sent to telle hem of his passing, þei knew
36 veryly þat þis was þe houᵽ in whech he passed. It is ful likly

*Side notes:*
Then she thought that Gilbert arose and began to sing in Latin,

and that she interrogated a man about it,

Leaf 83, back.

who told her Gilbert was like St. John the Evangelist. The nun said she knew St. John's life nigh by heart.

She entered the church,

and saw many processions meet St. Gilbert's.

Leaf 84.

When she awoke her sisters were going to matins, and she told them her dream, which was soon corroborated by a messenger.

---

¹ I *crossed through.*   ² *is written more plainly above in red,*
³ i *added in red.*   ⁴ MS. his.

Such visions occurred at other times.

þat þis visioñ was soth, for we rede þat þe deth of Martyn was knowe to many sundry persones whech dwelt fer, in þat same houȓ of his passing, as to Seynt Seueȓ, bischop of Coleyn, and to Seynt Ambrose, bischop of Melan. Eke Seynt Benet say his sistir*is* soule 4 boȓ on-to heuene þe houȓ of hir deth. And Seynt Ierom alsoo appered on-to Seynt Augustyn in þat same houȓ.

[CHAPTER XXXI.]

Another woman thought she saw a flock of angels,

LIch on-to þis vision was schewid a-noþir to a noble woman 8 of vertuo*us* condicione*s* & wif on-to a man lich in vertu on-to hire. Sche þoute in hir slep þat sche say a grete multitude of au*n*gellis, with grete noyse of praysing and ful swete song, flye up in-to heuene. And aftyr þei were go sche say too grete cumpanies 12

Leaf 84, back.[2]

and a choir of angels holding a sheet, in which were three children.

‖ of blissed spirites[3] wech were so ordeyned þat ech of hem had face to face, lich as þei haue þat stand in a qweer. Thei held a-mongis hem a fayre white schete, and in þis schete were thre naked childirn. On of hem sche myth see fro þe nowle vpward; 16 he was balled, and ȝet had he a childis face; þe oþir too say sche

She learnt that one of them was Gilbert of Sempringham, new-born to God.

but þe schulderis and þe face. Sche inqwired of on in þe cumpany what maner þing þis myth be, & it was answered to hir þat he in þe myddis was maystir Gilbert of Sempingham, whech was ded to 20 þe world and þus born to God. Sche inquyred eke if þese to were chanones of his ordre, and it was answered, nay. Thei [are] not of his ordre, he said, but good and holy men whech were take oute

This she saw the night that the Saint died, and told her husband.

of þe world and þus led to heȓ Lord. This same vision say þis 24 woman[4] þe same nyte oure maystir deyid, and whan sche wook sche[5] told þis visioñ to hir husbond; þei both noted þat day and founde aftir þat it was þe same in whech ouȓ mayst*er* went fro þe world: whidir he was born or wheȓ he was sette, was schewid aftir 28

A canon of Gilbert's

Leaf 85.

order saw in his sleep one of his dead brethren,

in visioñ to on of his chanones. For a grete tyme aftir þat ouȓ mayst*er* was ded a chanon of his ordȓ say in his sleep ‖ on of his breþerin þat was ded long be-fore. He þoute þat he inqwyred of

---

[1] *In margin*, 31.
[2] *The embellishment of capitals in red omitted from this page.*
[3] Soules *crossed through and* spirites *written above.*
[4] n *crossed through.*   [5] l *crossed through.*

him many sundry þingis, and had answeȓ ful *conuenient* on-to his
questiones. Tho inqwired he of þe astate of heȓ maystir, what he
dede or wheȓ he was, & his broþir answerd in þis maneȓ : He is
4 not with us ; a hyer place holdeth him. For fro þat tyme in
whech he was take fro þe world, a-non was he set a-mongis þe
dauns of virgynes.

*whom he
asked con-
cerning Gil-
bert, and who
said that
the Saint sat
high in
Heaven with
the virgins.*

[CHAPTER XXXII.]

cap. xxxij.

8 OVre blessed Lord, as he magnified Seynt Gilbert in his
lif with grete *meruelous* werkis, rith euene soo wold he
schewe þe ioye of him aftir his deth with grete & manifest
tokenes. And alle þese tokenes, who þat þei cam to þe lite of
12 ouȓ knowlech, þat þei þat lyue now and eke þei þat schal come
aftir us haue no doute in þis matere, schortly, as þei were doo,
we wil reherse here. Whan þis man, wel be-loued with God,
was passed fro þe world, þat men schuld know wel his lyf and
16 his merites weȓ acceptable to God, in þe first ȝere of his deposicioñ
and so forth oþir ȝeres,[1] weȓ many myracles doo at his graue.[2]
But at þat tyme þei whech he had left at Sempingham ‖ were
men drawen in-to secret[3] *contemplacioñ* and had ful lytyl deynte
20 with grete aqweyntauns of þe world, &[4] were necligent, if I schuld
say so, to dyuulge þese grete myracles whech were dayly wrout
a-mongis hem. Thus þoute þei, of very *humilite*, be-cause þei
weȓ his childyr, if þei weȓ þe first þat schuld puplysch þese grete
24 myracles of heȓ *mayster*, men myth sey of hem, as Crist ded of
þe Pharisees,[5] þat þei[6] magnified heȓ owne hemmys. For þis
cause, xj ȝeȓ aftir his deth was no gret pupplicacion mad, not-
with-stand þat in many sundry place[7] were wroute many sundry
28 myracles ; and þan þe breþerin at Sempingham þoute þat þe
hidyng of þese glorious werkis was displesauns to ouȓ Lord,
deregacioñ on-to seyntis, and wrong a-geyn þe worchip of þe
cherch ; þei as wise men and gouerned be þe councell of wise

*As during his
life, so after
his death,
Gilbert was
magnified,*

*and miracles
were done at
his grave.*

*Leaf 85,
back.*

*But those of
his order were
reticent,*

*so that till
eleven years
after his
death no pub-
lication of his
miracles was
made.*

---

[1] MS. ȝes, *with s crossed through and res over in red.*
[2] MS. gra *with* ue *over in red.*   [3] c *added above in red.*
[4] *added above in red.*   [5] *In margin in red,* M[t] 23.
[6] a *added in red.*   [7] ce *added in red.*

Hubert, archbishop of Canterbury, was then told.

men, went up to þe archbischop of Cauntyrbyry, cleped þat tyme Hubbert, and told him aîî þis þing. Whan þe man herd aîî þis he wept for very ioye, and þankid God with ful grete deuocioñ þat he wold schewe swech myracles in his dayes. And þouȝ it were 4 so þat he had no doute of þe holynesse of þis Seint Gilbert, ‖

Leaf 86.

be-cause he had know þe man & herd gret reporte of his holy-nesse, ȝet for to satisffye þe opynyon of oþir men, he þoute best to put þis mateȓ in dilacion and tary a-while, in whech he 8

He commanded certain abbots to hold inquiry,

myth heȓ more to confermacion of his entent. Vp-on þis poynt þis same archbischop sent down on-to certeyn abbotes of þis same prouynce, comaundyng hem be his letteres þat in þis mateȓ þei schuld make bysy inquysicioñ, and here inqwisicion, 12

and write the results,

in what forme it was mad, he wold þei schuld write it on-to him, þat he, þus instruct be her informacioñ, myth write þe

that he might get Gilbert canonised.

more sikirly[1] on-to ouȓ fader þe Pope to haue leue of him for to[2] puplysch þe canoniȝacioñ of þis Seynt, aftir þe Pope had 16 doo his part. These abbotes deuoutly receyued þis comaundment, and ioynend on-to hem for moȓ auctoryte many oþir persones

These abbots and others went to Sempringham on January 9, 1201, when King John was there. There they held inquiry.

of þe cherch, both reguleȓ and seculeȓ. Thus came þei aîî to þe place of Sempingham, þe ix day of Ianuary, þe ȝere of ouȓ 20 Lord a M ccj, and þat same day þe kyng of Ynglond, Ion, with many of his lordis, visited[3] þe same place. There þei dede rede þe myracles and discussed hem with grete diligens and streyt examinacioñ; þei wrote hem þanne ‖ in her letterys, both 24

Leaf 86, back.

on-to þe seid archbischop and to þe Pope. Alle þese letteris

Hubert sent their letters to the Pope,

sent þe seid Hubbert on-to þe Pope with his owne episteles,[4] in whech he comended þe grete dedes wroute be þis man, and prayed þe Pope to graunt leue þat he schuld be lyfte fro þe 28 erde and leyde in more honourable place. Eke, be exhortacioñ of þis same man, many notable persones of Ynglond and prelates

to whom many wrote also asking for Gilbert's canonisation.

wrytyn comendatyf letterys on-to þe court, besekyng þe Pope of þe same. The kyng eke wrote on his side and many of his 32 lordes þat þe Pope schuld þe soneȓ performe here entent.

---

[1] ly *added in red.*   [2] canoni *crossed through.*
[3] MS. vsitcd.   [4] l *crossed through.*

[CHAPTER XXXIII.]

Capitulum xxxiij.[1]

TO of þe lettered men of þis ordre þoo weᵽ sent with all þese letteris to þe court, to whom fel a grete myracle, þat
4 not-withstand þei went in þe hoot someᵽ in ful grete distemper wedir, in whech mech folk deyid of pestilens caused be þat same hete, for al þis þese men went and cam heyl and sound, not hurt with þat pestilens. A-noþir þing fel eke in þat iornay, þat
8 þei went þorw a buschment of malandrynes, and not aspied, for ouᵽ[2] Lord sperd þe sith of þoo þeues with a seknesse cleped acrisia,[3] whech is a febilnesse þat a þing schal ly be-foᵽ ‖ a mannes eye and not be seyn. Þus weᵽ þei saued be meryte of Seynt
12 Gilbert. Thus serued ouᵽ Lord[4] þe kyngis men of Surre þat be-seged Dotaim to kylle Helise, and he appered on-to hem, & þei knew him nowt.[5] Thus ar þei come hom in good prosperite fro þe court, brynging with hem þe bulle of ouᵽ holy fader þe Pope,
16 with his comaundment to þe archbischop of Cauntyrbyry, to þe bischop of Hely, to þe abbot of Borow, and þe abbot of Wardon, in wheche bulle was enioyned on-to hem þat þei schuld goo to þe place of his sepultuᵽ and þere schuld þei comaunde to þat
20 college of his ordre to faste iij dayes solemply, and in all þoo dayes þei schuld pray deuoutely to God þat he schuld open in þis mateᵽ to hem þe weye of treuth, and more-ouyer, þat þese bischoppes with þe abbotes schuld ransake stretly þe witnesses
24 and þe fame opene in þe cuntᵽ, &[6] summe scriptuᵽ autentik of þe vertue of þe maneres of þis man and of þe vertue of þe myracles doo in his name, all þis schuld þei inqwire bysyly, treuly write it, and aftir send it up to þe court seled with her seles,[7] be wise men
28 and trewe, whech men must swere in þe presens of ouᵽ fader þe Pope þat all þis ‖ informacioᵑ was trewe. All þis comaundment of þe Pope was fulfillid in-dede.

Margin notes:
Two Gilbertine clerks were sent to Rome with the letters, and passed safely through pestilence and ambush.

Leaf 87.

The Pope commanded the archbishop and others to go to Sempringham, where, after three days' fast,

all witnesses should be examined and a record made of Gilbert's life, &c., and all this should be taken to Rome and sworn to.

Leaf 87, back.

---

[1] *In margin,* .3.   [2] ha *crossed through.*   [3] *in margin.*
[4] *above in red.*   [5] *In margin in red,* 4 Reg. 6.
[6] þe *crossed through.*   [7] I *crossed through.*

[CHAPTER XXXIV.]

Capl. xxxiiij.[1]

On St. Cyprian's day the archbishop and many others

THe sexte kalend of Octobyr, þat is to sey þe day of Seint Cipriane and Iustine, þis same archbischop, with þe bischopis of Bathe, of[2] Hely, and of Bangore, with many abbotes & prioures, 4 with summe archdekues, chanones and officeres of þe cherch of Lyncoln, with many famous maysteres and grete puple, came

went to Sempringham

to þe hous of Sempingham; and aftir þei had fastid iij dayes, þei cleped first þe Holy Goost, as men doo at elecciones; þoo 8

and called all the witnesses.

cleped þei þe witnesses, or witnesseres, religious and seculeres, clerkis and lewed men and women, mad hem to swere þat þei schuld say soth in þat mater in whech inqwisicion schuld be

All their testimonies were sent to Rome.

mad. And all her testimonies þei writyn ful treuly in a dewe 12 forme, and sent hem to þe Pope closed vndir her seles. Ferþermor, þei writyn certeyn proues of his holy lyf and conuersacion and of þe fame of þe cuntr. And whilis þei taried þere iiij dayes

At the same time a young man whose head was turned with

þe treuth was opened of þe mater whech þei soute, be a grete 16 myracle do at his graue, of a ȝong man whos heed with seknesse turned round, of whech turnyng he was oute of hys mynde, and,

Leaf 88.

for uery || peyne, loked euery hour to be ded. Ther was he mad

pain, was cured there, and went to Rome with five priests and others,

hool in here presens, and with þe messageres went in good helth 20 to Rome, and in good helth cam hom a-geyn. For þei sent in þis ambassiat to Rome v. of þe same ordre, prestes, sex simple on-lerned, of whech noumbr summe wer holed fro certeyn seknesse be þe merites of þis Seynt, summe were present whan certeyn men 24

who testified to the truth of the letters.

wer holed. For þis cause wer þei in special sent, þat þe Pope schuld knowe be þe men whech wer þer[3] þat þe suggestion of þe letteres sent was soth. The messageres go forth with gret[4] ioye, trostyng on our Lordes help and þe Seyntes prayer for whom 28 þei goo, mech more with þe betir chere, for þei hadde mery dremes be-fore her iornay, and in her iornay grete prosperite in þe weye, & many oþir good tokenes. And þus, with no grete difficulte, þouȝ it wer so þat Sathanas wold a letted her wey, 82 ȝet, as we saide, with-outen any grete difficulte, þei come to Rome

---

[1] *In margin, 34.*
[2] *inserted above.*
[3] *in margin.*
[4] MS. grt.

on Newȝere euen, and aftir þat þe secund day of Ianuari þei come
to Anagniam, wheř þe Pope dwelt þat tyme. Ouř Lord gaue
hem so grete grace in þe site of ouř holy fader and of þe cardinales,
4 þat þe x day aftir þei weř come þei were sikyr of all þat euer
þei desired. ‖ For ouř fader þe Pope had his deliberacion of
þis mateř a-mongis þe cardinales, and say þe wytnesse and þe
iurates what þei weř, apposed hem a-sundyr, and fond gret acord
8 betwix hem ; and þouȝ, as be mannes reson,[1] þe Pope and þe cardinales þoutȝ þis mateř myth be performed a-non, ȝit plesed it to
þe councell of ouř Lord þat it schuld be dilayed, for he wold þat
his councell and his help schuld be cleped to þis mateř.

From Rome
the mes-
sengers went
to Anagnia,
where the
Pope was.

Leaf 88,
back.

The Pope and
cardinals
consented to
the canonisa-
tion, but
delayed it.

[CHAPTER XXXV.]

12   cap. xxxv.[2]

O nyth with-inne þese[3] ten dayes lay ouř fader þe Pope stodiand
on [4] þis mater and myth not slepe. He þoute mech [5] of þis
man Gilbert, & was gretly in doute what he schuld do in þe mateř.
16 Thoo prayed he God [6] þat he wold schewe him sum tokne be which[7]
he myte haue knowlech of Goddis wil. In þis þoute slep fel up-on
him, and in þat same slep swech a vision was schewid on-to him.
He þoute he say be-fore him [8] a grete and a hy touř, to whech
20 touř he had gret appetite to goo,[9] and þedyr he went with many
folk aboute him, as he was wone. Whan he was come with-inne
þe touř, he say a bed ful of stre and arayed at þe best ; a-boute
þe bed a curteyn of silk, precious I-now, he say hanging, and
24 þis curteyn, as he þoute, was embrowded with ‖ many ymages
of seyntes. He stood and merueiled longe on þe beute of þis
curteyn, for he had no swech a-boute his bed, and for þat cause
he gan to pulle þe curteyn to him, for he þoute he wold sowe
28 it new and make mete to his bed. And in al þis besynesse he
sey a-noþir chambir moř inward and mech folk þere. Whann
he was com þidir he inqwyred what he schuld do in þe cause,
for whech þe chanones of Sempingham were come and in þe
32 canoniȝing of þis Seynt. Tho al sodeynly he herd a voys crying
þus : Michael þe archangel, he schal be þi help in þis bisinesse.

One night
the Pope

dreamt he
saw a high
tower,

where he
found a bed
with a rich

Leaf 89.

curtain em-
broidered
with saints'
images.

He asked
men in
another
chamber what
he should do
for St. Gil-
bert.

The answer.

---

[1] b *crossed through.*   [2] *In margin,* 5.   [3] C. 33 b. thesse.
[4] C. studeant of.   [5] C. much.   [6] C. good.   [7] C. wiche.
[8] *above in red.*   [9] C. for to go.

Whan þe Pope had seyn al þis in his slep, sodeynly he wook,[1]
gretely coumforted of þis reuelacioñ, for he vndirstood[2] be þis
þat ouꝝ Lordis[3] comaundment and plesauns was þat þis materꝝ
schuld be broute to parfite ende. And a-non, with-oute letting, 4

he mad a special orison of ouꝝ fader Gilbert with a secrete and
postcomun aftir þe forme of þe missale, and whañ he had mad
hem he comaunded þat þei schuld be seyd openly in his com-
memoracioñ. Ferþermoꝝ, þe Pope, as a wise man[3] desiring[4] for 8
to haue þe very certeyn of þis materꝝ, cleped on-to him a ful

wise man and holy, an abbot, þei cleped hym Reyner, and
commaunded him, be vertue of obediens, þat he schuld ‖ be-þink
him of his dreem and telle him þe coniectuꝝ of þat same. The 12
cause why þat þe Pope uttered his vision to þis man rather
þan to a-noþir, was for he led a solitary lif in þe mountes, and
was in gret opinion both to þe Pope & þe court. Tho answered
þe abbot a-gayn on-to þe Pope, and sayde þat þis mater neded 16
non auysement, for both þe drem and his interpretacion was

open i-now. So as a-nothir Daniel on-to Nabugodonosor, or lich
a-noþir Ioseph on-to Pharao, he expowned it[3] in swech declaracioñ :
The fayre touꝝ he seid and þe hye, whech þou say, Ser Pope, 20
is þe grete excellens of þi dignite, to whech þou aspirest ; not as
ded many bi-fore þe, but[5] be trew eleccion þou enterest in-to
þe same, and þat is ment in þi drem wher þou þoutist þat þou
werꝝ led in-to þis place witȝ[6] þe handis of many men. The bed 24
so wel arayed is a clene consciens, in whech a man restith as in
his bed, lich[7] as þe prophete Dauid said in þe Psalme : I schal
wasch, he seith, or ellis, water[8] my bed with my teres. For euene
as cloþis in whech we rest be mad clene witȝ watyr, so is ouꝝ 28
consciens clensed with repentauns of ouꝝ synnes. The curteynes

a-boute þis bed in whech be impressed ‖ þe faiꝝ figures of seyntes
are þe commemoraciones of holy seyntis used in þe cherch, be
whech we be schadowyd fro wyndes of temptaciones. These 32
corteynes aray ful wel ouꝝ consciens whan we, both with hert
and with werk, fulfille heꝝ desir, eþir to honouꝝ hem in God or
elles to folow her steppes. Thou fader Pope be-gan to sowe þis
curteyn whan þou þout first to sette þis man Gilbert in þe 86

---

[1] C. 33 woke.   [2] C. vnderstode.   [3] *inserted above.*   [4] C. desieryng.
[5] t *added above.*   [6] C. 34 b. wᵗ.   [7] C. lech.
[8] C. I shall wech the feꝛch or ellis water.

kalendeꝛ of seyntes, and I suppose, veryly, he is ful worþi to
be annoted a-mongis hem.   Eke swech þing as þou desyred
waki*ng*, þou asked in þi slep, and þin answere was goue, þat
4 Mychael schuld be þi help.   Noþing a-geyn reson.   Michael is
þe prouost of Paradys and pri*n*ce ordeyned be God to receyue
þoo soules whech schul be offered to God.   This same Michael
hatʒ receyued þis ma*n*ne soule and led it to the hye court of
8 blessed spirites, and in þat same court it is determyned þan þis
ma*n* Gilbert, fro þis tyme forward, schal be halden in honour [1] and
reuerens as a Seynt.   Sowe him In, þerfor, with þi nedel, with
þis poweꝛ no ma*n* hath þat in hand but þou.   Ioyne him on-to
12 þe felauchip of seyntis, for it is conuen*i*ent þat þe cherch in erde
folow þe ‖ cherch a-boue in heuene.

Leaf 90,
back.

[Chapter XXXVI.]

THis interpretacion of þis drem, whan̄ it was þus expressid be
16 þe abbot, plesed þe Pope gretly, for he, with-oute ony tary,
mad calle al̄ þe court of Rome, whech was grete at þat tyme,—and
in special þe archbischop of Reymes was þere present at þat tyme
and bare witnesse of þe holy lyf of Seynt Gilbert, for in his ʒong
20 age he had be in Yngland and knew both þe persone and þe fame.
In þis gret congregacio*n*, whan al̄ men weꝛ sette saue þese
messageres of Sempingha*m*, þe Pope sayde a grete and solempne
sermon of þe holynesse and þe myracles of Seynt Gilbert, rehersing
24 þe witnes þere present, and aftir certeyn wordis whech be pertinent
to þis offise, þere he solemply & openly canoniʒed Seynt Gilbert
with þe comou*n* assent of al̄ þe cherch, and þeꝛ eke he mad a [3] decre
þat þe fest of Sey*n*t Gilbert schuld be seid and songe i*n* þe cherch
28 lich as þe festis of oþir seyntis be.   Thus whan þe Pope in his sete
had þus openly schewid on-to puple þis canoniʒacion̄ of þis holy
man, aftir-ward he comau*n*ded þat letteris schuld be mad of þe
same sentens to þe archbischoppis of Ynglond & to þe chapetir of
32 Sempingha*m*, in whech ‖ letteris he rehersed al þe mateꝛ fro þe

The Pope
called his
court, and the
archbishop of
Rheims testi-
fied to Gil-
bert's holy
life.

The Pope
then delivered
a sermon,
and canonised
Gilbert,

and sent
word of all
this to Eng-
land,

Leaf 91.[4]

---

[1] C. 84 halden in honor.   [2] *In margin*, 6.   [3] dc *crossed through.*
[4] *The embellishment of capitals omitted from this page.*

beginnyng on-to þe ende; with aÍÍ þe inquisicion of his lif and his
myracles he rehersed eke who discretly, who sadly, with what
circumstauns, þis mateř had be [1] treted, wher-for he comaunded in
þe ende of þe bulle þat swech þing as þe Pope with solempnite and 4

and ordered his feast to be kept. with auyse had ordeyned to be kept, þei, as good subiectis, mekly
schuld fulfille and comaunde þe fest of þis holy man to be
solempnized be aÍÍ her prouinces.   A special comaundment sent

He also commanded the archbishop to perform the ceremony, he eke on-to þe archbischop of Cauntyrbyry, be-cause þe place of 8
Sempingham stant in his prouince, þat whan-so-euer þe breþerin
or chanones of Sempingham required him, þat he schuld goo þidyr
and left up fro þe ground þe body of þis holy confessouř, and with
dew reuerens ley it þere whech as þe same breþerin had ordeyned 12
it schuld be leyd.   This comaundment of þe Pope was receyued of
þe archbischop and of þe seid chanones as þouჳ it had come fro
heuene; wherfore þei, desiring as good childyrn to fulfiÍÍ her faderes
comaundment, aÍÍ þing þat was neccessarie to swech solempnyte 16

and as the Saint was passing out of þei purueyed in aÍÍ hast.   And þouჳ þe mynde of þis Seynt, as
haue be of many oþir, was mech oute of rememberauns, eþir for

Leaf 91, back. age or elles, ‖ for necligens of men, or vnkunnyng, or sum oþir

remembrance, all haste was made. cause; ჳet, as we hope, it was sufficient to us for to be-gynne þis 20
werk, be-cause we had reuelacioñ first fro God and comaundment
fro ouř holy fader þe Pope, to whos comaundment we be bounde
to obeye as þouჳ it had come fro God.   Eke for þe man [2] in his lyf
comaunded us to do þis þing and we eke desired it schuld be do 24
whil we lyue, þis was þe grete [3] hast in þis mateř.   For þei þat
weř sent for þis mateř þoute it conuenient to fulfiÍÍ þe Popes
precept whil he was on lyue and þei eke.

[CHAPTER XXXVII.]

cap. xxxvij.[4]   28

In the vigil of the Holy Cross, 1202, the men of Sempringham ask the archbishop to be THe ჳere of ouř Lord Crist a M.cc.ij., þe forseyd breþerin of
Sempyngham, in þe vigil of þe holy crosse, with þe moost
famous men of aÍÍ þat religion came on-to þe said archbischop
with heř maystir, makyng grete instauns þat þe next Sunday aftir 31.

---

[1] tred *crossed through.*   [2] *in margin.*
[3] of *crossed through.*   [4] *In margin,* 7.

þe feest of Seint Denys, he wold vouchsaf of his faderhod to be at at the trans-
þe translacioñ of þis holy confessouꝛ Gilbert. The archbischop lation of Gilbert.
receyued hem not but in þe best maneꝛ, and saide he was glad of
4 þese tydannes and redy to fulfille[1] þat solempnyte whech þei aff He invited
desired, and up-on þis he wrote to þe bischoppes of his prouynce his bishops to attend.
þat if þei myth haue leyseꝛ þei schuld[2] come to him and ‖ honouꝛ Leaf 92.
þis holy day. Ferþermoꝛ, he desired of hem þat þis schuld be
8 notified þorw-oute her diocise, þat aff men whech had deuocion to
þis Seynt myth come to þis fest if þei wold. Thus in þe same day
prefixid, þat is to seyn, þe iij ide of October, aff þis mateꝛ is put in So it all hap-
execucion. And be-side aff þe myracles rehersed be-foꝛ in þe Popes pened, and
12 presens, eke be-side reuelaciones had fro heuene, and be-side þe seid
witnesses, newe þingis fel þat same day. The nyth of his translacioñ, þat is to sey, þe nyth be-twix þe Satirday and þe Sunday, þe
noble man, þe archbischop with oþir bischoppes and ministres came
16 on-to þe graue wheꝛ þe holy membres of Gilbertes body was hid,
and with grete worchep þei lifte up þat holy uessel of God, þat, so
waschid and arayed þe next day aftirward, he myte with lesse
tariing be laid in his schrine. Whilis þat þis seruise was do to þe wonderful miracles were
20 body with swete ympnis and songis, summe religious men þere done at the time.
present, and eke summe seculeres, seyn a grete knot of fyꝛ al
round, as þou3 many candeles had be ioyned to-gidyr, or ellis lich
a grete schinyng sterre ones, twyes, þryes, com down fro heuene
24 and eft-sones goyng up to heuene aboue þe roof of þe cherch,
euene ‖ ouyr þe sepultuꝛ. And at þe þird comyng it semed as Leaf 92, back.
þou3 it had þirled þe rof & falle in-to þe cherch. Thei þat sey
þis site with-outen told it hem with-inne, þat þei myth goo owte
28 and se þe same, þat is to sey, þe lite of ouꝛ Lord aboue þe cherch.
Lich þing sey oþir men whech had waked at þe graue certeyn
nytes in her prayeres a litil be-foꝛ þis translacioñ, þat is to sey,
a grete lite entꝛ þorw þe rof and thries entre in-to þe graue wheꝛ
32 þe holy body was layd. Swete sauour eke felt þei þere whan þe
stones were remeued be masones for to make space wheꝛ the newe
scryne schuld be sette.

---

[1] MS. fulfulle.   [2] d *added afterwards.*

[CHAPTER XXXVIII.]

cap. xxxviij.[1]

More miracles
were done at
the transla-
tion,
Nowt only þese myracles rehersed weȝ doo at þis tyme but
many oþir testimonies weȝ had in whech men myþh know
þat þis translacion was plesauns to God.   Thus whan þei had lifte 4
þe ston fro þe graue þere was founde fayre red pouder of his
flesch,[2] swech as þei sey as virgines[3] haue whan þei aȝ ded.   The
chesible eke in whech þe body was woundyn, of silk, was found
hool with-oute corrupcion.   Whan all þese relikes were lift fro þe 8

Leaf 93.
ground and waschid þe[4] archbischop went a-gayn ‖ to chambyr for
and the arch-
bishop be-
came sud-
denly ill,
to take a rest, for it was fer fro day.   Whan he had leyn a litil
tyme on his bed sodeynly fel up-on him a greuous seknesse, and þe
peyne vexed him so sore þat he stood in grete dowt, and in maner 12
dispeyr, þat he myth not fulfill þat office for whech he was come,
and to whech he had cleped so many persones in special of swech
reuerens.   For þis secund cause was he moȝ sory þan for his bodely
seknesse.   He leyd medicynes to his body, swech [5]as þei[5] tawt 16
him, but al þoo profited nowt.   Tho turned he his trost and his
deuocion to God and to Seynt Gilbert, þat ouȝ Lord[6] at mediacion
of þat good Seynt wold send him myte and strength to performe
þis office for whech he was come and many oþir persones.   A-non 20
but was cured
through
devotion to
St. Gilbert.
as þis prayer was fulfilled so sone left him all þis peyne, for aftir
þat same peyne was goo he felt his body moȝ myty and strong þan
it was be-fore.   At þis same chaunge cam þe houȝ in whech þe
couent rang to mateyns.   A-non as þe archbischop herd þe belle 24
he roos him-self and cleped all his clerkys, and all in fere þei go
on[-to] þe chanones mateynis, whech, for þe worchip and loue of
Leaf 93,
back,
þat Seynt for whom þai ‖ were gadered, were ful solemply songe.
In þe morownyng þe archbischop[7] roos heyl and sound, and all þat 28
euyr God and Seynt Gilbert had schewid on-to him þat same nyth,
with grete ioye he told hem, praysing þe vertue of ouȝ Lord and of
þis holy Seynt, whech vertue he felt notablely fulfillid in him.
The houȝ is come of þe day þat þis solempnite schal be doo; the 32

---

[1] *In margin, 8.*   [2] wh *crossed through.*
[3] *s added afterwards.*   [4] pope *crossed through.*
[5]–[5] *inserted above.*   [6] *inserted above.*
[7] MS. pope *crossed through and* archbishop *written over in red.*

bischop is arayed with his mynystres; þe watir is halowed þat
schal serue in þe office; þe schrine eke is halowed and born
a-boute on þe schulderis of princes and lordis whech be þere
4 present: a solempne procession is ordeyned, in whech procession
first go þe clergie, nexte princes, lordis and oþir, many beryng þis
halowid uessel in whech þei wil ley him; last of all folow þe
bischoppis. Certeyn seke men þat wer ny and touchid þese relikes
8 wer mad hol þat same hour, as was veryly proued. Ther saide þe
archbischop a ful notable sermone grounded al up-on þe holynesse
and þe myracles of þis holy man Gilbert, and þere mad he rehersaile
of all þe processe, who it[1] was sent on-to þe court of Rome, what
12 answer þei had fro þe Pope & mech oþir þing. Tho be-gunne þei
a messe of þis same Seynt with ful swellte concent, and in þe last
ende[1] of þat masse, aftir þe bischop had receyued þe holy sacrament, er þat þei song þe postcomoun, þe seide relikes were wounde
16 in fayr silk and þan in a cloth of silk precious I-now whech our
fader archbischop had ʒoue to þat same entent, and all þese[2] þus
wounden wer layde in þat same vessel mad for þe same cause.
Thei layde eke with him a grete chartour in whech was wretyn al
20 his lif, his canoniʒacion eke, and his translacion seled with þe seles
of þe bischoppis & abbotes whech wer þere present. Ther was put
in with him eke a plate of led, in whech plate was wrytyn al þis
þing more compendiously, as I suppose, þat þe rememberauns of al
24 þis werk schuld last euyr. Thus was þat uessel sperd and sette
up-on a wal of marbil in þe same place where þe seint lay be-for.
Tho mad þei an ende of þe masse, and aftir þei had refreschid her
bodies euery man with ful gret ioye turned a-gayn on-to his owne
28 place. Our maystir is layd now in his rest; lete us folow þerfor
þe steppes of his good lyf þat we may be translate fro wrecchid-
nesse to ioye and þorw his ledyng come ‖ to þat cuntr wher we
schul haue ioye euyr.

Marginal notes:
Everything is ready for the ceremony,

more miracles are performed; the Archbishop preaches;

mass is said:

Leaf 94.

the relics are wound in silk

and laid in their vessel,

with a charter of the Saint's life, duly sealed.

The vessel is closed, and mounted on marble.

And so the Saint is at rest.

Leaf 94, back.

---

[1] *inserted above in red.*   [2] *þis crossed through and þese written above.*

[CHAPTER XXXIX.]

cap. **xxxix.**[1]

Gilbert's miracles attest his greatness.

Of these we will tell as the Archbishop inquired and discovered.

How a clerk, going to school in another town, lay down and slept, and woke with a withered leg,

Leaf 95.

which was without feeling;

NOw of our̃ fader Gilbert, who holy was his lyf, who holsom was his doctrine, who grete rewardes wer̃ sent fro God on-to his blessed merites, witnesse þe grete myracles whech aftir his deth 4 wer wroute be our̃ Lord God. And of þese myracles now wil we telle all þe maner̃ lich as þei fell and lych as our̃ wel be-loued fader in God, þe[2] said archbischop of Cauntyrbyry, at þe comaund-ment of þe Pope Innocent þe þird with his suffraganes ransaked 8 and inqwired. Lich þat inquysicion̄ in sentens & in̄ termes, whech inqwysicion̄ þei sent þat tyme to Rome,—þorw whech sond þis canonizacion̄ was performed,—lich þat forme wil we write here.

Ther was a clerk whos name ne place is now on-knowe þat used to 12 go to skole fro o town to a-noþir as in þis lond is grete custom. This clerk in his weye to skoleward fell in grete heuynesse, so þat he must nedis slepe. He layd him down and slept, and aftir slep whan he wook he felt al his rith legge, foot and all, so sered and 16 dryed þat he myth not goo þeron in no maner. So with his staf and his oþir legge he hipped forth as he myte tyl he cam to þe nexte ‖ town. Fro þens was he caryed to a monasterye whech þei clepe Hauyrholm, for þer̃ dwelled he iij monthes, euyr vexid with 20 þe same infirmite. That legge, in al þat tyme, down to þe foot was soo insensible and all þe myth þerof go, þat if men had prikkid him with a nedyl or ony oþir scharp þing, he felt no mor̃ þerof þan a man had put þis scharpnesse on-to a stoon or a tre. Eke þe vse 24 of þat legge was as lost, for whan he schuld walk he schuld drawe it after him as þouȝ it had be a braunch of a sere tree, for he was more greued with þe birden þan esed with þe offise. Be-cause he myth not lyft þat foot fro þe ground, but draw it euyr fro þe erde, 28 þe toos were flayn and blody to grete peyn of him & gret pite to all þat seyn him. The prouost of þat place ded make him a hose al of ledir, and þat was wered a-non, in special at þe ferþest ende whech trayled so on þe ground. Aftir þis he ordeyned him a-noþer 32 remedy, for he teyhid his legge fro þe ground with a roop on-to his schulderis, and þus bare he þe legge whech schuld a born him.

---

[1] *In margin,* 9.   [2] MS. þei, *with* i *dotted underneath.*

To þis same clerk slepyng on a nyte appered a *person*e of grete how the clerk was told in a dream to go to St. Gilbert.
worchip, as he þoute, and saide þus on-to him : If þou wilt be hool
þis same day, loke ‖ þou visite þe graue, or ell*es* þe sepultuꝛ, of Leaf 95,
4 maystir Gilbert at Sempyngha*m*.   At þat same houꝛ þe man gat back.
him a cart and with on¹ of þe breþerin of þat same hous he was He went to the Saint's grave and slept ; had a vision ;
brout to þis sepulture, and sodeynly, as he prayed, he fel on slep.
In his slep, as he þout, þe same *person*e whech appered to him
8 be-fore appered a-gayn and sayde on-to him swech wordes : For
what cause liggist þou here so longe ?   Be-hold þou art mad hool.
With þis visioꝬ he swette meruelously and be-gan to wayle fyue
sithes, þoo wook he and roos be him-self, loked on his foot and
12 trad with it on þe ground for to asay wheþir he myth go with þat
or nowt.   Be-cause of þe sodeyn chau*n*ge whech was come so
newly, he stood in grete dowte what he schuld doo.   The sexten
þat stood by and *per*auentuꝛ knew not of þis sodeyn chau*n*ge mad
16 tokenes on-to him þat he schuld rest a-gayn.   He lay down eft-
sones, and aftir a litil slep wook a-gayn, and þanne he roos and and awoke whole.
felt both feet, thy and legge al hool ; þus he þrew a-way þis staf
a*n*d forsook his cart, and with ful grete lithnesse¹ went wheꝛ he
20 wold.   And in tokne þat þis helth cam to him be myracle, i*n* þat
place whech he myth not fele a ‖ nedel prikkid be-fore, now, whaꝬ Leaf 96.
þe natural hete is come a-gayn, he felt sumwhat a peyne in þat same
place wheꝛ þat þe wou*n*de was.   A-mong*is* aꝛ oþir þat boꝛ witnesse This man went to Rome and gave his evidence to the Pope.
24 of þe myracles do be Sei*n*t Gilbert þis man was on, for he went to
Rome & ² confessed al þis be-foꝛ þe Pope, and aftir, wha*n* he cam
hom, was mad chanon and prest in þis same ordre, þankyng God
aꝛ his lyf and Sei*n*t Gilbert of his gracious cure.

[CHAPTER XL.]

28   **Cap*itulum* xꝛ.³** The legs of a maid were contracted,

A Mayde was þere eke in þe strete at Sempyngham þat in
   both leggis, in þat part whech is be-hinde þe knees, was so
contract þat sche myth not stand ne goo, for in-stede of hir feet

---

¹ *in margin.*   ² *inserted above in red.*
³ *In margin, 4, another figure having been cut away at edge of leaf
perhaps.*

and her left
foot dis-
torted,
whan sche wold remeue hir body fro o place to a-noþir, sche crap
with hir handys and with hir lendes, or buttokkes. Eke with
grete rankouꝛ of þe soor hir left foot was meruelously disfigured,
for iij grete peces of flesch grew up-on hir foot, ech of hem 4
departed fro oþir, whech semed as þouȝ it had be cut. More-ouyr
like her left
arm,
hir left arme[1] had lost þe vertue of felyng and þe hand of þat
arme[1] was lych þe left foot with swech þre cuttyngis of flesch as
Leaf 96,
back.
we sayde be-fore. Thus hyng it as a[2] onprofitable ‖ byrden fro þe 8
schuldyr downward. This woman herd telle who þat þis clerk[3] of
whom we told last was cured and so cured þat he was strong to
She also went
to the sepul-
chre, and lay
there seven
days,
take his iornay to Rome. So mad sche grete instauns to þem þat
dwelled[4] in þat strete þat þei schuld lede hir to þis sepultuꝛ of 12
Seynt Gilbert and leue hir þere. Ther lay sche seuene days
continuely perseueraunt in hir prayeris, and as sche slept on
a nyth sche þout þat þe ston vndir whech Seynt Gilbert was
closed claf a-sundyr, and he roos up and sat þerupon with ful 16
In a dream
she saw Gil-
bert, who
gave her a
host ;
grete lite. Sche þoute eke þat he had in his hand many hostes
and þoo multiplied fast, as to hir site so fast and to so grete
noumbyr þat he myth vnneth hold hem. Too of þoo same hostes
he put in hir mouth, as sche þoute, and aftir þat gaf hir his 20
blessyng. Aftir þis sche a-wook sodeynly and fonde hir body al
on a swet so habundaunt þat it dropped fro hir body and mad þe
pauyment weet; sche felt euene at þat tyme a new chaunge in hir
body, for þat whech was heuy and contract be-fore now sche felith 24
it of swech disposicion þat, as it semeth to hir, sche myth flye for
litenesse. In þis same chaunge sche say who þe lites þat stood
Leaf 97.
a-boute þe sepultuꝛ of Seint Gilbert ‖ and brent felle down sodeynly,
and þo sche gan to crepe as hir vse was for to amende þoo lites. 28
In hir creping þe senewes whech were contract be-fore in hir[5]
lendes, þei brak and streyned oute to swech largenesse þat sche
and she
awoke, and
stood up.
roos and stood on hir feet and myth walk and in þat brekyng sche
herd a grete noyse, who þei craked and had ful grete meruayle 32
who þat þe senewes craked whan þei be-gunne to extende hem-self.
In þis same tyme þat þis woman standith þus merueylyng, þe

---

[1] MS. harme. h crossed through in red.   [2] inserted above.
[3] b crossed through.   [4] Word blotted in text and re-written in margin.
[5] but crossed through.

nunne, þe sextenesse, rang to mateyns; þe sisteres be come down

and se þis woman standyng be þe sepultur: first þei[1] be a-ferd

be-cause many of hem wist not þat sche was þere, for sche was not

4 þere at euen whan þei went to bedde, as it semeth; þei walk on-to

hir and sche confessith al þe circumstauns of þe myracle euene as

it fel. Þere þank þei God and Seynt Gilbert all with o *consent*

for þe grete cur whech now[2] is don. The woman was kept with

8 hem a certeyn tyme for declaracion of þe myracle and on-tyl[3] hir

arme[4] and legge had parfitly here use; aftyr þat tyme sche went

hom to þe strete and leued þer with hir frendis in good helth of

body, þankyng our Lord of þat sodeyn chaung. ∥

[CHAPTER XLI.]

12

cap. xlj.

A Knytys wyf þere be-side, a lady of ful noble fame, had swech

sekncsse and peyne in spe*cial* dury*ng* *in* hir lyft[5] arme þat

sche myth not meue þat arme ne do with-al no man*er* werk. This

16 peyn lastid up-on hir fro þe feest of Seynt Petyr, whech þei clepe

in Latyn, 'ad vincula*m*,' in Englisch, 'Lammesse,' on-to þe nati*u*ite

of our Lady. Be-side þis had sche oþir sores whech we name not

now. With al þis infirmyte sche is come on-to þe sepultur of þis

20 holy man and aftyr sche had wecchid in deuoute prayeres al a nyte

sche went hom hol fro· both sores, euyr-mor hauy*ng* grete trost in

þis holy Seint.

¶ A-noþir woman was þere be-side con*tract* & croked whech myt

24 not go, ne sitte, ne stand, with-oute help of hem þat wer waytyng

up-on hir. The fader and þe moder of hir, hauy*ng* gret sorow for

þat desese, brout hir on-to þe sepultur·of our maystir. The first

nyte sche was þere, at instau*ns* of hir frendes, þe chanones put

28 up-on hir þe scapulary of Seynt [6]Gilbert, and þe woman confessed

þere be-for hem all þat in doi*ng* on of þat cloth sche felt gret

alleuyau*ns* of hir sore. The nyte folowand appeared on-to hir

a fayre old man with gray her, as sche þoute in hir sleep, and

---

[1] i *added above.*   [2] her *crossed through and* now *in margin.*

[3] to *crossed through and* tyl *written above.*

[4] MS. harme, h *crossed through in red.*   [5] b *crossed through.*

[6] a *stroke crossed through.*

Leaf 98.
Gilbert ap-
pears in a
dream and
tells her to
walk.

She awoke
whole.

in his hand he had a staf, as men walk for age. Thus ‖ he saide
on-to hir: Wilt þou be hool? Sche answered þať gladly sche wold.
Tho he blessed hir and said, Thou schal be hool. Sche inqwyred of
him what man he was & he answered þat he was maystir Gilbert 4
of Sempyngham. Aftir þis dreem sche a-wook and felt hir-self
hool in euery part and þus in helth lyued many ȝeres.

[CHAPTER XLII.]

cap. xlij.

A clerk had
a great
swelling,

A clerk was þere eke in þat cuntř þat in his breest and in his 8
wombe had a meruelous risyng whech bolned soo with-inne
his breest þat he fered gretly it schuld drawe on-to ydropesy.
Thus al in dispeyř of helth he lay in his bed [1] up-on fiftene dayes
with-oute hope of ony recuř. Certeyn men whech cam to visite 12
hym told him of þe grete myracles whech ouř Lord wroute at
Sempingham þorw þe merites of ouř fader Gilbert. Whan þe seek
man herd of þese noueltes he mad a-vow openly þat þat place
schuld [2] he visite [2] whan ouř Lord wold sende him disposicion and 16
leyser. Sone aftyr þis avow was mad þe man felt him sumwhat
amended, þat he myth ryse and walk. For whech cause in grete

and went to
Sempring-
Leaf 98,
back.
ham, where
he lay on the
grave and
said devo-
tions.

hast he took his iornay on-to Sempyngham, and þere in grete
deuocioñ he lened up-on þe graue and sayde swech deuo‖ciones 20
as he coude, praying with bittyr teres þat God schuld send him
sum reles of his peyne. In þis tyme of prayeř he felt þat alł þe
boweles of his body weř gretly meued and turned, as þei had
drawe on-to a-noþer kynde þan þei [3] weř be-fore. Tho rose he 24

And when he
arose the pain
was gone.

fro þe graue and felt him-self in oþir plite, for alł þe bolnyng and
eke þe peyne is a-voyded. Thus walkith he in þe cherch, assaying
him-self if [4] al be weel, and whan he say veryly þat he was hool he
took leue and walkith on-to his wonyng.   28

Another
priest became
ill after
bathing ;

¶ A-noþer prest was waschid in a batth up-on a Fryday and
on þe Satirday folowand he fel in so greuous seknesse whech
continued a hool ȝeř and more, þat alł þe membris of his body
had lost her offise; he myte not ete but if he weř fed, not goo but 32
if he weř led. Thus as a man alł contract with a maneř of a

---

[1], [2-2] *in margin.*   [3] i *added in red.*   [4] MS. it, *with f written on the* t.

palesie, he kept his bed, neuer remeuyng þens but with help. he too went to the sepulchre,
Thus was he fed and norchid lich a child with his seruaunt ordeyned
to his seruyse, for he myth nowt do him-self. This man was brout
4 with grete besinesse on[-to] þe cherch of Sempyngham in a cart,
be-twyx þe myd-day and euensong. Ther at þe graue he mad his
deuoute prayer þat our Lord ‖ be þe merites of Seint Gilbert schuld Leaf 99.
releue him. That same day was he so hool þat with-outen cart or and was cured.
8 hors he went hom to his owne place.

[CHAPTER XLIII.]

Capitulum xliij.[1]

In þat same cuntr[2] and in þat same place at Sempyngham was a A nun going to the kitchen, stumbled,
nunne whech, at þe comaundment of hir prioresse, went on-to[3]
12 þe kychyn, and be-cause sche went with grete hast and took no gret
consideracion what þing lay in hir weye, sche stombeled at a blok
whech was hid with straw, and þus fel sodeynly. In whech fal sche
was so greuously hurt þat hir foot was fro þe ioynt, and þus[4] sche and injured her foot.
16 lay crying and waylyng for grete peyne þat sche felt. Hir cry
was herd þorw þe place and a-non hir sisteres cam on-to hir,
coumforted hir, lyft hir up with many handis and grete heuynesse,
and bar hir on-to þe infirmarie. Thus bolned þe foot and ranked,
20 þat þei wer compelled to kit hir schoo, elles had þei not gote it of.
Many remedies wer ordeyned to þis foot; it was drawen with All remedies failed to cure her.
grete peyne to bryng it in ioynt ageyn, but it a-vayled not. Thei
layde eke to it playsteres of dyuers herbis, but it profited not, for
24 euyr þe peyne grew mor and mor. Thus lay þe nunne in þat
peyne ‖ at þat ȝer and þe next, on-to þe day whech we clepe þe Leaf 99, back.
annyuersarie of Seint Gilbert. Than was sche so febyl þat þei
þoute best to gyue hir þe holy anoyntyng whech is last of all þe
28 sacramentis. Tho sche reqwyred hem to make a kandel of wax[5]
aftir hyr length, and þat same kandel and hir-self eke sche desired She was taken to the sepulchre,
þei schuld bere on-to þe sepultur of Seynt Gilbert. This was doo
in dede, for whan sche was broute þedyr þe prioresse took þe same
32 lynand cloth in hande whech lay up-on þe breest of þis holy con-

---

[1] *In margin, 4 and part of 8 at edge of leaf.*
[2] *was crossed through.*
[3] *to above in red.*
[4] *s written above.*
[5] *in margin.*

and her foot was wound in Gilbert's linen cloth.

fessour̃ swech hour̃ as he schuld dey. In þis same cloth wonde þe prioresse þe soor foot of hir sister often rehersed. Thus lay sche wakyng þere be þe sepultur̃ all pat anniuersary day, þe nyte folowand, and þe next day tyl it was noon, for þan fel sche in sleep. 4 And in þat same sleep sche þoute þat sche say many men, clad al in white, comand in-to þe monasterye and bysy to araye þe auter̃ as þouȝ a preest schuld go to masse. Be-hynde hem al came Seynt Gilbert, as sche þoute, arayed lich a prest, and his chesibile was al 8 red. He turned him to þat woman whech lay þus seek; he blessed

Gilbert in a dream bids her rise,

Leaf 100.

hir̃ þryes, and at euery blessyng he mad a tokne on-to hir þat sche schuld ryse. ‖ Sche þout in hir slep þat sche roos and wold haue hold him be þe clothis, but hir hold fayled and sche fel down gruf 12 up[1]-on þe ground. As sche þoute in hir slep so fond sche whan sche a-wook, for sche lay þus still on þe pauyment sor̃ astoyned. In þis mene-tyme come þe prioresse and hir sisteres fro mete with

and she is made whole.

her̃ grace, and a-non þis same woman told hem who sche was 16 mad hool be þe help of Seynt Gilbert, eke[2] of al hir dreme and appering of þe Seynt sche mad at þat tyme open declaracion. Tho þe prioresse took hir be þe hand and felt wel þat sche was hool, for hir-self, with-outen ony leder̃, sche went agayn to þe 20 infirmarie, and euyr aftyr was þat foot as fayr̃ and as hool as ony foot myth be. ·

[Chapter XLIV.]

cap. xliiij.[3]

Virtue of the water in which Gilbert's dead body was washed.

WE rede eke þat, be touching of þe clothis of our̃ fader 24 Gilbert, and eke be drynkyng of þat water in whech his ded body was waschid, þat many vertues wer̃ wroute þerby and many sores holed. For þere was a prioresse of þat same ordre whech was vexed with seknesse xv dayes and þat greuous maledy. 28 Remedye cowde sche non haue of no bodely medycynes, wherfor̃

How a prioress was

Leaf 100, back.

cured by drinking it;

sche turned hir trost to þe help of God and þis Seynt, and with a gret feyth drank of þat water ‖ in whech his body was waschid, and sone aftyr was sche hool, for þe cuppe was not so sone fro hir 32 mouth þat hir body was hool, as many of hir sisteres bore witnesse whech were þere present.

---

[1] MS. ut.   [2] *in margin.*   [3] *In margin,* 44.

¶ A-noþir woman eke was þere fast by whech trauayled in byrth and a woman in child-birth;
of a child too dayes, so greuously vexed with peyne þat euery man
had pite of hir. Sche drank eke of þat[1] watyr in whech þe tonsure
4 of his berd was wette, and sche was mad hool.

¶ Eke þe same ȝere þat oure fader deyid, on of þe nunnes, as and a nun who had swallowed a fish-bone.
sche sat in þe[2] refectory and ete fysch with hir sisteris, þe bon of
a fisch left in hir þrote and stood so fast þat sche myth be no weye
8 remeve it, not-withstand þat sche myte touch it with hir fynger.
Sche drank often sithes be þe councelt of hir sisteres, but it
a-mended nowt, for þe penauns was so grete in hir drynkyng þat
sche cast þe likour, but þe boon a-bode stille. Hir felawes ded alt
12 her craft to drawe it owt, and al a-vayled not. This cur, as myn
auctour seith, was reserued to a-noþir maner drynk and an-oþir
werk. Thus lay sche, hir peyne euyr encresing fro myd-day tyl
euen. Hir sisteres þan, takyng a sadder councelt, ledde hir in-to
16 þe cherch, ‖ broute hir on-to þe auter and þere alle þei felt down Leaf 101.
on knees, deuoutly praying to God and to Seynt Gilbert for helth
of hir.[2] Tho mad þei hir to drynk of þat water in whech þe body
of þat holy confessour was wasch in. A-non, as sche had dronk
20 þat watyr, sodeynly sche was delyuered of þat peyne, but sche
coude nevyr haue knowlech wher þis bon be-cam.

[CHAPTER XLV.]

cap. xlv.[3]

O F þat same ordre eke a chanon had swech peyne in his nek A canon wraps his sore head
24 and þe aftir part of his hed þat he myte not suffir þat place
be touched, not with his owne handes. This peyne lastid eyte
dayes, þat he myth neuyr turne his hed but if he turned al his
body. On of his breþerin, whech was his keper,[4] gaf him þis
28 counsel, þat he schuld wynde his hed with a certeyn cloth of in a linen cloth of Gilbert's,
lynand whech Seynt Gilbert wered. I suppose veryly it was his
awbe, for my auctor her setteth a word 'subucula' whech is both
an awbe and a schert, and in þe first part of þis lyf þe same
32 auctour seith þat þis holy man wered next his skyn non hayer,
as for þe hardest, ne lynand, as for þe softest, but he went with

---

[1] *was crossed through in red.*
[2] *In margin,* 45.
[3] *in margin in red.*
[4] r *added in red.*

wolle, as with þe mene. Whan þis man had wounde þus þis

Leaf 101, back. cloth a-boute his hed,[1] whech cloth Seint ‖ Gilbert had used at
solempnite of messe, as we seid, a-non and sodeynly þis man was
and suddenly became whole, hool. This was at euen, for on þe morow he was purposed to entï 4
þe infirmary þat he schuld not inqwyet his breþerin with[2] clamouï
whech he mad for peyne. For þis cloth was not so sone put
a-boute his hed, and he þat wond it a-boute his hed was not
go fro him thre or fouï passe, or he cleped him a-geyn, saying þat 8
al his peyne was goo and he felt no maner greuauns. He leyd his
hand to þe place whech was sore, groped it, and touchid it with sad
felyng, and he felt no sor. His hed myte he turne on what side he
wold, not mevyng his body; flesch, skyn and nek, al was hool. 12
and followed his usual course of life. The same nyte he slept quyetely, and, to merueyle of aft his
felawchip, roos to mateyns, þere fulfillid aft his office[3] in redyng
and synging as he of vsage was wone to doo. In þe morownyng
and non er he told his breþerin al þis myracle, who he was mad 16
hool be þe[3] lynand cote of Seynt Gilbert.

[CHAPTER XLVI.]

cap. xlvj.

A woman with a swollen knee Eke a woman of good report dwelled þere be-side, whech in hir
kne and legge had swech a passioñ þat a month hool sche 20
Leaf 102. myte not goo on þe rite foot, so bolned and rankyd was hir ‖ kne.
Thus with grete bysynesse of hir seruauntes sche was horsed, for in
sykyrnesse þis is hir desire, þat sche wol be caried to Sempyngham,
trosting in þe merites of þis holy confessouï þorw whech sche 24
goes to Sempringham, wears Gilbert's hose, and is cured. schal be hool. Whan sche was come on-to Sempyngham aftir hiï
desire, þei broute hir þe hose of Seynt Gilbert; sche put hir legge
in þat same hose and sodeynly sche was hol, so parfithly cured
þat sche went þat same day a myle on hir feet hom to her owne 28
hous.

A woman was sick after childbirth; ¶ A-noþir woman eke aftir delyuerauns of a child had a greuous
seknesse fourty wekys and too. For hir womb was bolned to swech
quantite men supposed sche schuld deye. Many holy places visited 32

---

[1] in *crossed through in red.*   [2] ch *crossed through.*
[3] *inserted above.*

sche for hir helth and was not hool. So was sche inspired at þe she visited Sempring.
last to visite þe sepultuꝛ of ouꝛ fader Gilbert, and þeꝛ was sche ham and was cured.
mad hool. For sche was cured þere sone aftir sche was com, euene
4 in þe fest of Seynt Cruce, þe ix houꝛ of þe day. And þan with ful
glad hert sche went hom, schewing to hir frendis hir body wheꝛ þei
myth parceyue þat al þat swellyng was goo.

[CHAPTER XLVII.]

capl. xlvij.

8 THe þrote and eke the hed of a-noþir man þere be-syde was Another
so risyn and bolned with seknesse whech þei ‖ clepe þe Leaf 102, back.
swynesye, and eke so greuously knottid, þat viij dayes *continuely* man's throat
he was compelled for very peyne with-outen mete or sustenauns to and head were swollen,
12 kepe his bed and suffyr þe maledye. The last too dayes was his
drynk secluded fro him, so closed weꝛ his pipes with violens of þat and he had to fast.
soꝛ. Than fel on-to him moꝛ greuauns, for in þe myd houꝛ of þat
last nyth of þoo viij days he lost his spech, whech *priuacion* lastyd
16 on-to þe euyn of þat day folowand. Thañ supposed þei all whech
weꝛ aboute hym þat he schuld dye. For to heꝛ coumfort and
consolacioñ he myte in no wyse gyue non answeꝛ. The small
issewes of his þrote myte ful euel receyue wynd in-to his body.
20 Than, at grete instauns of his wyf, þe girdill of Seynt Gilbert was The girdle of Gilbert was
broute, and water eke, whech he halowyd. With þe girdill þei brought, and water which
girt his nek ful deuoutly, and þe watyr þei pored in-to his mouth. he hallowed ;
Eke þei waschid þe bolnyng of his þrote with þat same watyr, and
24 þan be-gan þe man fele sumwhat reles, for wyth þat wasching he
voyded wynd, and aftyr þe wynd o grete blody drope went oute fro and through
his mouth. Thus be-gan he to releue in so mech þat or euen he these he was healed.
spak and ete, and ‖ wyth-inne iij dayes he receyued parfite hele, so Leaf 103.
28 sodeynly cesed his peyne.

[CHAPTER XLVIII.]

Cap. xlviij.

ON of þe nunnes of þat same ordꝛ xxx. ȝere *continuely* twyes[1] A Gilbertine nun was fre-
or thries in þe ȝere had meruelous seknesse with-inne quently sick,
32 hir body, for a-bowte hir hert and in hir left syde was swech

---

[1] *ones crossed through, and* twyes *written above.*

and at such times went out of her mind.

pressuꝛ þat whan it cam, þe woman, ny ded for uery peyn, lost hir mynde. And in þis peyne sche had swech strength þat many of hiꝛ sisteres myth not at þat tyme hold hiꝛ ne kepe hir in rest. Thus on a day whan þe seknesse had caute hir þus violently 4 þei sent aftir prestes of þe same ordre for to be a-boute hiꝛ in tyme of hir deth, for aff loke þei whan sche schal passe.

The Master of Sempringham goes to her;

A-mongis þese prestis cam in þe maystir of Sempingham, þat same mayster whech was next successouꝛ aftir Seynt Gilbert. 8 Theꝛ fond he þe woman bownden and holden as a furiose person is wone to be seruyd. Tho he inqwyred of hem þat weꝛ þere [1]

she is given the water of St. Gilbert,

if ony part of Seynt Gilbertis watyr weꝛ in þat hous. Thei had it redyly, and at þe comaundment of heꝛ prelat, þei pored 12 of þe same watyr in-to hir mouth. A grete merueyl was seyn þere, for þat watyr was not so sone entered in-to hir þrote but sche be-gan to chaunge aff þat wode rage, and hir veyl, whech

Leaf 103, back. and is made whole.

was pul|led down to hir schulderis, in ful religious maneꝛ sche 16 redressid, and hid hir face and hir eyne as sche was wone to doo. And þoo in þe presens of þe maystir & many folk whech stood with him, sche cryed in þis maneꝛ: O moder of mercy,—What schuld we teff long tale?—As þouȝ sche had be in a trauns 20 sche be-gan to knowe hir-self, and be processe of tyme sche was restored to parfite helth, for aftyr þat tyme had sche neuyr more þat seknesse.

Another woman had dysentery and gout,

¶ A-noþir woman was þere with dyuers seknesse vexed, þat 24 is to seyn dissentyrie, govte, and vomyte dayly folowand. Dissentryye þe Grekys clepe þis sekenesse whan a mannes guttys be hurt so þat þei be slitte or cutte. Othir sekenesse had þis woman dyuers, whech sche was a-schamed to confesse and for 28 whech sche was compelled be debylite to kepe hir bed fro þe

and hearing of her neighbours being cured,

fest of Aff Seyntis on-to iij dayes be-foꝛ Candeff-masse. Than was told hir þat too of hir neybouris, women bothe, on def, a-noþir bedred, infect with a maner of palesie, þat þei weꝛ led 32 on-to þe toumbe of Seint Gilbert and þere weꝛ þei mad parfitly hool. Of þese tydanes sche caute a coumfort, and a-non sche let [2] make a candel aftir hir mesuꝛ, and in a cart with þat same was

---

[1] *inserted above.*

[2] led *crossed through in red, and* let *in black in margin.*

sche caried on-to þe sepultuꝛ of ouꝛ fadeꝛ. ‖ Theꝛ wook sche **Leaf 104.**
in prayer al þat nyte, & þe next day a-boute nyne of clok was **went to the sepulchre and**
sche mad hool of alł þoo maledies rehersed be-fore. **was cured.**

[CHAPTER XLIX.]

4   **Capitulum xlix.**

A noþir woman was þere whos kne was soo *contract* þat too **Another woman had**
monthis sche myth not goo. Sche was brout eke in a cart **a contracted knee, went to**
on-to þe toumbe of Seynt Gilbert wheꝛ sche wook to nytes in **Sempring-ham,**
8 ful devoute prayeres. The secund nyte sche þoute in hir dreem
þat oute of a ymage mouth whech stood be þe graue, mad in
worchip of ouꝛ Lady, felł a fayꝛ red flouꝛ, and eke þat same **had a dream of Our Lady,**
flouꝛ, as sche þoute, felł up-on hir soꝛ kne. Sche a-wook and
12 felt hir kne hool, for þis sodeyn helth, as sche vndirstood weel, **and was healed.**
was goue hir be þe mediacion of ouꝛ Lady and þe merites of Seint
Gilbert. Than with ful grete deuocioñ sche kissid þe feet of
þat same ymage, and þus in parfite helth sche is goo hoom.

16   ¶ Theꝛ was a-noþir woman eke in þat cuntꝛ whos rite eye **A woman with bad eyes**
be-gan to wax seek, þat is to sey, al red of colouꝛ with peyne **prayed by the tomb,**
folowand. Sone aftir þe lift eye was in þat same plite, for þat
eye in special bolned soo þat iij dayes sche myth se no lite.
20 In all þis peyne sche cam to þe toumbe of ouꝛ fadeꝛ Gilbert,
with a candelł brennaund and a petous hert. Theꝛ ‖ a-bode **Leaf 104, back,**
sche stedfastly in prayeꝛ whilis þat þe priouꝛ of þat same place
sayde masse þere. Aftir sche had herd þat masse sche went
24 hom in hope of helth, and þere felł sche on sleep. Aftir hir
sleep sche felt neythir passioñ in eye ne hed, and or þe sunne
went to rest þat bolnyng was voyded and hir site restored. Day
be day aftyr þis hir site wex bettyr and bettir tyl it cam to þe **and was healed.**
28 same perfeccioñ whech it had be-foꝛ.

[CHAPTER L.]

Capitulum l.

A conuerse of þat same ordꝛ, in þe vigile of Seynt Mathie **On a Saint's vigil a weaver**
þe apostelł, whech was a weueꝛ of cloth, aftyr þe euensang **continued weaving,**
32 sayd of þe same apostel, sat stille in his craft weuyng. Othir of

his felauchip warned him þat at reuerens of þat feest he schuld sese, but he wold not. The same nyte, aftir his first slep, he felt þat al þe myte of his rite arme was lost fro þe cubyte on-to þe hand; eke þe same rite hand was turned wrong, and myte 4 in no maneꝛ haue recors on-to his natural office. This peyne lastid iij wekys and iij dayes. So in þe feste of Seynt Benet he asked leue of þe priouꝛ of þat place in whech he was conuerse þat he myte goo visite, with oþir too felawes ioyned on-to him, 8 þe sepultuꝛ of ouꝛ fader Gilbert. Thidir he cam with a hand ‖ of wax, and mad his offeryng; þere abod he certeyn tyme in prayeꝛ & wakyng, lynand euyr in hope þat he schuld haue reles of his peyne. The fyrst nyte folowand his hand was rather apeyred þan 12 amended, so was þe hand of ouꝛ Lord agreued up-on him. The man be-þoute him and remembred þat þe soꝛ of his soule, per-auentuꝛ, as often is sene, was cause of his bodely seknesse; wherfor he þoute best to þrowe a-wey his synnes, þat he myte 16 þe soneꝛ purchase grace of his desire. Vp-on þis he went to a prest, & with good rememberauns he confessid his synnes fro his ȝong age on-to þat same day, took his penaunce mekely and ful-fillid it deuoutely. So aftir þis up-on þe nyte next þe anun- 20 ciacion of ouꝛ Lady he set his hope only in him [1] þat wold þat same day be incarnate for ouꝛ helth, and in hir eke, þat blessed virgine, of whom. he took both flesch and blood; moꝛ-ouyr he put his trost in his fader Gilbert, whech in his lyf exercised þe 24 weyis both of chastite & of mekenesse: in al þis trost he desired with certeyn lite for to wake al a-lone at þe sepultuꝛ of his fader Gilbert. Ther lay he & sayde his seruyse swech as is assigned on-to ‖ conuerses of þat order. He prayed instantly for helth 28 on-to his fader and many oþir seyntes, and in his prayeꝛ as he lened up-on a ston þat lay ouyr þe graue, he fel on slepe, and so rested a tyme. Whan he a-wook he felt certeyn prykkingis in his arme ny his cubite; he drow his hand on-to him, and say 32 wel þat þe crokednes þerof was a-mendid, for he myte strecch it oute as he wolde. Aȴ þe senewis & aȴ þe fyngeres weꝛ so restored on-to helth þat he myte meue hem; eke in his arme felt. he no moꝛ peyne.   36

Marginal notes:

and his right arm was smitten.

Leaf 105.

He went to the sepulchre of Gilbert,

and at first became worse.

He then con-fessed his sins,

and after-wards watch-

Leaf 105, back.

ed by the grave, and fell asleep.

He awoke healed.

---

[1] MS. þat wold þat wold, *the first two words crossed through in red.*

[CHAPTER LI.]

cap. lj.

There was a woma*n* eke þat for seknesse fel in a frenesie, _{A woman behaved as if mad.} or ellis in swech mane*r* passio*n* whech was lich frenesie.

4 For as a[1] wod creatu*r* sche spak, gnacching with hir teth, and voydyng hir spatil in oþir me*n*nes faces & wome*n*. So was sche vexed in swech wilde rage þat þei bounde hir fast, and þus lay sche bownde fully a monthe. Sche was broute þus bownde in _{She was brought to the sepulchre, and was cured.}

8 a carte be labou*r* of hir husband and hir frendis on-to þe toumbe of Seynt Gilbert, and þere abood in prayeres iij dayes and nytes; þoo co*m*plet sche went hom heyl and sou*n*d, euer þankyd be God.

12 ¶ Lich on-to þis myracle fel on-to a-noþer woma*n* þat too _{A similar miracle.} monthis and a half was ‖ distraut, and whan sche was broute _{Leaf 108.} on-to þe graue and lay þere too dayes and nytes, þe þird day a-boute þe þird ou*r* sche was mad hool.

16 ¶ Eke at a monastery cleped Wathone a pore man, kept in _{At Watton a madman} þe hous mad for po*r* men, had swech a seknesse too monthis þat he fel in-to a mane*r* of frenesy so was his mynde alienat. The s*er*uauntis of þat infirmarie had ful grete pite and co*m*passion

20 up-on him and leyd him[2] in an old hors bere i*n* whech ou*r* fader _{was laid in St. Gilbert's bere,} Gilbert was caried su*m*tyme whan he myte not wel walk for grete age and febilnesse. Many seke men had be layde in þat same bere, and caut he*r* helth be þe merites of þis ma*n* whech

24 used it su*m*tyme. The man was layd þer-in, and be-cause he was wilde þei bond him to þe bere; so lay he too dayes and _{and so was cured.} too nytes, and on þe þird day was he mad hool and turned on-to helth a-geyn.

[CHAPTER LII.]

28   cap. lij.

Eke a noble woma*n*, as þei sey, dwelled not fer þens, and _{A noble-woman had great pain in her eyes.} sche had a greuous passio*n*[3] in hir eyne, so greuous þat sche myte se but litil or ellis nowt, speci*a*li on day lite. Be-side

---

[1] *inserted above in red.*   [2] *inserted in red above.*

[3] *s crossed through.*

9–2

þis had sche oþir seknesse, so þat sche was compelled to kepe hir

bed.   There had sche a vision, þat if sche wold goo on-to ‖ þe tumbe of þis holy fader, sche schuld be releued of þat peyne.

Sche mad a candeʒ be þe mesuꝛ of hir body, and to þe graue 4 sche is come, wheꝛ sche drank of þat same watir in whech þe holy confessouꝛ body was wasched ; sone aftir þat drynk sche was mad sodeynly hool.

¶ The sun of þis same woman eke receyued helth of his eye,[1] 8 whech was ny ouyrspred with a webbe, be drynkyng of þat same watyr.

¶ Eke a-noþir woman þat myte not heꝛ no maner þing, not þe sound of grete bellis, aftir sche had wakid in deuocioñ at 12 þis sepultuꝛ o nyte, first receyued coumfort þat sche myte heꝛ þe noyse of bellis, and aftyr, þe speche of men.

¶ A-noþir man of ful grete fame, cleped Herry Biset, a ful long‧ tyme was seek, and aftir þat seknesse had a grete & greuous 16 bolnyng of his wombe.   This same peyne lastid him too ʒeꝛ or moꝛ.   The bolned womb roos on-to so grete quantite þat whan he was sette he myte not se passing too vnch of his thy.   Thus

in dispeyre of aʒ helth, for medycynes myte not help, he sent 20 his wif and his douteres to Sempingham, to dwelle þere and

haue a-qweyntauns, for he supposed not elles but ‖ for to deye.

The wif cam hom a-geyn to se hir husband and broute with hir a lynand[2] girdil with whech ouꝛ fader Gilbert was sum-tyme 24 girt ; sche broute eke of þat same watir in a crowet in whech þe holy confessouꝛ body was wasched.   And whan þe man had drinkyn of þat watyr and was girt with þat girdiʒ, a-non he bo-gan to qwake & gnach with teth, but he wex no þing hoot. 28 Thoo fel he in a sleep, and in þat same sleep, merueyl to here, he fel on a swete, for he had no swete of al þe tyme in whech he was seek.   But now swetith he horribily.   His wif, þat sat by, sey þe ʒelow dropes who þei[3] stilled fro him and þoo were 32 grete and had ful euel sauouꝛ.   Whan he wook he aspied þis him-selue, and felt þe same sauouꝛ.   He loked up-on his wombe

and say wel þat al þis bolnyng was fled downward fro þe girdiʒ ny half a fote.   For þe skyn whech was be-forn his sleep so 36

---

[1] wa *and part of* s *crossed through.*   [2] gil *crossed through.*
[3] i *added afterwards.*

pressed oute þat he was aferd it wold brest, now is it voyde as
a empty bagge. Aftir al þis not long tyme þe man recured all
þis seknesse and cam to *parfite* helth, myte ryde and goo as ma*n* and finally cured him.
4 of armes, for as it semeth be my*n* aucto*ur* he was a knyte. ‖

[CHAPTER LIII.]

Cap. liij.   Leaf 107, back.

A Woman eke was in þat cunt*r* whech had a greuo*us* sekenesse Another woman cured
with-inne hir boweles all a hool ʒere. Hir wombe bolned of an internal complaint
8 not, ne no mane*r* risy*ng* had sche of skyn ne flesch, but fretyng
and prikkyng, spec*i*ali a-boute hir hert and sum-tyme in hir sides,
þat sche supposed veryly for to deye. Wherfor[1] sche was schryue
and hoseled and took all mane*r* obseruau*n*ces whech lo*n*g to men
12 whan þei schal passe, and be-cause sche abode still in lyf aftir
all þis do, þerfor hir husband, of grete deuocion, caried hir in
a cart on-to þe hous of Sempyngham, trostyng in þe merites of
þis holy confessou*r*. Whan sche was come on-to þat place sche
16 receyued þe sacrament newly a-geyn, and þan þei mad hir to by means of the water.
drynk of þat watir in whech þe body was waschid of þis holy
confessou*r*, Gilbert. Thus a-bode sche stille praying at þe graue
of þis Seynt iij dayes; in þe þird day sche had a great vomyte
20 of corupte blood, and with þis corrupcion ca*m* oute a grete long
worme. Thus iij dayes & ij nytes had sche þis purgacion. Aftir
þis went sche hom, and þus day be day þe vomyte sumwhat cesed,
and þe gre‖te peyne was fully relesed.   Leaf 108.

[CHAPTER LIV.]

24   capl. liiij.

I n þat same hous of Sempi*n*gham was a nu*n*ne[2] whech ou*r* A nun at Sempring-
fader Gilbert had receyued him-self. This woma*n* was infect ham had leprosy.
with leprosite, whech encresed in hir so horibily þat all hir body
28 was infect. The her fled fro hir hed, hir browes and hir eyne
we*r* so infect þat sche myte not lift hir ey-ledes for to loke.[3]

---

[1] l *crossed through.*   [2] non *crossed through and* nunne *in margin.*
[3] his *crossed through.*

She lay years
without use of
her limbs, Hir handes eke so sore þat sche myte in no maneꝛ put mete
or drink on-to hir mouth.   Thus lay sche in þe infirmarye xij
ȝere, euyr serued be a woman whech was hir bodely sistir, whech
woman ofte tyme wold[1] sey[2] þat sche sey[2] neuyr man ne woman 4
so horribily infect.   Be-cause þat þis same woman was so conuersaunt with hir and had often tymes vsed to a-noynt hir naked
body with certeyn medycynes, þat þe soꝛ schuld be moꝛ tollerable,
and was
isolated. for þis cause, þe nunnes of þat hous fled þe comunicacion of þis 8
same woman, so weꝛ þei aferd for to be infect.   To þis woman
þat ley þus greuously hurt with þis horible seknesse appered
in sleep a worchipful lady, comaundyng hir þat sche schuld
She sleeps by
the sepulchre,
Leaf 108,
back. be caried to þe sepultur of Seynt Gilbert, for þere schuld sche 12
receyue helth.   Thus ‖ is sche brout on-to þe graue and þere, aftir
deuoute prayeres, sche fel in a slep, in whech slep þe same
has a dream, honourable lady appered to hir and saide þese wordes: A-rise, for
þou art hool; and be-for þese wordes þe lady, as sche þoute, sprad 16
a fayre mantell of purpill a-boute þe graue, with[3] whech mantel
sche cam in, and eft-sones sche sayde on-to þe sek woman: A-rise,
for þou art hool.   Than in þat same dreem semed it to þat seek
woman þat sche was hool, and sche herd þe couent syng Te Deum 20
Laudamus for hir helth.   Thus lay sche dremyng on-to þat tyme
awakes as the
matins are
rung, whan þe conuent rang to mateyns; þan sche awook and returned
a-gayn to þe infirmarie.   In hir rising sche voyded gret humores
and in grete quantite, but with-inne iij dayes sche was parfitely 24
hool, for al a weke aftir, þe swames fell fro hir body as þei had
and is subse-
quently cured. be scalis of a fisch, & þus with-inne fewe dayes aftir, hir flesch
was restored lik þe flesch of a ȝong child.

[CHAPTER LV.]

Some men
crossing the
Channel were
becalmed, CErteyn men of þis lond sayled ouer þe see whech is be-twix
Inglond and Normandye.   In her sayling ros a grete tempest
whech þei skaped with ouꝛ Lordes mercy.   Whan þe tempest ‖
Leaf 109. was sesed and down, þan had þei no wynd for to sayle, but likly 32

---

[1] *inserted above.*
[2] MS. *say with a dotted underneath and e written above.*
[3] *in margin.*

weꝑ þei al þat nyte for to trauase þe se. Many þat weꝑ þeꝑ drede *and many dreaded the peril of the sea.*
mech þe perel of þe se, specialy be nyte cared mech, but remedy
coude þei non. A man was a-mongis þem¹ þei cleped Ion, con-
4 stable of Chestir, a man of noble birth & grete fame ; he cleped
a prest on-to him whos name was Ancelme, whech was his *Anselm brings out Gilbert's scapulary,*
chapeleyn, and prayed him þat he schuld bryng forth þe scapularie
of Seynt Gilbert whech þe successouꝑ of Seynt Gilbert had² ȝoue
8 him,³ and whech he kept for a gret relik. This Ancelme ful
deuoutly arayed him in holy uestimentis lich a prest, waschid
his handes, and oute of his lordes cophre took oute þis scapulary, *and, holding it aloft,*
lyft it up in þe eyre, and þus he prayed þat þei all myte here : *prays for wind.*
12 Lord God omnipotent, Lord Almyty, if it be so þat þe lif and
þe conuersacion of Seint Gilbert weꝑ wroute on-to þi plesauns,
schewe now þat þorw his merites we may come to sum hauene
in³ whech we may be saf fro perel. A-non, as þese wordes weꝑ
16 said, a fayre soft wynd blew in þe scapulary, and fro þe scapulari *A wind arise.., and they 'oversail' other ships.*
it ascendid on-to þe sayl and euyr multiplied, þat in þat same
day⁴ þei ouy[r]took schippes ‖ þat sailed with hem and ouyrsailed *Leaf 109, back.*
hem, were eke in Normannye long or þei ; for summe schippis
20 þat were in þat viage cam not to Normanie neythir þat day ne
þe next day. Many oþir tokenes were do be þe myracles of ouꝑ *Many other miracles are forgotten, and some are not attested.*
fadeꝑ Gilbert whech be not touchid in þis present werk, for summe
of necligens ar forgotin, summe were not approued be swech
24 notable witnesse as þese were, summe weꝑ eke wroute aftir tyme
þat þis book was mad, wherfor þei be not ȝet browte in-to þis
forme. And be-cause þat we be in no dowte þat þese weꝑ do
in þe same forme, þerfor haue we wrytin hem in swech langage
28 as we coude, to þe praysing and ioye of ouꝑ Lord God in whos
name þei were wroute, to þe worchip of holy cherch and profite
of hem þat schul rede or here þis lif, for whom þese notable þingis
weꝑ do, to þe worchip eke of þis holy man be whom þese myracles
32 weꝑ doo, whech man with his merites and pray[er]es schal com-
mende us to þat Lord whech is hiest of all Lordes, and bryng
us eke on-to þoo ioyes þat be eterne, wheꝑ we may rest fro all
labouꝑ with-outen ende, Amen.

---

¹ *inserted above.*   ² *in margin.*
³ *ne in inserted above.*   ⁴ *h crossed through.*

[CHAPTER LVI.]

Capitulum lvj.‖

OWre holy fader, þe Pope Innocent þe þird, ordeyned þat þe canoniȝacion of þis same fader Gilbert schuld be solempniȝed in þe cherch, and eke his translacion, of whech canoniȝacioñ he 4 him-self at Rome, be-foŕ al þe clergye and þe puple, mad a ful solempne sermoñ, whech sermoñ he comaunded it schuld be wretyn and sent on-to þe archbischoppis and bischoppis of Ynglond in bullis, and eke on-to þe chapiter of þe hous of 8 Sempingham, of whech sermon þis is þe sentens: For-as-mech as treuth seith in þe gospeŀl þat no man litith a lanterne & hidith it vndyr a buschel mette, but settith it up-on heith, þat aŀl þat dwelle in þat hous may haue coumfort of þat lite, for þis cause, 12 we þink þat it is a dede of grete pite and of equyte þat þoo men whom ouŕ Lord God hath crowned for her merites & goue to hem honour in heuene, þat we in erde schuld worchep hem, prayse hem & make ioye of her exaltacioñ, specialy whan ouŕ Lord, for 16 swech worchip as we do hem, is þe more magnified of us, be-cause þat scriptuŕ seith: Our Lord is preisable, or praysid, and glorious in seyntys.   To þe grete vertue of pite longith ‖ þe grete behest, nowt only of þis present lyf but of þe lyf eke þat is eterne, as ouŕ 20 Lord saith be þe prophete on-to hem þat deye in holy lyf: I schal make ȝou þat ȝe schal stand in swech opinion of þe puple þat þei schal gyue to ȝou praysyng & honouŕ, þe ioye þat ȝe haue schal I gyue ȝou.   And in a-noþir place of scriptuŕ þus is seide of[1] 24 seyntis: Ritefulmen schul schyne as þe Sunne in þe kyngdam of her Fader.   For ouŕ Lord oft-tyme, þat he schuld schewe[2] meruelously þe myte of his uertu, and þat he schuld werk merci-ablely þe cause of ouŕ helth, þoo same trewe seruauntis whech 28 he rewardith in heuene often-tyme he honourith in þis world, and at þe places where heŕ bodies rest þere reysith he grete tokenes and myracles be whech[3] þe wikkidnesse of heresies is confundid and þe trew cristen feith confermed.   32

---

[1] MS. seide of seynt of seyntis ; *only* seynt *crossed through in red.*
[2] MS. schewe þe uertue meruelously ; *only* uertue *crossed through.*
[3] *a character crossed through.*

[CHAPTER LVII.]

capł. lvij.

THerfor we, as we may not as we schuld, sende þankinggis on-to Almyty God þat in oure dayes to þe confirmacion of 4 cristen feith and confusion of wikkid heresie hath mad now his tokenes newe and chaunged hem meruelously, makyng þe seyntis now in oure dayes to schyne with myracles, whech seyntis as is now sene kept þe trewe cristen ‖ feith, not only with mouth but 8 with werk. A-mongis whech seyntis maystir Gilbert, fundouꝛ and be-gynneꝛ of þe ordꝛ of Semyngham, whech in þis world was myty in grete merites, now liuand in heuene, schynyth with grete miracles, for it is ful conuenient þat his holynesse schuld be 12 approued with open & manifest tokenes. And þouȝ it be soo þat fynal perseuerauns is sufficient i-now to proue þat he or ony oþir þat deyith in goodnesse schuld be a seynt be-for God in þat cherch a-boue whech hath ouyr-come her enmyes, witnesse of treuth þat 16 seith: He þat is perseueraunt in goodnesse, in-to þe last ende schal be saf. And in þe Apocalipse wheꝛ he seith þus: Be trew on-to þe last ende, and I schal gyue þe þe crowne of lyf; ȝet þat a man schuld be hold holy in þe opinion of men, and here in þis cherch 20 whech lyueth in continuel batayle with hir enmies, too þingis to þis mateꝛ be ful necessarie: Vertue of good maneris, & vertue of tokenes, þat is to sey, good werkys and myracules, þat ech of hem schuld bere witnesse to oþir. For good werkis be not sufficient 24 with-oute myracules, ne myracules sufficient with-oute good werkys to bere very witnesse of ony ‖ mannes holynesse; for as we rede, sumtyme þe deuele, whech is cleped þe aungel of Sathan, may transfiguꝛ him-self lich to aungel of lite, and summe men as we 28 rede ałł heꝛ good werkis whech þei do, þei do hem for þis entent þat þei schuld be knowe a-mongis men as for holy leueres. Eke of þe wicchis þat dwelled with Pharao rede we, þat þei wroute meruelous tokenes; and Anticriste whaɲ he comth schal werk so 32 meruelous þingis þat, if it myte be, þoo soules þat be chosen to heuene schuld be meued and led in-to errour be þe same tokenes. Wherfor we conclude þat þe testimonie of good werkis be him-self a-lone is sumtyme fals and deceyuable, as may be sen openly in 36 þese ypocrites, eke þe testimonie of myracles be him-self sumtyme

The Pope's sermon on Gilbert.

Leaf 111.

Leaf 111, back.

is deceyuable, as is sene in þese wicchis þat dwellid with Pharao. But whanꝺ good werkis go be-foꝛ in ony persone, and aftir þoo folowyn glorious miracles, þan haue we[1] a very certificacion of mennes holynesse, þat þoo too þingis schuld lede us þe rite wey to 4 honouꝛ þat persone whom þat ouꝛ Lord hath offered on-to us to be worchiped, with good werkis going be-foꝛ and miracles folowand.

Leaf 112. These to ar notabely touchid in þe ‖ Euangelist Mark wheꝛ he writith þus of þe aposteles: Thei walkid forth in þe world and 8 prechid, ouꝛ Lord werkyng and helpyng her sermones and signes or ellis myracles folowid aftir þat.

[CHAPTER LVIII.]

Capꝑ. lviij.

Continuation of the sermon. And þou; it be soo þat oure weel be-loued childyrn in God, þe 12 priouꝛ and þe couent of Sempingham, haue instauntly mad heꝛ postulacion on-to us þat we schuld graunt þat maystir Gilbert schuld be wrytyn in þe cathaloge of seyntis and be a-noumbered a-mong seyntes, whech Gilbert was be-gynner of her ordre,[2] and 16 whech man, as þei sey, be-foꝛ his deth had exercise of good werkys, and aftir his deth wroute many grete myracules, ;et wold we not **The Pope will inquire into Gilbert's life ;** graunt heꝛ peticion but we wil be fully enformed of[3] his lyf and of his myracles, not-with-stande[4] þat ouꝛ noble & worchipful son 20 in Crist, Ion, kyng of Yngland, with his lordes, and ouꝛ broþir,[5] archbischop of Cauntybyry, Hubert, with his suffraganis, eke þe priouꝛ of þe seid couent, with oþir abbotes and prioures, wrote on-to us in þis mateꝛ of þe vertuous lif of þis man and of þe 24 tokenes do at his graue.   Wherfor we wil in þis mater do grete **Leaf 112, back.** diligens to haue þe very treuth, ‖ and for þis cause we haue writyn **and has written to various clerics to proclaim three days' fast at Sempringham,** and comaunded be oure letteris to ouꝛ welbeloued breþerin, archbischop of Cauntirbyri, þe bischop of Hely, and to ouꝛ welbeloued 28 sones, abbot of Borow & abbot of Wardon, þat be ouꝛ auctorite þei schal go to þat place of Sempyngham and, in vertu of obediens, comaunde al þat college of men and women þat þei schul fast iij dayes and crien on ouꝛ Lord God whech is weye, treuth and lyf, 32

---

[1] *inserted above in red.*   [2] *inserted above in red.*
[3] MS. of of.   [4] *a character crossed through.*
         [5] *er crossed through.*

þat he wil open þe treuth of þis mateɼ on-to þe knowlech of his
seruauntis. Ferþermore we wil þat þei ransake þe wytnesse and
þe fame spred in þe cuntɼ, and make al þis to be writyn be scriptuɼ
4 autentik of þe¹ vertue of þe maneris, of þe vertue of þe myracules
of þis man, and al þis þing þus writyn, seled with heɼ sealis, send
up on-to us be feythful and trewe men whech may swere in ouɼ
presens þat al þis þing be trewe, þat we, þus pleynly informed,
8 may þe moɼ sikirly procede in þis mateɼ,—whech is to moring of
þe ioye of oure Lordis name and a grete confirmacion of cristen
feith.   And if it be so þat alle þese men assigned may not be at
þis examinacioꝼ, we wil at þe lest þat iij of hem schul fulfille þis
12 dede.

and to gather
and examine
evidence,

and send it
with witnesses
to Rome.

[CHAPTER LIX.]

Capitulum lix. ‖²

Thus þese same men fulfillid ouɼ comaundment ful treuly, and
be-cause on of hem myte not be þeɼ for a grete and a
16 neccessarie cause, þerfor iij of hem had þis examinacion in ouɼ
name, þat is to seyn, þe forseid archbischop, and þe bischop of Hely,
with þe abbot of Borow ; þese iij went on-to þat place and fulfillid
al þat was conteyned in ouɼ comaundment, for with gret diligens
20 þei examined all þe witnesse and mad hem for to swere þat þei
schuld non informacion make but soth; þei mad clepe religious
men, seculeɼ men, clerkis, lay men, men and women generali, whos
attestaciones and witnesse þei wrytyn treuly, and vndyr her seles
24 closed, sent al þis þing to us, whech sondes þouȝ þei were euydent
and certeyn, be-cause þei wery many and dyuers, we wil not at þis
tyme sette hem in oure wrytyng.   Thei mad eke grete inqwysicioꝼ
of his conuersacion and of his maneres, whech was open on-to alle
28 men ; þei cleped in dyueres religious men, whech were famyliar
with him at dyuers tymes, and whech knew of his pryuy conuersacion : all þese men with on acord bore wytnesse þat his lyf was ‖
ondefyled and holy.   For he was a meruelous man in abstinens,
32 a clene man in chastite, a deuoute man in orison, mech vsed to
wakyng; ouyr þat flok of his congregacion with grete prouision

Leaf 113.

The clerics
did as they
were bidden,

called wit-
nesses, and
examined
them,

and recorded
their evi-
dence.

They inquired
into Gilbert's
life,
and learnt of
his virtues.

Leaf 113,
back.

---

¹ MS. þe þe, *the first dotted underneath in red.*
² *Leaf 113 has heading.* Item lix.

and discrecio*n* eue*r* bysy ; certey*n* hou*r*is wha*n* he myte haue o*n*y leyser in co*n*templacio*n*, quiete. So as it semeth, whil he was in erde he departed treuly his lyf, sumtyme in good werkis of actyf lyf, sum in holy rest of *con*templatif, lich on-to þe patriarch Iacob 4 þat sey au*n*gelle*s* in þe ladde*r* goyng up and goyng down.   And whan he had o*n*y collocucio*n* with his breþeri*n* or sisteres, it myte be seid of him, as it was seid of Samuel, þere feɫɫ not a word of his on-to þe erde. For aftir þe doctrine of þe holy apostel, ydil wordes 8 were ful seldom in his mouth, but þoo wordes whech he spak were to edificacio*n* of ou*r* feith, for he was good in þat same, and þerfor his wordes we*r* ful of grace on-to þe hereres. And þou3 many oþir þingis mad his lyf to be i*n* grete comendacio*n*, þis was 3et a pri*n*cipal 12 þing longi*n*g to his perfeccio*n*, þat he wold chese wilful pouerte, and aɫɫ his possessiones whech we*r* left him be herytage, he wolde assigne

for euyr ‖ to meyntey*n* þe breþeri*n* and þe sistery*n* [1] whech he had institute and set vndyr a vertuou*s* reule of religion. For his 16 succession in processe of tyme grewe, be þe goodnesse of ou*r* Lord, to so gret a nou*m*byr þat he byled nyne monasteries of wome*n* and fou*r* of chanones regule*r*, in whech monasteriis þat tyme þat he deyid he left, be-side þe religiou*s* men, a þousand and fyue hundred 20 sisteres þat se*r*uyd God ou*r* Lord with-oute vylonye.

[Chapter LX.]

MOre-ouyr, to strength of þis mat*er* and to a gretter cautel, fyue of þoo breþerin of þat forseid order whech we*r* sent 24 on-to ou*r* *p*resens, we haue charged hem with grete oþis þat þei schuld informe us with þe soth, & þei haue told us mech mo*r*, both of his meke werkys and of his gloriou*s* myracules. Wherfor we,

of þis ma*n*nes lyf and myracules be sufficie*n*t witnesse þus informe 28 and set in a man*er* of sikirnesse, aftir þe testimonie of þe aungel þat seid to Tobie, it is good to hydy*n* þe sacrame*n*t of þe hy kyng, but þe werkis of God to open and confesse is gret worchip,—eke for þe Psalme seith [2] þat God schuld be praysed in his seyntis,—for 32

þese causes ‖ haue we ascribed and anou*m*byred Seynt Gilbert in-to

---

[1] whom *crossed through.*
[2] *inserted above and written again in margin.*

þe cathaloge of seyntes, and ordeyned þat his memory schal be   So Gilbert is
songyn a-mongis oþir seyntes. Aíl þese be þe Popes wordes; now   canonised.
folowith þe autouꝶ. Thus aftir þe comaundment of ouꝶ fader þe
4 Pope, whaīn þe translacioīn of Seynt Gilbert was broute to an ende,
and þe holy relikes weꝶ layd in þe vessel arayed for hem, but or it
was closed þe bischoppes and þe abbotes þat weꝶ *principal* fufilleres   The clerics
of þis werk, layde a char*tour* up-on his breest, in whech chartoꝶ   put a charter
with his body,
8 was *conteyned* aíl þe maneꝶ of his translacioīn, of þe myracles and   and a plate
describing
of þe canoniȝacion; eke þei layde þere a plate of led, in whech led   him.
was wrytyn certeyn þing whech schuld neuyr be oute of mynde.
The scripture of þat plate was þis : Heꝶ lith Seynt Gilbert, þe first
12 fader and foun*dor* of þe order of Sempyngha*m*, whech was translate
in-to þis schrine[1] be ouꝶ fader & lord, Hubert, archbischop of
Cauntyrbury, be þe comaundment of ouꝶ holy fader, Pope I*n*nocent,
[2] þe þirde yde of October, the ȝere of ouꝶ Lord, a þousand, too
16 hundred and on. This is þe wryti*ng* of þe chartoꝶ layde be him
in his schryne : In þis schryne ar *conteyned* þe relikes of ‖ Seynt   Leaf 115.
Gilbert, prest and confessouꝶ, þe first fader and begy*n*neꝶ of þe ordꝶ   The charter
tells of his
of Sempyngha*m*, whos lyf, þouȝ it be so þat many þingis mad it   life,
20 comen*dable* & honourable, þis was þe *principal* and moost excellent
cause whi he schuld be i*n* mynde, þat wilfully he chase honest
pouerte and aíl his temporal goodes þat God had sent him he freely
relesid to þe neccessite and sustentacion of þoo breþeri*n* and sisteres
24 whom he sette vndyr reguler discipline and kept hem ful bysily.
And to þis same Gilbert in *processe* of tyme ouꝶ Lord God graun*ted*
swech grace and uertue þat he mad fouꝶ houses of chanones and   his work,
nyne monasteries of nu*n*nes, in whech houses þat tyme þat he
28 deyid and went to ouꝶ Lord, be-side al þoo þat were ded be-fore,
he left of religious men on-to a vij hundred, of sisteres a þousand
and fyue hundred, whech ful bysily ded ser*uyse* to God. He deyid   his death
in his best age,[3] more þan a hundred ȝere old, þe ȝere of þe incarna-
32 cioīn of ouꝶ Lord Ihe*su*, a þousand, a hundred[4], eyty and nyne, þe
day be-foꝶ þe nonas of Februari, þe tyme of þe worchipful kyng
Herry þe Secu[n]d. And þus, be-cause of his owne merites and be   his miracles,
‖ testimonie of many myracles folowand, and reuelaciones eke, þat   Leaf 115,
back.

---

[1] *in margin in red.*
[2] MS. þe þird þe þirde ; þe þird *crossed through in red.*
[3] *a stroke crossed through.*   [4] *final d added in red above.*

and his
canonization, cam fro God, he was canoniȝed and wryten in þe cathaloge of
seyntes of ouꝛ holy fader Pope Innocent þe þirde, be þe general
cort of Rome at Anagniam, be-for þe clergy and þe puple, þe ȝere [1]
of þe incarnacioꝝ of ouꝛ Lord a þousaud too hundred and too, þe 4
þirde idus of Ianuari, þe ȝeꝛ of þe kyngdam of þat [2] worþi man,
Ion, kyng of Ynglond, þe þirde, *president* to þe see of Cauntirbury
þe worchipful archbischop Hubert, whech aftir þe comaundment of
þe said Pope, with his felawis as in [3] þat act, bischop of Hely, 8
Eustace, & abbot of Borow, Acarius, had mad diligent inqwisicion
up-on þe miracules wroute be þis man, and wrytyn alle þis mateꝛ
treuly, and sent it up to þe court.   Be whech examinacioꝝ ouꝛ
fader þe Pope receyued þe very treuth, both of þe holynesse of þis 12
man Gilbert and eke of his tokenes, and for þis cause he anoumbered
him a-mongis seyntis, þe ȝere of his papate, þe fourte.   [4] And þat
same ȝere, be þe comaundment of þe seide Pope, he was translate of
þe seid archbischop in-to þis schryne, þe þirde ide of Octobir, 16

Leaf 116. standyng by, þese wor‖chipful men, bischop of Norwich, bischop of
and who offi-
ciated at it. Hereforth, bischop of Landaue, and oþir abbotes and prelates and
nobel-men of Ynglond, with mech prese of [5] clergy and puple.
And to *per*petuel memory of þis þing þus don, þe seid archbischop 20
and þe oþir bischoppis & abbotes sette her seles on-to þis chartoꝛ,
and in þis schrine þei put it, to þe praising of ouꝛ Lord God
Almyty, whech schal enforme us with þe exaumples of þis man, and
reise us fro synnes to grace with help of þe prayeres of þis man; 24
and eke þe same Lord schal lede us fro peyne to ioye wheꝛ he
So ends this
book, trans-
lated in A. D.
1451. lyuyth and regnyth euyr moꝛ.   Amen.   **Thus endith þe lif of**
Seint Gilbert, translat in-to ouꝛ moder tonge, þe ȝere of þe
incarnacioꝝ of ouꝛ Lord a M cccc lj.   28

---

[1] re *added above.*   [2] MS. þat þat, *the first crossed through.*
[3] *inserted above.*   [4] E *crossed through.*   [5] MS. of of.

A Treatise of the Orders under the Rule of St. Augustine

FROM A SERMON PREACHED BY

JOHN CAPGRAVE

AT CAMBRIDGE IN 1422.

And here begynnyth a tretis of tho[1] orderes þat be
vndyr þe reule of oure fader Seynt Augustin, drawe oute
of a sermoñ seyd be freɼ Ion Capgraue at Cambrige,
þe ȝere of ouɼ Lord a M cccc xxij.

WE may likne ouɼ fader Seynt Augustyn on-to þe holy Augustine is like Jacob.
patriark Iacob for many causes. On is for interpreta-
cion of his name, for Iacob is ‖ as mech to say as a supplanteɼ Leaf 116, back.
4 or a deceyuour, for he, at þe comaundment of God, supplauted his
broþir, bying his fader blessing for a mese of potage and aftirward
apperyng to his fader in Esaues cote. So may ouɼ blessid fader
Augustyn be cleped a supplanter of þe Deuel, for whan þe same
8 Deuel ha hold him in his seruyse xxx ȝere, þañ ran he fro þe
Deuel and took up-one him þe swete ȝok of ouɼ Lord Iheѕu Crist.
For xxj ȝere was he in paganite, and ix ȝere in þe heresie of þe
Manychees. He may[2] be cleped Iacob also, for euene as Iacob
12 sey ouɼ Lord God fas to[3] fas, so ouɼ maystir, with secret contemplacioñ, was as ny God as ony erdely man myte be, as may be
wel perceyued be þe labouɼ whech he had in inuestigacion of þe
godhed in þe bokes whech he mad of þe Trynyte. This Iacob
16 had xij sones, to whom all þe lond of byhest was distribute and
departed be Moyses & Iosue. And þis Augustin hath xij religious He founded twelve reli-
cumpanies, be whech xij all holy cherch heɼ in erde is replecchid. gious bodies like the twelve
We wil at þis tyme on-to ȝouɼ deuoute eres open þese Hebrew sons.
20 names of þese xij tribus, and referɼ hem to dyuers religions ‖ whech Leaf 117.
lyue vndir Seynt Austyn reule.

¶ The first be-goten child hite Iudas. ⁴For Iudas is as mech
to sey as a preyseɼ, and þese men preise God nyte & day in holy
24 songis & ympnis whech þei continuely be vsed too.⁴ And þis

---

¹ MS. who crossed through and tho written above.
² b and part of l crossed through.   ³ inserted above.
⁴⁻⁴ passage written at top of page and marks of insertion made.

Judas like the
Heremits. Iudas eke[1] may be referred on-to þoo heremites þat Seynt Augustin
mad ny iij ʒere be-for þat he was bischop[2] at Ypone, and mad þere
chanones. This mater is proued with grete euydens in þe book
Capgrave's
English and
Latin books
on the sub-
ject. whech I mad to a gentil woman in Englisch, and in þe book whech 4
I mad to þe abbot of Seynt Iames at Norhampton in Latin, whech
boke I named Concordia, be-cause it is mad to reforme charite
be-twix Seynt Augustines heremites and his chanones. In þese
same bokes may men se þe names of þe first faderes of þis order of 8
heremites, whech heremites Simplician sent witʒ Augustin on-to
Affrik.

Reuben like
the Secular
Canons. ¶ The second child of þis Iacob, he hite Ruben, and þis Ruben is
referred on-to chanones seculer swech as be in cathedral cherchis. 12
For Ruben is as mech to sey as seing in þe myddis, or seing be þe
myddis. What schal we calle bettir þe myddis þan þis present
lif? What was be-for þis lif ordeyned for us is on-knowe. What
we schal haue aftir þis lif it is in doute, saue we hope veryly, be þe 16
good menes of þis myd lif, to come sumtyme to Goddis mercy.
Leaf 117,
back. But ‖ men wil merueyle perauentur whi þat I sette seculer chanones
be-for reguler, and þis [is] my cause. Thoo chanones þat dwelled
with Seynt Augustin whan he was bischop went in cloþis of dyuers 20
colouris and in precious furres and with girdel[3] & barres of[3] syluer
and gilt, as is manifestly writyn in his sermones,[4] Ad fratres in
heremo, and þis aray long not to reguler chanones.

Gad like
Canons Regu-
lar. ¶ The þird son of Iacob he hite Gad, and his name is as mech to 24
sey as a man þat is[5] wel girt. Girdyng in holy scriptur is take
for restreynyng of our body fro uices, and þis may be applied in
þe best maner to chanones reguler, whech, with holy obseruaunces
girdyn her bodies fro sinful werkis & here soules fro foule desires. 28
If þese men be-gunne with Augustin in his cherch in þe same
degre as þei stand now, sum men haue doute; but I wyl not
stryue. I be-leue wel þat þere had þei her beginnyng but þe
harder distinccion fro þe first ordr was mad sithe be oþir holy 32
Monks of the
Charterhouse. faderes,[6] as þe munkis of Charturehous cam oute of þe blake
ordr.[7] Many euydens haue I mad [8] in my book *Concordia*[8] þat

---

[1] *inserted above.*   [2] MS. preest *crossed through and* bischop *written over.*
[3-3] *in margin.*   [4] wri *crossed through.*   [5] *inserted above.*
[6] s *added above.*   [7] *in margin.*   [8-8] *in margin.*

Seint Ruffus not be-gan þis ordr̃, but þat he reformed þis ordre.
So may I wel be-leue þat her first fundacion cam fro Augustin.

¶ The iiij son of Iacob, he hite Aser. Aser is as mech to ‖ sei Leaf 118.
4 as blessed, and þis blessing is referred to þe grete noumbir of þat Asher like the Dominicans.
holy congregacion whech Seynt Dominice gadered and ordeyned,
to þis entent, þat þei schuld labour̃ in þe world and with here
preching distroy synne in þe puple and plant vertue. This ordre
8 be-gan Seyn Dominice þe ȝer̃ of oure Lord a M cc xvj.

¶ The v. son of Iacob hite Neptalim, as mech for to sey as Naphtali like the
gret brede; be þis vndirstund we þe knytes of Seynt Ion whech Knights of St. John.
begunne first at Ierusalem, and now ar þei spred þorw-oute all þis
12 world. Her institucion is to defende Cristen feith a-geyn Turkes
and Sarsines. And all þoo possessiones whech þei haue in londis
of pees pay tribute to þe hous of Rodes.

¶ The sext son hite Manasse, and he is for [to] [1] sey as obliuious. Manasseh like the Knights
16 This son be-tokneth þe heres of Pruce whech wer̃ institute to þe of Prussia.
same entent to defense of þe bordures of cristen men a-geyn þe
enmyes of þe crosse. Obliuious be þei cleped be-cause þei must
forȝete þe delectable lyf of þis world and put [2] her̃ bodies in grete
20 perel for þe honour of Crist. The differens of þe habite of þese
too knytes is þis, þat þei of Seynt Iones haue blak mantell with
a crosse, and þei of Pruce white mantell with a crosse.

¶ The vij son of Iacob, he hite [3] Simeon, whech ‖ soundith in our̃ Leaf 118, back.
24 tonge heuynesse or pencifnesse, and þis may be applied with grete Simeon like the Gil-bertines.
conueniens on-to þat ordre þat was founded at Sempyngham be
þe solicitude of Seynt Gilbert, of whech Seynt, be-cause I mad
a special tretis on-to þe maystir of þat ordr̃, þerfor in þis place
28 I touch no mor̃ of him.

¶ The viij son of Iacob, he hite Leui, þat soundeth in owre Levi like the Premonstra-tensians.
langage a moryng or a multipliyng of þing þat was be-gunne,
and be þis name we vndirstande þe ordr̃ of Premonstracenses,
32 whech be-gan in Fraunce vndir a holy man þei cleped Norbertus,
þe ȝer̃ of our̃ Lord a M and a hundred, and be-cause þat I mad
his lyf in Englisch to þe abbot of Derham þat deyid last, þerfor as
now I wil no lenger̃ tarie in þat fundacion.

36 ¶ The ix son of Iacob, he hite Ysacar; he soundeth in our̃ Issachar

---

[1] MS. a *crossed through*.   [2] MS. but.   [3] se *crossed through*.

like the
Brothers of
the Cross.
langage grete mede for laboure; þis wil we applie to þat ordre whech þei clepe þe Freres of þe Crosse,[1] for þis cause, for þat crosse on heꝛ breest schul make hem so to labouꝛ in þe weye of Crist þat þei schuld come aftir heꝛ labouꝛ to euyrlasting mede. 4 Off þis ordre haue I as ȝet no certeyn knowlech, who was heꝛ foundoꝛ, or vndir what Pope, or kyng, þei be-gunne.

Leaf 119.
Zebulun like
the order of
St. Bridget.
¶ The x son of Iacob, he hite ȝabulon, and in ouꝛ langage it may be cleped a dwellyng-place of strength. ‖ Ful wel longith þis 8 interpretacion on-to þe ordꝛ of Seynt Bryde; þei haue a mansion of strength, for þei be sperd fro vanites of þe world, whech vanytes ar ouyr open to many men. This holy woman Bryde be-gan þis order and went to Rome for confirmacioñ; who wil se hir lyf and 12 hir reuelaciones he may diffusely se it in hir book, as now I haue no tyme to tary lenger in þat mateꝛ.

Joseph like
the order of
St. Victor.
¶ The xj son hite Ioseph, and he is to sey[2] a moring or augmen-tacioñ; þis is applied to certeyn chanones of þat hous whech be[3] 16 of þe ordꝛ of Seynt Victoꝛ. This hous of Seynt Victour is in Paris, to whech I trowe þei longe. We haue in ouꝛ libraries many sundry bookes þat to chanones of þat hous mad; on of hem hite Hewe, þe oþir hite Richard, notabel clerkis þei weꝛ and men of 20 holy lyf.

Benjamin like
the order at
Peterston in
Norfolk.
¶ The xij son hite Beniamin; he is þe son þat longith to þe rite hand, as euery religious man with þe mercy of God doth. This son, be-cause he is ȝongest of age, is likned on-to an ordre whech 24 is not in þe world, as þei sey, but in Northfolk. Fouꝛ houses had þei and on of hem is faꝂ on-to þe[4] kyngis hand, & he gaue it to Walsingham; þe hous hite Petirston: oþer informacioñ of hem haue I not at þis tyme.   28

---

[1] O *crossed through.*   [2] y *in red above.*
[3] *inserted above in red.*   [4] *inserted above in red and written in margin.*

NOTES

p. 3, l. 14. *Comagene,* the region north of Syria and Cyrrhestica between the Euphrates and the Taurus Mountains.

p. 3, l. 15. *Nussie,* perhaps Tuscany or Russia. Achay is Achaia, properly the northernmost part of the Grecian peninsula; Macedonia, north of Thessalia and Epirus; Dalmatia in Illyricum on the Adriatic seaboard.

p. 3, l. 18. *ʒeugis,* i. e. Zeugitana, the northern part of modern Tunis, and east of ancient Numidia. Tripolitane is Tripolitana, modern Tripoli, minus Fezzan; Getuly is Gaetuli, south of Numidia; Gaetuli Darae was on the Atlantic coast south of the Atlas mountains, and part of Mauritania.

p. 3, l. 27. *hated þe Greke letteris and loued weel þe Latyn.* Confessionum, ed. P. Knöll, Lipsiae in aedibus B. G. Teubneri, 1909, Book i, p. 14, l. 21 : 'Quid autem erat causae, cur graecas litteras oderam, quibus puerulus imbuebar, ne nunc quidem mihi satis exploratum est. Adamaveram enim latinas, non quas primi magistri, sed quas docent qui grammatici vocantur.'

p. 4, l. 3. *Cathegories,* or 'Predicamentes', see 11/28; not by Aristotle. Augustine says he understood the book freely and without master. *Confessionum* iv, p. 70, l. 29.

p. 4, l. 10. *good and rich kynrod.*—Not so; in the *Confessions,* ii, p. 26, l. 13, Augustine describes his father as a poor freeman of Tagaste: 'municeps Thagatensis admodum tenuis.'

p. 4, l. 18. Conversion of Patrick, *Conf.* viiii, p. 182, l. 27.

p. 4, l. 23. A brother is mentioned in *Conf.* viiii, p. 185, l. 25.

p. 5, l. 25. *redy eke on-to ire. Conf.* viiii, p. 181, l. 6 : 'erat vero ille praeterea sicut benevolentia praecipuus, ita ira fervidus. Sed noverat haec non resistere irato viro, non tantum facto, sed ne verbo quidem. Iam vero refractum et quietum cum opportunum viderat, rationem facti sui reddebat, s forte ille inconsideratius commotus fuerat,' etc.

p. 6, l. 18. The mother-in-law, *Conf.* viiii, p. 181, l. 28.

p. 6, l. 29. The orison, *Conf.* viiii, p. 190, l. 19.

p. 7, l. 8. *Seint Gregorie telletʒ in his Dialoges:—Dialogues,* Book iv, ch. xix. The tale is told by Robert of Brunne, *Handlyng Synne,* p. 161, from William of Wadington's *Manuel des Pechiez,* which follows St. Gregory. The child in this tale was torn away from his father's bosom and carried to hell, when five years old, for cursing.

p. 7, l. 17. Childhood's sin, *Conf.* i, p. 5, l. 23, p. 6, l. 10, p. 8, l. 1, p. 8, l. 17.

p. 7, l. 27. *put to skole, Conf.* i, p. 10, l. 22.

p. 8, l. 5. *lerned lesse þat he schuld or myth a lerne, Conf.* i, p. 11, l. 20 : ' et peccabamus tamen minus scribendo aut legendo aut cogitando de litteris, quam exigebatur a nobis . . . delectabat ludere et vindicabatur in nos ab eis qui talia utique agebant.'

p. 8, l. 8. *Mandauris,* i. e. Madaura, *Conf.* ii, p. 26, l. 9.

p. 8, l. 11. *sekenesse in his stomake, Conf.* i, p. 12, l. 29.

p. 8, l. 12. *þe fader wold not suffir it, Conf.* i, p. 13, l. 11—p. 14, l. 2.

p. 8, l. 20. Goes to Carthage, *Conf.* ii, p. 26, l. 11 ; iii, p. 35, l. 1.

p. 8, l. 22. Tullius Cicero, &c., *Conf.* iii, p. 38, l. 26. Cicero is mentioned only in connexion with *Hortensius.* See note to 9/13.

p. 8, l. 26. *tauernes and stewis.* Capgrave's interpretation of Augustine's reference to the ' cauldron of shameful loves '—' sartago flagitiosorum ' (iii, p. 35, l. 15)—and to the stage-shows—' spectacula theatrica ' (iii, p. 36, l. 12) ; and to his joys of passion (iii, p. 36, l. 8).

p. 9, l. 7. *an appil-tre, Conf.* ii, p. 29, l. 12.

p. 9, l. 13. *Hortencius, Conf.* iii, p. 39, l. 21 : ' liber ille ipsius [Cicero] exhortationem continet ad philosophiam et vocatur Hortensius.'

p. 9, l. 18. *name of Crist, Conf.* iii, p. 40, l. 24.

p. 9, l. 22. *holy scriptuꝛ, Conf.* iii, p. 41, l. 1. The reference to St. Paul is not in *Confessions.*

p. 9, l. 27. *þe Maniches, Conf.* iii, p. 41, l. 14 : ' Itaque incidi in homines superbe delirantes, carnales, nimis et loquaces,' &c.

p. 10, l. 1. *ix ȝere, Conf.* iii, p. 51, l. 2.

p. 10, l. 11. *a faiꝛ tre, Conf.* iii, p. 50, l. 4.

p. 11, l. 1. *consolacioꝛ be an holy bischop.* The bishop is not named. *Conf.* iii, p. 51, l. 11.

p. 11, l. 22. *imprended sche.* ' The Latin is, *Conf.* iii, p. 52, l. 5 : ' quod illa ita se accepisse inter conloquia sua mecum saepe recordabatur, ac si de caelo sonuisset.' This ends Book iii.

p. 11, l. 28. *Predicamentis.* See note to 4/3.

p. 11, l. 31. *bokes of philosophie,* &c. In *Conf.* iiii, p. 72, l. 30, Augustine speaks only of the ' so-called liberal arts '.

p. 12, l. 3. *he cam first hom.* The chief dates of Augustine's life are as follows : born, Tagaste, 354 ; lived at Carthage, 371-373 ; went to Rome, 383, and taught rhetoric for a short time ; went to Milan and met St. Ambrose, who baptized him in 387. In 388 he returned to Tagaste, and lived in quietude for awhile. He became bishop of Hippo in 395. The date of the *Confessions* is 397. He died in August, 430, at Hippo.

p. 12, l. 7. *resorted a-geyn to Cartage. Conf.* v, p. 82, l. 16 : p. 83, l. 7.

p. 12, l. 9. *Hermes.* Capgrave's misreading of Hierius, *Conf.* iiii, p. 66, l. 23 : ' Quid est autem, quod me movit, domine deus meus, ut ad Hierium, Romanae urbis oratorem, scriberem illos libros ? ' [*De Pulchro et Apto*].

p. 12, l. 11. *þei are not in hand now.* Cf. *Conf.* iiii, p. 66, l. 21 : ' non enim habemus eos [libros de P. et A.], sed aberraverunt a nobis nescio quomodo.'

p. 12, l. 14. *Faustus, a grete snare of þe deuele. Conf.* v, p. 74, l. 7 :

'Iam venerat Carthaginem quidam Manichaeorum episcopus, Faustus nomine, *magnus laqueus diaboli*.' The latter phrase is one of St. Paul's, 1 Timothy iii. 7, and 2 Timothy ii. 26. It is also used by Augustine elsewhere in the *Conf.* concerning the *Manichees*, iii, p. 41, l. 15, ' *laquei diaboli*.'

p. 12, l. 18.　*Contra Faustum*.

p. 12, l. 20.　*Conf.* v, p. 79, l. 26.

p. 12, ll. 32–33.　*a fayr̄-spoke man eke, but not grelly grounded in sciens*, *Conf.* v, p. 8, ll. 26–31; p. 81, l. 5; p. 81, l. 18.

p. 13, l. 2.　Defeat of Faustus.　*Conf.* v, p. 81, l. 29: 'Quae tamen consideranda et discutienda protuli, modeste sane ille nec ausus est subire ipsam sarcinam. Noverat enim se ista non nosse nec eum puduit confiteri.'

p. 13, l. 6.　*no deynte in her̄ bokes, Conf.* v, p. 82, l. 11.

p. 13, l. 11.　Augustine goes to Rome, *Conf.* v, p. 83, l. 5.

p. 13, l. 17.　*more liberte ȝoue on-to skoleres, Conf.* v, p. 83, l. 14.

p. 13, l. 22.　*His modir folowid him, Conf.* v, p. 84, l. 12.

p. 14, l. 8.　*greuous seknesse, Conf.* v, p. 85, l. 13.

p. 14, l. 11.　*bryng him forth*, &c., *Conf.* v, p. 86, l. 9.

p. 14, l. 13.　*not for to telle veyn tales, Conf.* v, p. 86, l. 20.

p. 14, l. 14.　*sche prayed for him, Conf.* v, p. 86, l. 13.

p. 14, l. 17.　Augustine whole again, *Conf.* v, p. 87, l. 3.

p. 14, l. 21.　Goes to Milan, *Conf.* v, p. 91, l. 7.

p. 14, l. 23.　*meyr̄ of Rome, Conf.* v, p. 91, l. 8 : ' ad praefectum urbis.'

p. 14, l. 28.　Ambrose. *Conf.* v, p. 91, l. 13 : 'et veni Mediolanium [Milan] ad Ambrosium episcopum, in optimis notum orbi terrae, pium cultorem tuum,' &c.

p. 14, l. 31.　Augustine hears Ambrose preach, *Conf.* v, p. 91, l. 24.

p. 15, l. 9.　*þe incarnacion̄.* Cf. *Conf.* vi, p. 97, l. 24.

p. 15, l. 24.　*þe feith of Crist, Conf.* v, p. 93, l. 18.

p. 15, l. 27.　*his moder sowt him, Conf.* vi, p. 94, l. 2.

p. 16, l. 3.　*Beth of good coumfort*, &c. Capgrave's embellishment of the incident. *Conf.* vi, p. 94, l. 2 : 'Iam venerat ad me mater pietate fortis, terra marique me sequens et in periculis omnibus de te secura. Nam et per marina discrimina ipsos nautas consolabatur, a quibus rudes abyssi viatores, cum perturbantur, consolari solent, pollicens eis perventionem cum salute, quia hoc ei tu per visum pollicitus eras.'

p. 16, l. 9.　*sche hopped*, i. e. leapt. But Augustine says distinctly that she was not unduly excited. *Conf.* vi, p. 94, l. 17 : Nulla ergo turbulenta exultatione trepidavit cor eius,' &c. Later on, after the *Tolle lege* passage, she does ' leap for joy '. *Conf.* viii, p. 166, l. 2 : 'exultat et triumphat et benedicebat tibi.'

p. 16, l. 18.　*Sche loved Ambrose*, &c., *Conf.* vi, p. 94, l. 30.

p. 16, l. 20.　*fluctuation̄.* Direct from the Latin, *Conf.* vi, p. 95, l. 2.

p. 16, l. 25.　*for-bode hir̄ be þe keper̄.* In the Latin, *Conf.* vi, p. 95, l. 8, ' ab ostiario,' by the door-keeper.

p. 17, l. 4.　Alipius and Nebridius, *Conf.* vi, p. 103, l. 21 ; p. 110, l. 1.

p. 17, l. 11.　*wyues.* The idea was to form a society of about ten. Some however, already had wives; and some, including Augustine, intended to have : hence the difficulty. *Conf.* vi, p. 115, l. 14.

p. 17, l. 17. Augustine's maid. *Conf.* vi, p. 114, l. 26.

p. 17, l. 23. Alypius arrested. The story appears somewhat mutilated in Capgrave's text. Alypius was studying under Augustine at the time, and was repeating, as he walked in the market-place, some rhetorical exercise. The thief was a youth, not the boy who recognized the axe. The friend who intervened was an architect (p. 108, l. 4).

p. 18, Chapter xiii. In this chapter Capgrave goes on with Book viii, making practically no use at all of Book vii.

p. 18, l. 30. Simpliciane, *Conf.* viii, p. 144, l. 18.

p. 19, l. 11. Victorinus, *Conf.* viii, p. 144, l. 22.

p. 19, l. 12. *a statua.* From the Latin. *Conf.* viii, p. 145, l. 7.

p. 19, l. 27. *sette to serue God, Conf.* viii, p. 150, l. 15.

p. 19, l. 30. Pontitianus, *Conf.* viii, p. 153, l. 13.

p. 20, l. 17. *grete Antonie, Conf.* viii, p. 153, l. 28. The story of Anthony's conversion, as told by Capgrave, follows.

p. 21, l. 5. Augustine's sorrow, *Conf.* viii, p. 155, l. 26.

p. 21, l. 14. 'What suffir we?' &c. *Conf.* viii, p. 157, l. 17: 'Quid patimur? Quid est hoc, quod audisti? Surgunt indocti et caelum rapiunt, et nos cum doctrinis nostris ecce ubi volutamur in carne et sanguine! An quia praecesserunt, pudet sequi et non pudet nec saltem sequi?'

p. 21, l. 21. *labou?' of his tunge, Conf.* viii, p. 157, l. 24.

p. 21, l. 32. *a figge-tre, Conf.* viii, p. 164, l. 16.

p. 22, l. 1. *O blissed Lord, who longe? Conf.* viii, p. 164, l. 20: 'et *tu, domine, usquequo? Usquequo, domine, irasceris in finem?* ... Iactabam voces miserabiles : "Quamdiu, quamdiu, 'cras' et 'cras'? Quare non modo? Quare non hac hora finis turpitudinis meae?" ' The italicized portion is from Psalm vi. 3 (4 in Vulgate).

p. 22, l. 5. *whil he lay pus, Conf.* viii, p. 164, l. 26.

p. 22, l. 8. *Tak and rede. Conf.* viii, p. 164, l. 29: 'Tolle lege, tolle lege!'

p. 22, l. 15. *Non in comessacionibus,* &c. *Conf.* viii, p. 165, l. 13. Capgrave's text does not exactly follow the Augustinian. The passage is from Romans xiii. 13.

p. 22, l. 20. *schalful dedis,* 'wantonness' in authorized version, 'non in impudicitiis' in *Conf.*

p. 22, l. 32. Monica. *Conf.* viii, p. 166, l. 1. This ends Book viii.

p. 23, l. 3. Leaving the rhetoric school, *Conf.* viiii, p. 167, l. 15.

p. 23, l. 10. *heruest dayes. Conf.,* vintage vacation, viiii, p. 167, l. 21: 'ad vindemiales ferias.'

p. 23, l. 18. *a feld pei cleped Cassiate. Conf.* viiii, p. 169, l. 29, a country-seat called Cassiciacum, or villa (*Conf.* viiii, p. 171, l. 27).

p. 23, l. 26. Plato. This expression of Capgrave is based on a statement made by Augustine concerning the 'Academics, as they are considered, doubting everything and fluctuating between all.' *Conf.* v, p. 93, l. 9: 'Itaque Academicorum more, sicut existimantur, dubitans de omnibus atque inter omnia fluctuans . . .'

p. 24, l. 26. *Psalmis of Dauid.* *Conf.* viiii, p. 171, l. 24.

p. 24, l. 29. *In pace, in idipsum,* &c. *Conf.* viiii, p. 174, l. 20, from Psalm iv. 8.

p. 25, l. 4. *seknesse . . . of þe teth.* *Conf.* viiii, p. 175, l. 6 : 'dolore dentium,' &c.

p. 25, l. 14. Letters to St. Ambrose, *Conf.* viiii, p. 175, l. 23.

p. 25, l. 20. *Ysaie, Conf.* viiii, p. 175, l. 27.

p. 25, l. 25. Goes to Milan. *Conf.* viiii, p. 175, l. 19, then ending his rhetoric teaching.

p. 25, l. 26. Baptism, *Conf.* viiii, p. 176, l. 3.

p. 25, l. 35. Te Deum. This story of the making of *Te Deum* is, of course, quite apocryphal.

p. 26, l. 4. Adeodatus, *Conf.* viiii, p. 176, l. 7.

p. 26, l. 11. *he had neuer no woman but hir.* Not so ; in Book vi Augustine relates how when his concubine left him for Africa, he turned to another woman ; p. 115, l. 30 : 'et illa in Africam redierat vovens tibi alium se virum nescituram relicto apud me naturali ex illa filio meo. At ego infelix nec feminae imitator, dilationis impatiens, tamquam post biennium accepturus eam quam petebam, quia non amator coniugii sed libidinis servus eram, *procuraui aliam,* non utique coniugem.'

p. 26, l. 27. *De Quantitate Animae.* The book mentioned in this connexion by Augustine is *De Magistro, Conf.* viiii, p. 176, l. 16.

p. 27, l. 1. Songs of St. Ambrose and Justina. *Conf.* viiii, p. 177, l. 1. The remarks concerning the hymnology of Ambrose, ll. 11–12, are apparently a specimen of Capgrave's 'pertinent' ideas. Augustine himself quotes from one of Ambrose's hymns in this same Book viiii, p. 89, l. 6 : 'Deus, creator omnium,' &c. Augustine describes, in connexion with Justina, the discovery of the bodies of Gervasius and Protasius, and the consequent miracles. This Capgrave leaves unmentioned.

p. 29, l. 10. Monica desires to go home. Augustine says, *Conf.* viiii, p. 178, l. 20, that he and Euodius and others desired to go where they might best serve God, and so started to return to Africa ; and that on the way, at Ostia Tiberina (Ostia), Monica died. In Chapter xx, p. 28, our text is first made up by systematic use of the Sermons, which henceforward continues to the end of the narrative, except for Chapters xxii–xxvi.

p. 30, l. 31. Monica, 'a very moder,' &c. *Conf.* viiii, p. 183, l. 3.

p. 31, l. 2. *Tussie,* i. e. Tuscany.

p. 31, l. 15. Wyclif. 'Was there ever,' writes Mr. G. M. Trevelyan on a card to me, 'a persecuted sect of whom that was *not* said ! ' 'Be thou as chaste as ice,' &c. : it is an old story.

p. 31, l. 29. Ostia. *Conf.* viiii, p. 183, l. 15.

p. 32, l. 2. The window. *Conf.* viiii, p. 183, l. 13. The garden did not belong to Monica, as Capgrave says, but to the house where Augustine and his party rested.

p. 32, l. 11. *Son, as to my part,* &c. *Conf.* viiii, p. 185, l. 11 : 'fili, quantum ad me adtinet, nulla re iam delector in hac vita. Quid hic faciam adhuc et cur hic sim, nescio, iam consumpta spe huius saeculi. Unum erat, propter quod in hac vita aliquantum inmorari cupiebam, ut te Christianum catholicum viderem, priusquam morerer. Cumulatius hoc mihi deus praestitit, ut te etiam contempta felicitate terrena servum eius videam. Quid hic facio?'

p. 32, l. 18. Fever. *Conf.* viiii, p. 185, l. 20.

p. 32, l. 33. *No-ping is fer fro God. Conf.* viiii, p. 186, l. 29.

p. 33, l. 1. *reise me,* i. e. resurrect me. *Conf.* resuscito.

p. 33, l. 12. *Thi seruaunt, Lord. Conf.* viiii, p. 190, l. 1: 'famula tua,' l. 3.

p. 33, l. 23. *Entyr not with hir in-to þi dom. Lete þi mercy flete above þi dom. Conf.* viiii, p. 190, l. 28: 'ne intres cum ea in iudicium. Superexultet misericordia iudicio.' From Psalm cxliii. 2, and James ii. 13.

p. 33, l. 30. *Inspire, Lord,* &c. *Conf.* viiii, p. 191, l. 29. Here ends the debt of our text to the *Confessions.*

p. 35, l. 15. *De Magistro.* See note to 26/27.

p. 37, l. 6. *Euodio,* &c. Notice the retention of the Latin case-ending.

p. 46, l. 33. Cf. note to 4/10.

p. 52, l. 27. Donatists, called from Donatus, one of their leaders. These men rebaptized converts from the Catholic Church, hence the 'Rebaptiȝatores' of l. 30.

p. 53, l. 2. *wepun.* Note the plural without the plural ending, a survival of O.E. neuter *wæpen.*

p. 54, l. 9. *leuand.* The early Midland form of the present participle ending was *ende,* later *inge. ande* was characteristically Northern, but was fairly common in Midland.

p. 54, l. 30. *þe other tonge,* i. e. Greek.

p. 56, l. 6. St. Thomas Alqwyn, i. e. St. Thomas Aquinas.

p. 61, l. 1. This ' maystir of þe order' was Nicholas Resby, or, as Capgrave spells it, Reysby, known to be master in 1445, and receiver in that year of Henry VI's exemption of the houses of the order from aids, subsidies, and tallages, &c. See Rose Graham's *St. Gilbert of Sempringham & the Gilbertines,* 1903, p. 155.

p. 61, l. 7. See before, p. 1/15.

p. 61, l. 12. See after, p. 145.

p. 62, l. 31. Gilbert's father was Joceline, a wealthy Lincolnshire land-owner; his mother, a Saxon woman of inferior position,—*inferioris conditionis;* the 'non' prefixed to this in Cotton Cleop. BI f. 37, being an interpolation. Dugdale retains the *non,* vi, pt. II, p. vi*. (See Graham, 3.)

p. 63, l. 28. *þaȝ despised of þe world.* Gilbert was afflicted with some sort of deformity, which rendered him repulsive, and was despised even by the serving-men.

p. 63, l. 30. Gilbert was not a very willing pupil in his young years; and he left England for France to study letters—a fact which Capgrave omits to mention.

p. 64, l. 28. It may not be amiss to refer the reader to what Dean Stanley had to say concerning this 'Athanasian' *Quicunque Vult, Eastern Church,*

p. 247, Everyman edition: 'the ancient hymn, "Quicunque vult," . . . throughout the middle ages and by our own Reformers, was believed to be the Creed of S. Athanasius. The learned world is now fully aware that it is of French or Spanish origin. It not only contains words and phrases which to Athanasius were unknown, but it distinctly and from the first asserted the doctrine of the Double Procession of the Spirit, which never occurs in the writings of Athanasius.'

p. 65, l. 33. Of Robert Bloet, Miss Graham says, *S. Gilbert*, 7, 8 :—'Like many of the bishops of that age, Robert Bloet was a royal official who had received a bishopric as a reward, and he continued to serve the King rather than the Church. He was a chaplain of William the Conqueror, and was with him when he died at Rouen. Immediately afterwards he set out for England with William Rufus, to carry the letter sent by the Conqueror to Lanfranc, bidding him crown Rufus king. Until 1092 Robert served Rufus as chancellor. In the first week of Lent in that year the king lay sick unto death at Gloucester ; his bishops and nobles came to him and implored him to repent of his evil deeds. In terror of death, Rufus gave the archbishopric of Canterbury to the unwilling Anselm, Abbot of Bec, and the see of Lincoln to Robert Bloet. Robert resigned the chancellorship, but under Henry I he held the more important office of justiciar. He was famed for the splendour of his household. "When I beheld the glory of our Bishop," wrote Henry of Huntingdon, one of his archdeacons, "honourable knights, noble youths, costly horses, gold and gilded vessels, the number of dishes, the splendour of his servants, the purple raiment and the torches, I could think of nothing more happy." In the last year of his life he was twice impleaded by King Henry on the charge of an inferior justice ; he was disgraced and condemned to pay a heavy fine in both instances. He retired to his palace at Lincoln overwhelmed with grief. "As I reclined by his side at dinner," said Henry of Huntingdon, "I saw him shedding tears, and asked him the reason. 'Once,' he said, ' those who stood around me wore costly raiment ; now the fines of the king, whom I ever sought to please, have compelled them to put on lambs' wool.' ". Robert Bloet died on January 10, 1123. "The King was riding in his deerfold at Woodstock, and the Bishop Roger of Salisbury on one side of him, and the Bishop Robert Bloet of Lincoln on the other side of him ; and they were there riding and talking. Then the Bishop of Lincoln sank down, and said to the King, ' Lord King, I am dying.' And the King alighted down from his horse, and lifted him betwixt his arms, and caused him to be borne to his inn ; and he was then forthwith dead ; and he was conveyed to Lincoln with great worship, and buried before S. Mary's altar. And the Bishop of Chester, named Robert Pecceth, buried him." '

p. 66, l. 1. *Mad a chapeleyn.* Not so, at first. A chaplain, Geoffrey, was appointed by Bloet, as Gilbert was not ordained. It was Alexander, Bloet's successor, who made Gilbert a priest, against his will, and subsequently offered him the archdeaconry. See l. 23.

p. 67, l. 6. This is what the worthy Fuller, *more suo*, has to say of Gilbert and his order :—' *Gilbertine Monks*, may be the third, a *mongrel Order*, observing some *Select Rules* partly of S. *Bennet*, partly of S. *Augustine*. So named from *Gilbert* (son to *Joceline* a Knight) Lord of *Sempringham* in *Lincoln-shire*, where 1148, first they were planted. Whereupon, this Order may *boast*, that it alone is a *native* and *Indegena*, (whereas *Benedictines* are by original *Italians* . . .) pure *English* by the *extraction* thereof. This *Gilbert*, *unhandsome* but not *unlearned*, erected this order, (contrary to *Justinians* constitution, who forbade *double Monasteries*) wherein men and women lived together, (though secluded) under one roof. He survived to see *thirteen Houses* of this his own Order, and in them *Seventeen hundred Gilbertine Brothers and Sisters*. Yet I finde no *Writer* of this *Order*, conceiving them so well busied with their *Company* in their Convent, they had little leisure for the *writing of Books*,' pp. 268-9, Book vi. Fuller's *Church History of Great Britain*, fol. 1655. Not very generous this.

p. 67, l. 9. Of these maidens, one was the daughter of a poor parishioner of Sempringham, in whose house Gilbert, and Geoffrey, the chaplain, dwelt. (Graham, 6.)

p. 67, l. 12. St. Andrew's Church is the last relic of Gilbert's Sempringham. The picture of the south doorway forms the frontispiece to Miss Graham's *S. Gilbert*. The maiden's dwelling was by the north wall.

p. 69, l. 32. No 'veyn tales' by the way. Unlike Harry Baily, we presume, and his motley wayfarers.

p. 72, l. 21. This was Roger, Prior of Malton, one of Gilbert's first canons, at whose hands, as Capgrave remarks, l. 25, Gilbert received the canon's habit.

p. 73, l. 17. Gilbert suffered, however, from ague.

p. 76, l. 5. *Cadney.* This was on Christmas night, 1188. Miss Graham, quoting *Monasticon*, vol. vi, pt. II, p. xxii*, says Gilbert received extreme unction at the monastery of Newstead-on-Ancholme.

p. 76, l. 11. *sum man of gret myth.* The real danger feared was lest some other church or monastery should become the resting-place of Gilbert's remains.

p. 77, l. 21. *at laudes, at mateyns,* the phrase *at laudes* being added above. As *at mateyns* is not cancelled by Capgrave, we let it stand. See l. 26.

p. 78, l. 34. This was in the priory church of St. Mary.

p. 81, l. 20. *De Constructione Monasteriorum*, now lost.

p. 81, l. 28. Tyrington, i. e. West Torrington.

p. 82, l. 1. See note to 67/9.

p. 83, l. 32. Alexander, successor to Bloet, and nephew to Roger, Archbishop of Salisbury.

p. 85, l. 24. *þe auctouŗ of þis lif*, i. e. the canon of Sempringham who wrote of Gilbert's life and miracles at the command of Roger, Gilbert's successor.

p. 89, l. 13. *Cystewys*, the Cistercians, meeting in congress at Citeaux, in 1147.

p. 90, l. 5—p. 91, l. 24. The Latin text is as follows, Dugdale's *Monasticon*, vol. vi, Pt. II, pp. viii*-ix*, from MS. Cot. Cleop. B I :—

' *Quod commissum est ei a Domino Papa Regimen Ordinis sui.*

' Data est igitur et iniuncta beato Gileberto a sancto Papa Eugenio collecti gregis custodia, quia non inveniebatur, nec inveniri poterat melior conservator, quam is qui fuerat conquisitor, nec fortior esse poterat boni status zelator; quam qui primus et summus fuerat ad statuendum laborator. Verumtamen vir sanctus, ad tanti pondus regiminis virgentis aetatis causabatur importunitatem, ad honorem; indignitatem, ad magisterium; imperitiam ad praelationem suam praetendit humilitatem. Timuit namque suam, quibus praeferendus erat imparitatem; timuit placide mentis suae soliditatem dissipandam; timuit delecti sui secreti et assiduae contemplationis dulcedinem debellaturam occupationem: quae omnia devotae humilitatis apologetica intellexit, ut erat vir prudens dominus apostolicus, et eo proclivius et securius pastoris ei deputavit officium, quo nullum vidit illi inesse praelationis appetitum: propositum enim eius erat semper humilibus adhaerere (vel humilia appetere) et Domini fuit voluntas, illum se semper humiliantem amplius exaltare.

'Cognoscens autem beatus Gilebertus divinum circa se exactum iudicium, non est ausus diu supernae reniti dispositioni, quae illud ad hoc opus asciverat; sed ne caeteris, quibus pollebat, se privaret virtutibus, si pertinaciter obsisteret, amplexatus est devote obedientiam Dei, eiusque vicarii papae, ampliorem inde sperans mercedem, quia nullam ex hoc habuit delectationem; suique, solius postposuit utilitatem, ut multorum adipisceretur salutem. Contemplationis studiis iamdudum eruditus, piae actionis nunc consensit inservire operibus, ut utriusque vitae meteret fructus: Porro licite poterat earum rerum fieri dispensator, quarum pristinus fuerat possessor, quoniam pauperibus ea conferens, et ipse pauper effectus, ut minister sibi credita, non ut dominus propria gubernavit. Propter haec et huiusmodi sanctitatis signa, et multorum consona testimonia, doluisse fertur Papa Eugenius, quoniam virum antea non novisset, eo quod voluisset, ut dixit, illum sullimasse in archiepiscopum Eboracensem, cuius sedes tunc vacabat, si fama meritorum eius illi prius innotuisset. Beatis quoque Malachiae, Hyberniensi archiepiscopo et Bernardo Clarevallensi abbati, in illo itinere adeo factus est familiaris, ut illis solis praesentibus, ipse quoque praesens adesset, ubi per orationem eorum fertur sanitas collata cuidam aegroto. Insignia etiam amoris, baculum scilicet tam praesulis, quam abbatis, accepit ab utroque; in quibus quaedam factae sunt virtutes; et orarium cum manipulo ei dedit abbas in monimentum sui.'

p. 91, l. 17. *Clareualle*, i. e. Clairvaux. See the Latin passage above for the origin of Capgrave's form.

p. 93, l. 24. This was in 1164. For a full account of the incident see Miss Graham's *S. Gilbert*, pp. 16–19.

p. 97, l. 32. The debate among the lay-people. The leaders were Ogger and Gerard, who spread defamation throughout the neighbourhood, and demanded less labour and better food. They then left England, and journeyed to Alexander III, whom they convinced of the justice of their case. Henry II, Hugh the papal legate, William, Bishop of Norwich, however, and other influential men, stood by Gilbert in his adversity. Ogger and Gerard were seen to be false, finally returned to Gilbert, asking forgiveness and the mitigation of the harshness of the order. Gilbert received and forgave them. See MS. Cot. Cleop. BI. f. 89b, &c., and Graham's *S. Gilbert*, p. 21.

p. 98, l. 5. *Albyne*. This was Albinus, Gilbert's chaplain.

p. 99, l. 13. Oseney Abbey. See the *English Register* of the place, edited by Dr. Andrew Clark, pt. I, E. E. T. S., 1907. I find no mention of this particular cellarer.

p. 100, l. 5. *Beuyrle*, i. e. Beverley, in Yorkshire, 7½ miles north-west of Hull.

p. 101, l. 7. *wat* = was. The same form occurs in *Cursor Mundi*, ed. Morris, p. 1576, l. 29185 :

> ' Þar was a woman hight mari,
> Þat sum time *wat* wit me-selri,'—

again followed by a monosyllabic ending in the dental.

p. 106, l. 13. The dream of angels carrying the soul to heaven is not infrequently met with in mediaeval monkish books. Compare the story of how the Oxford student died, and of his friends watching the bier, and,

> ' As hi slepe, hem þoȝte boþe : þat hi angles meniee iseȝe
> Here felawes soule þat þer lai ded : to heuene lede heȝe
> Oure leuede as to teche þe weye : hire silue ȝeode bifore
> And openede þe dore of heuene : þat þe soule were in ibore.'

Early English Poems and Lives of Saints, ed. Dr. Furnivall, 1862, p. 41.

p. 118, l. 20. *Hauyrholm*, i. e. Haverholm, given to Gilbert in 1139 by Alexander of Lincoln.

p. 141, l. 16. The Latin text is as follows, Dugdale's *Monasticon*, vol. vi, pt. II, p. xix* :—

> ' *Rescriptum Cartae, in Feretro positae, hoc est.*

' In hac capsa continentur reliquiae beati Gileberti presbyteri et confessoris, primi patris et institutoris ordinis de Sempringham ; cuius vitam, licet multa praeclaram reddiderint et commendabilem : hoc tamen praecipue eum insignivit, quod spontaneam eligens paupertatem, omnia temporalia, sibi a Deo praestita, fratrum et sororum, quos sub regulari disciplina prudenter instituit et sollicite custodivit, necessitatibus deputavit : cui processu temporis tantam Deus adauxit gratiam et virtutem, quod quatuor canonicas regulares, et ix. monasteria sanctimonialium construit : in quibus eo tempore, quo migravit ad Dominum, praeter innumeros antea defunctos, circiter septingentos viros religiosos, mille et quingentas sorores iugiter Deo famulantes reliquit. Obiit autem in senectute plusquam centenaria ; anno incarnationis Domini MC. lxxxix, pridie nonas Februarii, tempore incliti regis Anglorum Henrici secundi. Exigentibus vero propriis meritis, attestantibus miraculis multis, et suadentibus revelationibus divinis canonizatus, cathalogo sanctorum est ascriptus a domino papa Innocentio tertio, per generalem curiam Romanam, apud Anagniam, coram clero et populo, anno Verbi incarnati MCC. ii, tertio idus Ianuarii, anno regni illustris regis Iohannis tertio, praesidente sedi Cantuariae venerabili archiepiscopo Huberto ; qui de mandato memorati summi pontificis Innocentii tertii, cum collegis suis Heliensi episcopo Eustachio, et abbate de Burgo, Achario, diligentem super miraculis per eum divinitus patratis fecerat inquisitionem, et ipsi eorum attestationes fideliter in scripturam redactas, sub sigillis suis, clausas, ad sedem apostolicam transmiserunt ; unde certioratus dominus papa de sanctitate eius, et signis, ipsum sanctis Domini decrevit annumerandum, anno pontificatus sui quarto. Et eodem anno per mandatum praefati papae, a praedicto archiepiscopo Huberto translatus est in hunc loculum tertio idus Octobris, assistentibus viris sibi venerabilibus Norwicensi, Herefordensi, et Landavensi episcopis; et abbatibus, aliisque ecclesiarum praelatis plurimis, cum maioribus et nobilioribus Angliae, magno ibi praesente coetu cleri et populi : ad cuius rei perpetuandam memoriam, iam dictus archiepiscopus, et coepiscopi sui, et abbates, sua signa huic scripto appenderunt, et in hoc loculo reposuerunt.'

p. 142, l. 9. *Acarius.* This is Acharius, Prior of St. Alban's, called Zacharias by Hoveden; he became abbot in 1200 and died on the 2nd of the ides of March, 1210. See *Monasticon*, I, p. 354.

p. 145, l. 1. The following is the account of this sermon in Tho. Gibbon's *Historical Collections*, Harley MS., 980; fol. 120 :—

' Gilbert (the son of a Norman knight that came in with the conquerour and of the Lady of Sempringham) was the first founder of the Gilbertines of the ordere of Sempringham. He builded nine monasteries of women & fower of chanons reguler in which monasteries he left at the time of his death of religious women 1500 and of men 700. He died ann. 1189 And was translated by the command of Innocent 3 Ann. 1201. Vid. Joh. Capgraue in Vit. Sti Gilberti manuscript ex Museo Rbt Kemp Milit. Gissing.

The religious which liued vnder the rules of St Augustine wer in number 12.

The first of Hermites made by St. Aug before his being bishop of Hippo.

The second of Cannons seculer when he was bishop.

The Third Canons reguler which were begun by him but a distinction hath been made since by others (as by St Ruffus) and so the monks of Charter-house came out of the black order.

The 4th The Dominicans begun Ann. 1216.

The 5   Knights of St Johns of Jerusalem.

The 6   Heres of pruce, the same with St John but that they of St John haue black mantles with a cross and they of Pruce white with a cross.

The 7   the Gilbertines of Sempringham order.

The 8   Premonstratenses begon in France by Norbertus ann. 1100.

The 9   the friers of the cross ther foundat incertan.

The 10   The order of St Bridget.

The 11   the canons of St Victor in Paris.

The 12   An order onely in Norff which had 4 house[s] one of them is faln into the Kings hand and he gaue it to Walsingham hite Peterston.

Joh. Capgrave in vii sermon at Cambridg Ann. 1422 et ex museo supra-dicto.'

p. 148, l. 20. Hugues and Richard de St. Victor, two of the most famous theologians of the middle ages. Richard was a Scotchman.

p. 148, l. 27. This appropriation of Peterston to Walsingham took place in 1449.

GLOSSARY

ABBREVIATIONS USED

adj., adjective.
adv., adverb.
comp., comparative.
gen., genitive.
imper., imperative.
inter., interjection.
n., noun.
np., noun plural.
pl., plural.
pp., past participle.

prep., preposition.
pres. p., present participle.
s., singular.
subj., subjunctive.
sup., superlative.
v. i., verb intransitive.
v. t., verb transitive.
1, first person.
2, second person.
3, third person.

A

a, *inter.* ah ! 24/30.
a, *v. t. inf.* have 8/5, 57/17, 68/5, 69/6, 84/22, 23. *See* have.
abiden, *v. i.* 3 *pl. pres.* abide 15/6.
abod, abood, *v. i.* 3 *s. p.* abode 8/23, 10/1, 28/2 ; abod, abood, *v. i.* 3 *pl. p.* 23/21, 27/26, 28/28 ; abood, *v. t.* 3 *pl. p.* awaited 32/1.
a-boue, *adj.* above 2/29.
absens, *n.* absence 29/4.
absolucioñ, *n.* 75/25.
abstined, *v. i.* 3 *s. p.* abstained 70/11.
Achay, *n.* Achaia, Greece 8/15.
acordith, *v. i.* 3 *s. pres.* accordeth 2/3 ; acorded, *v. i.* 3 *pl. cond.* accorded, agreed 17/14.
acrisia, *n.* 109/10.
Aduent, *n.* Advent 70/14.
aferd, a-ferd, *adj.* afraid 16/2, 32/34.
afore, *adv.* before 13/2.
aftir, *adj.* hinder, back 125/24.
aftir, *prep.* after 1/8.
a-gayn, a-geyn, *adv.* again 6/33, 19/16.
ageyn, *prep.* against 12/17.
a-knowe, *pp.* made known 47/5, 57/16. *See also* I-knowe.
akyng, *n.* aching 98/21.
al, *n.* all 19/23.
Alani, *np.* Alans 58/18 (Latin *A lani*).
a-legge, *v. t.* 1 *s. pres.* allege 63/4 ; alleggid, *pp.* 37/5.

alienat, *pp.* alienated 131/18.
Alisaundr̃, *n.* Alexandria 64/30.
allegaunce, *n.* 43/15.
alleuyauns, *n.* alleviance 121/30.
ambassiat, *n.* embassy 110/22.
ambicius, *adj.* ambitious 57/30.
amitted, *pp.* admitted 90/19.
a-mongis, *prep.* amongst 1/27.
a-mys, *adv.* amiss 10/26.
amyse, *n.* amice 46/30.
an, *conj.* and 19/4.
an, *prep.* on, at 64/22.
anachorites, *np.* anchorites 38/10.
and, *conj.* if 37/33, 69/5.
annexid, *pp.* annexed 21/24.
annoted, *pp.* recorded 113/2.
apeyred, *pp.* impaired 78/9.
aposteñ, *n.* apostle 1/7 ; apostoles, *np.* 30/1.
appechid, *pp.* appeached 17/20.
appelles, appillis, *np.* apples 9/9, 10.
appil-tre, *n.* apple-tree 9/7.
apposed, *v. t.* 3 *s. p.* opposed 111/7.
approximat, *adj.* approximate 3/29.
aproximacioñ, *n.* 64/7.
aqueyntauns, aqweyntauns, *n.* acquaintance, friends, 36/9, 52/2.
arayed, *pp.* arrayed 38/28.
archibischoprych, *n.* archbishopric 91/14.
aretten, *v. t. inf.* ascribe, reckon 66/18.
argew, *v. i. inf.* argue 26/19.
armur̃, *n.* armour 53/2.

arowys, *np.* arrows 2/24.
arsmetrik, *n.* arithmetic 11/32.
articules, *np.* articles 9/3.
a-schamed, *adj.* ashamed 21/11.
a-sikir, *adj.* safe 36/26.
asined, *v. t.* 3 *s. p.* assigned 19/3 ; assined, *pp.* assigned 9/2.
asken, *v. t. inf.* ask 26/19.
aspie, *v. t. inf.* aspy, perceive 11/11 ; aspied, *v. t.* 1 *s. p.* 11/15.
aspying, *n.* 31/8.
assoyle, *v. t. inf.* assoil 71/25 ; assoiling, *pres. p.* 71/28.
astate, *n.* estate, authority 66/5.
astates, *np.* estates 51/36.
astoyned, *pp.* astonished 25/13, 124/14.
attached, *pp.* apprehended 18/21.
aucter, aucter̃, auter̃, *n.* altar 14/12, 32/26, 124/6 ; aucteris, *np.* 16/24.
auctorite, *n.* authority 95/27.
auctour̃, *n.* author 38/10 ; auctoris, *np.* authors, 1/27, 2/27.
audiens, *n.* audience 53/24. '
auditorye, *n.* auditory, pupils, hearers 65/18.
aungellis, *np.* angels 1/6.
autentik, *adj.* authentic 109/24.
auysement, *n.* advisement 76/8.
a-vised, *adj.* advised 49/35.
a-vow, *n.* vow 20/37.
avowe, *v. t. inf.* 78/16.
avowid, *v. t.* 3 *pl. p.* dedicated 21/4.
awbe, *n.* alb 125/30.
axid, *pp.* asked 83/32.

B

bagg, *n.* bag 30/10.
bakkes, *np.* backs, 65/29.
balled, *adj.* bald 106/17.
baptem, *n.* baptism 8/15, 24/17.
baptisterie, *n.* baptistery 25/31.
bar̃, *adj.* bare 48/27.
barbar̃, *adj.* barbarian, foreign, 3/25.
barres, *np.* bars 28/21.
batayle, *n.* battle 8/20, 63/16.
be, *conj.* but, 40/31.
be, *prep.* by 4/19, 19/18.
be, *v. i.* 2 *pl. pres.* be 38/26 ; ar, ar̃, be, *v. i.* 3 *pl. pres.* are 2/10, 14/9, 23/7, 28/34 ; beth, *v. i.* 2 *pl. imper.* be 16/3, 52/10 ; was, wast, wat, *v. i.* 3 *s. p.* was 19/19, 101/7, 103/28 ; be, ben, *pp.* been 7/8, 15/16, 20/6, 27/4.
Beamoundis, *np.* Beaumonts 63/8.

bedred, *adj.* bedridden 79/19, 128/32.
be-forn, *prep.* before 132/36.
beginne, be-gynne, *v. t. inf.* begin 1/23, 20/30 ; begynnyth *v. t.* 3 *s. pres.* 5/11 ; be-gunne, *v. t.* 3 *pl. p.* 12/15.
be-had, *v. i.* 3 *s. p.* behaved 68/19.
be-hest, *v. t. inf.* promise 85/16 ; be-hestyng, *pres. p.* 95/34.
beleue, *n.* belief 10/30.
bellis, *np.* bells 132/14.
benyngly, *adv.* benignly 64/12.
ber̃, *v. t. inf.* bear 39/8 ; berith, *v. t.* 3 *s. pres.* 67/1 ; beren, *v. t.* 3 *pl. pres.* 62/23 ; bare, *v. t.* 3 *s. p.* bore 72/30, 84/29 ; bare, *v. t.* 3 *s. p.* 7/2 ; bor̃, bore, *pp.* born 3/2, 20/1, 26/12 ; bor̃, *pp.* borne 67/8.
ber̃ - baytingis, *nv.* bear - baitings 65/22.
berke, *v. i. inf.* bark 24/22 ; berk, *v. i.* 3 *pl. pres.* 52/26.
beryng, *n.* bearing, behaviour 66/6.
besekyng, *pres. p.* beseeching 108/31.
besi, bisi, *adj.* busy 6/23, 10/8.
besily, bisily, *adv.* busily 21/19, 24/16.
besinesse, bisinesse, *n.* business 13/28, 19/5.
bete, *pp.* beaten 7/27.
bettir, *adj.* better 1/20.
be-twix, *prep.* between 6/6.
beute, *n.* beauty 83/19.
Beuyrle, *n.* Beverley 100/5.
bittirnesse, *n.* bitterness 25/2.
blak, *adj.* black 28/21.
blasphemes, *np.* blasphemies 56/19.
blisse, *v. t. inf.* bless 78/1 ; blessed, *v. t.* 3 *s. p.* 75/3.
blodis, *np.* bloods 63/11.
blow, *pp.* blown 31/14.
bodely, *adj.* bodily 5/1.
bok, book, *n.* 5/2, 20/6, 8, 23/24 ; booke, bokes, bokis, bokys, *np.* 2/34, 3/31, 20/4, 53/33.
bolstering, *n.* bolstering (of bed) 71/20.
bon, boon, *n.* bone 125/6, 11.
bond, *v. t.* 3 *s. p.* bound 33/27 ; bounde, bounden, boundyn, bownde, *pp.* bound 6/13, 51/2, 100/2, 131/7.
bord, *n.* board 20/4, 47/23.
bordred, *pp.* bordered 91/23.
bordures, *np.* borders 147/17.
Borow, *n.* Peterborough, 79/28, 142/9.

bowt, *v. t.* 3 *s. p.* bought 92/13.

boystously, *adv.* boisterously 46/17.

breke, *v. t. inf.* break 20/38; brak, *v. t. i.* 3 *pl. p.* 120/30; broke, *pp.* 6/16.

brent, *v. t.* 3 *s. p.* burnt 21/11; brennyng, *pres. p.* 2/17; brennaund, brennyng, *adj.* burning, 1/28, 100/6, 129/21.

brest, *v. i.* 3 *s. p.* burst 96/31.

bringgist, *v. t.* 2 *s. pres.* bringest 5/5.

brith, *adj.* bright 16/17.

broches, *np.* 87/18.

broþir, *n.* brother 4/26.

brout, *v. t.* 1 *s. p.* brought 37/12; brout, brovt, browt, *pp.* 1/22, 16/19, 19/25, 21/8, 28/14.

brynk, *n.* brink, shore 14/3.

bullis, *np.* bulls (papal) 38/7, 95/7.

buscheℓ, *n.* bushel 93/2.

buschel mette, *n.* bushel measure, 136/11.

buschment, *n.* ambush 109/8.

buttokes, *np.* buttocks, 120/2.

buxum, *adj.* obedient 28/33, 103/15.

bye, *v. t. inf.* buy 49/31.

byled, *v. t.* 3 *s. p.* built 140/18.

byleue, *n.* belief 52/19.

biried, byried, byryed, *pp.* buried 16/25, 32/25.

byrrying, byryng, *n.* burying 32/28, 79/23.

Byȝance, *n.* Byzantium 3/19.

C

cacch, *v. t. inf.* catch 5/28.

Cam, *n.* Ham 3/9.

cam, *see* cum.

can, *v. t.* 1 *s. pres.* know 105/19; coude, *v. t.* 3 *s. p.* 39/10; coude, *v. i.* 1 *s. p.* could 1/26; cowde, *v. i.* 3 *s. p.* 30/12.

cap, *n. capitulum*, chapter 3/3.

capitle, capitule, *n.* chapter 1/2, 26/3.

capitoℓ, *n.* the Capitol at Rome 56/18.

carde, *v. i.* 3 *pl. pres.* card 55/18.

caryage, *n.* carriage, journey 76/12.

cast, *v. t.* 3 *s. p.* purposed 15/23, 25/26.

cathaloge, *n.* catalogue 80/1.

cathecume, *n.* catechumen 9/1.

caue, *n.* cave 20/25.

cautel, cautele, *n.* precaution 50/18, 140/23.

cedℓ, *n.* cedar 50/22.

celereℓ, *n.* cellarer 99/14.

celles, *np.* cells 67/13.

cenobites, *np.* 38/10.

cese, *v. i. inf.* cease 23/11.

cessacion, *n.* 23/13.

chalange, *n.* challenge 51/4.

chamel skynnys, *np.* camel skins 38/30.

chanones, *np.* canons, 5/15.

chapetir, *n.* chapter 113/31.

charite, *n.* charity 1/29.

chartoℓ, chartour, *n.* charter 141/7, 16.

chast, *adj.* chaste 83/14.

chateryng, *adj.* chattering 6/20.

chaundeleℓ, *n.* chandelier 93/3.

chekis, *np.* cheeks 21/21.

cher, chere, *n.* cheer, 10/13, 10/14.

chere, *v. t. inf.* cheer, entertain 44/27.

cherch, chirch, kirk, *n.* church 19/17, 19, 94/16; cherchis, *np.* 67/33.

chese, *v. t. inf.* choose 17/9, 39/16; chase, *v. t.* 3 *s. p.* 70/31; chase, *v. t.* 3 *pl. p.* 39/17; chose, *pp.* chosen 19/29.

chesibile, chesible, *n.* chasuble 116/7, 124/8.

childhold, *n.* childhood 4/21.

childyr, childyrn, *n.* children 4/23, 7/15.

chois, *n.* choice 30/2.

cite, cyte, *n.* city 2/30, 20/26, 31/15; cite, *n.* city, people 25/32; cytees, *np.* 87/22.

citeceynes, *np.* citizens 41/25.

clad, *pp.* 55/19.

claf, *v. i.* 3 *s. p.* cleft 120/16.

clamour, *n.* 64/18.

Clareualle, *n.* Clairvaux 91/17.

clatering, *adj.* 85/5.

clauseℓ, *n.* cloister 83/28.

clennesse, *n.* cleanliness 7/24.

clepe, *v. t.* 1 *pl. pres.* call 38/6; clepe, *v. t.* 2 *pl. pres.* 20/9; clepith, *v. t.* 3 *s. pres.* 23/30, 38/7; clepe, *v. t.* 3 *pl. pres.* 4/27; clepid, *v. t.* 3 *s. p.* 1/3; cleped, *v. t.* 3 *pl. p.* 12/9; clepyng, *pres. p.* calling 33/20; cleped, *pp.* called 3/7.

clepyng, *n.* calling 75/8.

clerkis, *np.* clerks, monks 36/20.

clopis, *np.* clothes 10/12.

cloystireℓ, *n.* cloisterer 66/8.

clyme, *v. t. inf.* climb 97/15.

coeterne, *adj.* coeternal 31/25.

cold, *n.* coldness 45/15.

collectes, *np.* collects 80/4.

college, *n.* brotherhood 29/18.

collocucioñ, *n.* conversation 140/6.
comendatyf, *adj.* commendatory 108/31.
comminaciones, *np.* commination 66/5.
comoun, *v. t. inf.* commune 11/4; comound, *pp.* 13/1.
compendiously, *adv.* 117/23.
complacens, *n.* 84/8.
compleynt, *n.* complaint 6/29.
compowned, compownyd, *pp.* compounded 2/27, 2/28.
comprehendid, *pp.* comprehended, contained 38/33.
compromisse, *n.* promise 58/5.
compunct, *adj.* constrained 20/28.
comyng, *n.* coming 19/30.
conceytes, *np.* conceits, ideas 33/34.
conclaue, *n.* 83/11.
condicioñ, *n.* behaviour, demeanour 5/26.
conformite, *n.* 70/32.
confundid, *pp.* confounded 136/31.
congrue, *adj.* congruous 77/16.
coniected, *v. t. 3 s. p.* conjectured 99/21.
consciens, *n.* conscience 9/8.
consent, *n.* accompaniment (of tunes to words) 27/14.
conservacion, *n.* conservation 69/4.
constrewyng, *n.* construing, grammar 8/17.
constriccioñ, *n.* constriction 100/34.
conuentual, *adj.* 67/33.
conuercion, *n.* conversion 21/1.
conuerse, *n.* convert 129/30.
conuicte, *v. t. 3 s. p.* convicted 41/21.
conyng, *n.* cunning 26/16.
coost, *n.* side, part 102/28.
cophre, *n.* coffer 135/10.
corage, *n.* courage, disposition 63/32.
corteynes, *np.* curtains 112/33.
cosyn, *n.* kinsman 5/13; cosynes, *np.* 5/7.
cote, *n.* coat 70/25.
couetyse, *n.* covetousness 36/3.
councell, *v. t. inf.* counsel 50/30.
coynoures, *np.* coiners 17/29; coynouris, *np. gen.* coiners' 17/32.
craft, *n.* ability 125/12.
craked, *v. i. 3 pl. p.* cracked 120/32.
crap, *v. i. 3 s. p.* crept 120/1.
credens, *n.* credence 78/2.
crien, *v. i. inf.* cry 138/32.
cristen, *adj.* Christian 2/18, 5/9, 29/13.
cristendam, cristendham, *n.* Christianity 20/12, 29/4.

croked, *adj.* crooked 70/28.
crokednes, *n.* crookedness 130/33.
crowet, *n.* cruet, phial 132/25.
cubiculeres, *np.* cubiculars 97/3.
cubyte, *n.* elbow 130/3.
cum, *v. i. inf.* come 12/19; comth, *v. i. 3 s. pres.* 5/19, 17/30, 42/7, 56/32; cam, *v. i. 3 s. p.* came 3/26, 13/36, 20/2; cam, *v. i. 3 pl. p.* 8/7; comand, *pres. p.* 63/30, 124/6.
cumpany, *n.* 24/10.
cunnyng, *n.* ability 13/3.
cuntr̄, cuntre, *n.* countiy 3/2, 12/4, 23/18.
cuntre-man, *n.* countryman 20/10.
cure, *n.* care, charge 48/18, 89/16.
cured, *pp.* covered 17/32, 96/27.
curs, *v. t. inf.* curse 51/1.
curyng, *n.* 74/25.
custumablely, *adv.* by custom, usually 4/29, 41/11.
cyssyng, *n.* kissing 79/7.
Cystewys, *np.* Cistercians 89/13.

D

daliauns, *n.* dalliance 16/6.
dar̄, *v. t. 1 s. pres.* dare 1/9; durst, *v. t. 3 s. p.* dared 18/4.
dauns, *n.* dance 77/30.
debate, *n.* strife 6/19.
debylite, *n.* debility 128/29.
deces, *n.* decease 79/26.
deceyued, *v. 3 s. p.* 13/31.
dedis, *np.* deeds 5/27.
dedly, *adj.* mortal, subject to death 25/28.
defautes, *np.* defaults 7/25, 75/26.
defenden, *v. t. 3 pl. pres.* forbid 92/20.
defouled, *pp.* defiled 36/7.
defraude, *v. t. inf.* 79/15.
del, *n.* part 70/19.
delectabily, *adv.* delectably 27/14.
delectable, *adj.* 23/23.
delectacionis, *np.* delectations, delights 19/9.
delicasises, *np.* delicacies 70/15.
delices, *np.* delights 96/4.
delite, *n.* delight 15/6.
delt, *v. t. 3 s. p.* dealt 65/17.
deme, *v. t. 3 pl. pres.* judge 41/17.
denouns, *v. t. inf.* announce 48/6.
departed, *pp.* divided 8/3.
dere, *adj.* dear 26/31.
deregacioñ, *n.* derogation 107/30.

desolat, *adj.* 23/10.
despect, *adj.* despised 4/9.
determyn, *v. t. inf.* determine, settle 58/3.
detour̃, dettour̃, *n.* debtor 1/3, 1/11.
dettis, *np.* debts 1/12.
deuele, *n.* devil 7/9, 56/30.
deuocyoñ, *n.* devotion 24/26.
deute, *n.* duty 33/26.
dew, *adj.* due 6/13, 103/3.
dewid, *pp.* dewed 24/23.
deye, *v. i. inf.* die 4/18, 27/27.
deyid, *v. i.* 1 *s. p. and* 3 *s. p.* died 5/4, 32/14, 35/17.
deynte, *n.* esteem 12/13, 13/6.
deynte, *n.* regard 107/19.
dialoge, *n.* dialogue 26/27.
diffuncioñ, *n.* conclusion 24/12.
diffusely, *adv.* 61/11.
dignyte, *n.* dignity 61/4.
dilacioñ, *n.* 86/23.
diosise, *n.* diocese 43/27.
dirkly, *adv.* darkly 57/14.
dirknes, *n.* darkness 77/20.
disceptacioñ, *n.* disceptation, debate 42/6.
discerne, *v. t. inf.* 7/12.
disciplens, *np.* disciplines 9/24.
disport, *n.* 20/22.
dissentyrie, *n.* dysentery 128/25.
disseyued, *v. t.* 3 *s. p.* deceived 13/23.
dissolue, *v. t. inf.* solve 54/10.
dissoluer̃, *n.* solver 54/9.
distraut, *adj.* distraught 131/13.
dite, *v. t. inf.* dight, prepare 70/16; dite, *pp.* 69/25.
diuturne, *adj.* diuturnal 71/16.
do, *v. t. inf.* do 6/13; ded, dyde, *v. t.* 3 *s. p.* 7/17, 27/28, 66/16; dede, *v. t.* 3 *pl. p.* 6/17; do, don, doo, *pp.* 4/16, 7/13, 33/25, 84/17, 67/17; doyng, *n.* doing 74/23.
dobiled, doblid, *pp.* doubled 87/15, 17.
dobyl, *adj.* double 67/4.
doctour̃, *n.* doctor 1/18, 7/17; doctouris, *np.* 2/10.
dom, *n.* doom, judgment 33/24, 89/7; dome-place, *n.* doom-place, judgment-place 18/1.
dor̃, *n.* door 31/33.
dormytori, *n.* 69/26.
dortour̃, *n.* dortor, dormitory 97/12.
Dotaim, *n.* Dothan 109/13.
doutir, *n.* daughter 6/24, 31/1; douteres, *np.* 132/21.

dowte, *n.* doubt 19/6; doutes, *np.* 13/1.
dramme, *n.* dram, drachma 82/4.
dred, *v. t.* 3 *s. p.* dreaded 34/12, 57/30.
dred, *n.* dread 16/1, 81/16.
drenchid, *pp.* drowned 21/17.
dronk, *v. t.* 3 *pl. p.* drank 16/33; drinkyn, *pp.* drunk 132/27; drynkyngis, *np.* drinkings 65/21.
dropesie, *n.* dropsy 79/19.
drow, *v. i.* 1 *s. p.* drew 29/24; drow, drowe, *v. t.* 3 *s. p.* 86/18, 130/32; drawe, *pp.* drawn, withdrawn 60/19.
dul, *adj.* dull (wit) 35/9.
dwolt, *v. i.* 3 *pl. p.* 21/2.
dysmittid, *pp.* dismissed (*Latin*: dismittere), 23/15.
dyuers, *adj.* divers 12/3, 20/15.
dyuulge, *v. t. inf.* divulge 107/21.
dyuynes, *np.* divines 56/3.
dyuynite, *n.* divinity 40/17.

E

ech, *pron.* each 1/8, 65/16.
edifie, *v. t. inf.* 29/33.
edifiyng, *n.* edifying 37/23.
eft-sones, *adv.* eftsoons, soon afterwards 115/24.
eke, *adv.* also 1/21.
eld, elde, *adj.* old 4/3, 6/22, 70/27.
ellis, *adv.* else 6/29.
elmes, elmesse, *n.* alms 14/13, 69/33.
elmesse-houses, *np.* alms - houses 67/29.
elmesse - ʒeuyng, *n.* almsgiving 82/15.
embrowded, *pp.* embroidered 111/24.
emolliment, *n.* emolument 60/20.
emperesse, *n.* 27/17.
emperour̃, *n.* emperor 20/21.
encenseris, *np.* censers 62/6.
encreser, *n.* increaser 2/33.
endewid, *v. t.* 3 *s. p.* endowed 41/13; endewid, endewyd, *pp.* endowed 1/9, 65/19.
endewred, *pp.* endured 49/16.
endyted, *pp.* indicted 93/26.
endytyng, *n.* inditing 12/16.
enforsyng, *pres. p.* enforcing 53/18.
ensaumple, *n.* example 41/5.
enspired, *v. t.* 3 *s. p.* inspired 19/20.
entent, *n.* intention 20/38.

entent, *n.* understanding 4/4.
enteŗ, *adj.* entire 95/26.
entŗ, *n.* entry 55/29.
epistil, *n.* epistle 2/11 ; epistoles,
 np. 20/9, 57/2.
equyte, *n.* equity 136/13.
er, *adv.* ere 68/4.
erdly, *adj.* earthly 32/7, 81/6.
eres, *np.* ears 14/4, 28/6.
ergo, *adv.* 19/18.
errouris, *np.* errours 19/6, 25/15.
eryng, *n.* hearing 67/14.
est, *adj.* east 8/9.
estern, *adj.* easter 28/29.
esy, *adj.* easy 1/13.
ete, *v. t.* 3 *pl. pres.* eat 47/15 ; ete,
 v. t. 3 *s. p.* ate 47/11.
ethimilogie, ethimologie, *n.* etymo-
 logy 2/1, 2/26.
eþir, *conj.* either 112/34.
euel a-vised, *adj.* ill-advised 5/31.
euyr, *adv.* ever 1/6.
euyr-lestyn, *adj.* everlasting 32/4.
ex, exe, *n.* axe 17/31, 18/3. '
excedid, *v. i.* 3 *s. p.* exceeded ; became wrathful 5/29.
excellens, *n.* excellence 1/28.
excusaciones, *np.* excuses 90/18.
exemplary, *n.* 61/23.
exequies, exequiis, *np.* exequies
 33/4, 78/23.
exhortacion, *n.* 19/8.
exorted, *v. t.* 3 *s. p.* exhorted 67/27.
experiens, *n.* 26/17.
experiment, *n.* declaration, proof
 73/28.
expounne, *v. t. inf.* expound 85/31.
eyer, *n.* heir 63/3.
ey-ledes, *np.* eyelids 133/29.
eyne, *np.* eyes 21/22.
eyr, *n.* air 9/30, 53/6.
eyty, *n.* eighty 77/25.

F

fader, fadeŗ, fadir, *n.* father 1/6,
 3/5, 4/17, 5/20 ; fader, fadir,
 faderes, *n. gen.* father's 7/10,
 63/11, 84/4.
faderles, *adj.* fatherless 66/29.
faderly, *adv.* fatherly 29/30.
falle, *pp.* fallen 8/25.
fals, *adj.* 19/9.
fantastical, *adj.* 9/29.
fas, *n.* face 145/12.
fast, *prep.* near 17/5.
fayr, *adj.* fair 13/5.
fayŗ-spoke, *adj.* fair-spoken 12/33.

feble, *n.* feeble (people) 66/30.
Februarij, *n.* 77/24.
fecch, *v. t. inf.* fetch 20/26.
fedyng, *n.* feeding 24/7.
feer, *n.* fear 16/1.
feest, fest, feste, *n.* feast 1/22, 2/11,
 4/30, 5/8.
feith, *n.* faith 19/23.
felauchip, felawschip, *n.* fellowship
 8/25, 12/29, 26/29.
felawes, felawis, *np.* fellows 2/22,
 20/18.
feld, *n.* field 23/18 ; feldes, feldis,
 np. 31/3, 101/5.
fennys, *np.* fens 94/2.
fer, ferŗ, *adv.* far 18/26, 28/34,
 38/13 ; fer, *adv.* far (dissimilar)
 4/6 ; feŗ, *adj.* far 21/27.
feŗ, *n.* fear 42/26.
feŗ, fere, *n.* comradeship 30/30,
 31/28.
ferd, *v. i.* 3 *s. p.* fared (?) 41/3.
ferforth, *adv.* farforth 55/21.
ferme, *adj.* firm 43/6.
feruent, *adj.* 80/9.
feuerys, ffevyrues, *np.* fevers 59/17,
 79/19.
feyne, *v. t. inf.* pretend 94/12 ;
 feyned, *v. t.* 3 *s. p.* 13/24.
feynt, *adj.* faint 94/19.
ffreŗ, *n.* frere 62/3.
figge-tre, *n.* fig-tree 21/32.
filt, *v. t.* 3 *s. p.* filled 14/4, 97/22 ;
 filt, *pp.* filled 100/10.
fistula, *n.* 100/13.
flayn, *pp.* flayed 118/29.
fle, *v. t. inf.* flee 70/33 ; fle, *v. t.* 3 *pl.
 pres.* 38/27.
fleschly, *adj.* carnal 24/7.
flete, *v. i. inf.* fleet, pass 33/24.
flouŗ, *n.* flower 129/10 ; flouris, *np.*
 62/24.
fluctuacioñ, *n.* 16/20.
folowand, *adj.* following 121/30,
 122/30, &c.
folowyn, *v. i.* 3 *pl. pres.* follow
 138/3.
fond, fonde, *v. t.* 3 *s. and pl. p.* found
 9/18, 20/3, 26 ; found, founde,
 founden, *pp.* 4/15, 28/31, 80/11.
forboden, forbodyn, *pp.* forbidden
 47/24, 94/10.
fore, *conj.* for 4/28.
for-gete, forgetyn, *pp.* 32/7, 27.
forgif, *v. t.* 2 *s. imper.* 33/22 ; for-
 3oue, *pp.* 52/15.
forhed, *n.* forehead 21/21.
form-faderes, *np.* forefathers 92/16.

fornays, *n.* furnace 95/18.
forsaid, *adj.* 24/6.
forsok, *v. t.* 3 *s. p.* forsook 27/4 ; forsok, *v. t.* 3 *pl. p.* 45/27 ; forsakyn, *pp.* 28/33.
foundour, *n.* founder 29/4.
fourt, *adj.* fourth 77/23.
fre, *adj.* free 5/25, 23/4.
fre-hertet, *adj.* free-hearted 36/34.
fremanly, *adj.* free, composed of freemen, 63/20.
frenesie, *n.* frenzy 131/2.
fretyng, *n.* fretting 133/8.
freyte, *n.* freight 104/4.
fro, *prep.* from 21/8.
frustrate, *v. t. inf.* frustrate 61/18.
frutes, *np.* fruits 2/16.
fulfillid, *pp.* replete 27/5 ; fulfilt, *pp.* fulfilled 16/12.
furris, *np.* furs 38/28.
fynde, *v. t. inf.* find 30/10.
fyred, *pp.* fired 1/29.
fytyn, *v. i. inf.* fight 51/4.

G

gadered, *v. t.* 3 *s. p.* gathered 21/29 ; gadered, *pp.* gathered 14/19, 21/10.
gaderer, *n.* gatherer 90/8.
gaf, goue, *see* ʒeue.
Galile, *n.* Galilee 3/14.
gardeyn, *n.* garden 21/24.
garmentis, *np.* 47/2.
gat, *v. t.* 3 *s. p.* got 11/29, 41/8 ; goten, *pp.* got 41/3.
gayler, *n.* jailor 84/28.
geaunt, *n.* giant 53/17.
gelosie, *n.* jealousy 42/27.
gemetrie, *n.* geometry 11/32.
gendres, *np.* genders, kinds 29/22.
gentill, *adj.* gentle 1/15.
gessid, *pp.* guessed 57/4.
gest, *n.* guest 66/29 ; gestis, *np.* 44/29.
gilty, *adj.* guilty 33/19.
girdil, *n.* girdle 28/21 ; girdilis, *np.* 38/29.
girdyn, *v. t.* 3 *pl. pres.* gird 146/28 ; girt, *pp.* 28/20.
glade, *v. t. inf.* make glad, gladden 70/3.
glorius, *adj.* glorious 2/8.
gnach, *v. t. inf.* gnash 132/28 ; gnacching, *pres. p.* gnashing 131/4.
go, goo, *v. i. inf.* 13/13, 13/25 ; go, *v. i.* 2 *s. imper.* 11/19 ; go, *v. i.* 1 *pl. imper.* 19/21 ; go, i-goo, *pp.* gone 16/7, 21/12, 77/20.

god, *adj.* good 29/27.
god, godis, *np.* goods 34/20, 37/23.
goost, *n.* ghost 12/28.
goostly, *adj.* spiritual 24/7.
Gothi, *np.* Goths 58/18.
gouernauns, *n.* governance, control, 5/27.
govte, *n.* gout 128/25.
gramer, *n.* grammar 2/2, 30/9.
greces, *np.* steps 97/14.
gret, grete, *adj.* great 1/1, 2/32; 4/30; gretter, *adj. comp.* 8/18.
gretly, *adv.* greatly, 6/31, 12/33.
greuauns, *n.* grievance, injury 8/14.
greue, *v. t.* 3 *pl. pres.* grieve, hurt 7/16 ; greued, *v. t.* 3 *s. p.* grieved, pained 7/1.
greuous, *adj.* grievous 14/8, 25/4.
griffid, *pp.* grafted 68/30.
groped, *v. t.* 3 *s. p.* touched, took hold 126/10.
grounded, *pp.* founded 117/9 ; grounded, *pp.* learned, versed 12/33.
groundes, *np.* foundation 56/7.
growen, *pp.* grown 68/22.
grucch, *v. i. inf.* grudge, murmur 50/10 ; grucch, *v. t.* 2 *s. imper.* 20/31 ; grucch, *v. i.* 2 *pl. pres.* 28/28 ; grucch, *v. i.* 2 *pl. imper.* 49/19 ; grucchid, *v. i.* 3 *pl. p.* 40/31 ; grucching, *pres. p.* murmuring, rebelling 15/8.
grucching, *adj.* grudging, complaining, 41/1.
gruf, *adv.* prone, face downwards 124/12.
guttys, *np.* guts, intestines 128/26.

H

ha, a, *v. t. inf.* have 8/5, 57/17, 68/5, 69/6, 84/22, &c. ; haue, *v. t.* 2 *pl. pres.* 18/18 ; hatʒ, *v. t.* 3 *s. pres.* hath 4/3, 19/28, 113/7 ; ha, had, *v. t.* 3 *s. p.* 19/2, 145/8.
hald, *v. t. inf.* hold 17/10 ; held, *v. t.* 3 *pl. p.* 74/13 ; hald, halden, hold, holden, *pp.* held 44/28, 63/29, 89/14, 113/9, 128/9.
halidayes, *np.* holidays 28/29.
halowid, *pp.* hallowed 25/31.
halsyng, *n.* embracing 83/8 ; halsyngis, *np.* embraces 83/14.
hambyr, *n.* hammer 52/10.
hand, *n.* handwriting 4/3.
hard-hertid, *adj.* hard-hearted 54/20.

hast, *v. t. inf.* haste 16/17 ; hasted, *v. t.* 3 *pl. p.* 20/35.
hattest, *adj. sup.* hottest 2/16.
hatyd, *v. t.* 3 *s. p.* hated 47/19.
hayir, her, *n.* hair 48/27, 70/31 ; herys, *np.* hairs 47/7.
he, it, *pron.* it 19/33, 56/33 ; his, hise, *poss. pron.* his, its 5/19, 28/3, 36/15.
hed, heed, *n.* head 15/7, 25/4.
hed, *n.* heed, 18/6, 55/16.
heith, *n.* height 81/3, 56/32.
hele, *n.* health 127/27.
Helise, *n.* Elisha 102/9.
Hely, *n.* Elijah 38/30.
hem, *pron.* them 1/10, &c.
hemmys, *np.* hems, borders 107/25.
hepes, *n. p.* heaps 21/29.
her, herys, *see* hayir.
heř, here, *v. t. inf.* hear 14/14, 15 ; heř, here, *v.t.* 2 *s. imper.* 33/19, 21 ; herd, *v. t.* 3 *pl. p.* 4/14 ; herand, *pres. p.* 76/28.
heř, *adv.* here 5/5.
her, heř, here, *pron.* their 1/6, 4/11, 6/2, 9/3, 12/21, 108/12, &c.
herborowid, *pp.* harboured 34/9.
heremite, heremyte, *n.* hermit 20/25 ; hermytes, *np.* 28/16.
hereres, *np.* hearers 140/11.
heres, *np.* knights 147/16.
hert, *n.* heart 1/29.
hertly, *adv.* heartily 10/6, 45/15.
heruest, *n.* harvest 23/10.
herying, *n.* hearing 47/10.
Heseleschop, *n.* Hessleskew Grange 103/23.
hethen, *adj.* 24/3.
heuene, *n.* heaven 1/5.
heuy, *adj.* heavy 10/14, 29/4.
hewe, *v. t. inf.* hew 17/33.
heyeř, *adv.* higher 66/6.
heyly, *adv.* highly 15/20, 43/14.
heyne, *v. t. inf.* exalt 68/17.
hie, *adj.* high 27/7 ; hyer, *adj. comp.* 107/4.
him-selue, hym-selue, his-selve, *pron.* himself 4/1, 54/18, 57/29.
hin, in, *n.* inn 13/26, 102/13.
hing, hyng, *v. i.* 3 *s. p.* hung 71/11, 120/8.
hipped, *v. i.* 3 *s. p.* hopped 118/18.
hiř, hiř, hire, *pron.* her 1/16, 4/21, 13/28.
his, hise, *poss. pron.* his 5/19, 28/3, 36/15. *See* he.
hith, *v. i.* 3 *s. p.* hight, was called 4/20, 5/7, 31/9.

hoggis, *np.* hogs 9/11,
hol, hool, hole, *adj.* whole 34/11, 14, 99/27.
hold, holden, *see* hald.
holed, *pp.* healed 75/4.
holpe, *pp.* helped 37/33.
holsom, *adj.* wholesome 80/9, 118/2.
hom, *n.* home 11/9, 20/3.
homward, *adv.* homeward 20/36.
hony, *n.* honey 24/22.
hoot, hote, *adj.* hot 2/24, 47/16.
hopped, *v. i.* 3 *s. p.* leapt, hopped 16/9. *See also* hipped.
horribil, *adj.* horrible 21/6.
hors bere, *n.* horse-bier 131/20.
horsed, *pp.* set on horse 126/22.
hose, *n.* hose 118/30; hosen, hosyn, *np.* hose 45/17, 74/29.
hositt, *n.* housel 76/6.
Hostie, *n.* Ostia 31/31.
hothous, *n.* 4/27.
housyng, *n.* housing 17/29.
humores, *np.* humours 134/23.
huscher, *n.* usher 30/8.
hydyn, *v. t. inf.* hide 140/30.

I

I, *pron.* 89/14.
Iaphet, *n.* Japhet 3/8.
idus, *n.* ides 142/5.
iff, *conj.* if 6/8.
Ihesu, *n.* Jesus 1/5.
impetuosnesse, *n.* 103/21.
implicat, *pp.* implicated 50/7.
importably, *adv.* insupportably 66/10.
imprended, *v. t.* 3 *s. p.* imprinted 11/21.
in, hin, *n.* inn 13/26, 102/13.
inclinacion, *n.* inclination (of the sun) 20/35 ; inclynacioñ, *n.* 3/28.
inexpert, *adj.* 85/15.
infancia, *n.* infancy 7/3.
infect, *pp.* infected 27/17.
inflawmed, *v. t.* 3 *s. p.* inflamed 54/19.
I-now, *adv.* enough 35/13.
inqwired, *v. t.* 3 *s. p.* inquired 19/14.
inqwyet, *v. t. inf.* disturb 126/5.
insolens, *np.* insolent deeds 9/6.
instauns, *n.* instance 1/16.
interfered, *pp.* interposed 96/11.
interogaciones, *np.* 26/28.
interrupt, *pp.* interrupted 57/26.
intituled, *pp.* entitled 12/10.
intollerablely, *adv.* intolerably 14/4.
inuecciones, *np.* invections, inveighings 18/3.

inuent, *adj.* literary, artistically composed (?) 14/15.
inuisibil, *adj.* invisible 35/6.
iocunde, *adj.* jocund 12/32.
iocundnesse, *n.* jocundity 46/16.
Ion, *n.* St. John Baptist 38/30.
iornay, *n.* journey 16/5, 98/5.
ioye, *n.* joy 23/7.
ioynend, *v. t. 3 pl. p.* joined 108/18.
ir̃, ire, *n.* ire, anger 5/24, 30.
irous, *adj.* subject to ire 6/7.
issewe, *n.* issue 63/8.
it, *pron.* it, 65/16. *See also* he.
Itaile, *n.* Italy 8/21.
iteration, *n.* 19/19.
Iubiter, *n.* Jupiter 56/12.
Iude, *n.* Judea 3/14.
iuge, *n.* judge 66/4.
iunctur̃, *n.* juncture 87/18.
iurates, *np.* sworn men 111/7.

K

kalende, *n.* calend 60/12.
kandel, *n.* candle 123/28.
kechyn, kychyn, *n.* kitchen 47/30,
123/12.
kende, *n.* kind 82/8.
kendly, *adv.* kindly, naturally 97/11.
kepand, *pres. p.* keeping 30/22.
keper̃, *n.* keeper 16/26.
kerchy, *n.* kerchief 91/22.
kirk, *see* Cherch.
kit, *v. t. inf.* cut 123/20.
knokkyng, *pres. p.* knocking 52/11.
knowest, knowist, *v. t.* 2 *s. pres.*
18/19, 33/13; knowe, *v. t.* 2 *s.*
imper. 19/15; knew, *v. t.* 3 *s. p.*
18/8; knew, *v. t.* 3 *pl. p.* 68/28;
know, knowyn, *pp.* 14/29, 87/26;
a-knowe, I-knowe, *pp.* made
known 47/5, 50/23. *See* a-knowe.
knowlech, *n.* knowledge 3/31, 52/3;
knowlech, *n.* knowledge, acquaintance 6/1.
knyt, *pp.* knit 81/15.
knyte, *n.* knight 62/33; knytys,
n. gen. 121/13; knytys, *np.* 38/29.
kyndeled, *v. t.* 3 *pl. p.* kindled 24/19.
kynred, kynrod, *n.* kindred 4/8,
36/9, 68/25.
kyrnel, *n.* kernel 85/11.

L

labourand, *pres. p.* labouring 50/5.
laboureres, *np.* laborers 4/10.

lak, *v. t.* 3 *pl. pres.* lack 7/12; lakkyn, *v. t.* 2 *pl. pres.* 46/22; lakkid,
pp. 69/16.
lamentable, *adj.* 22/1.
Lammesse, *n.* Lammas 121/17.
languor̃, *n.* 67/31.
laschid, *pp.* lashed 8/4.
Latyn, *n.* Latin 1/17.
laudes, *n.* lauds, the prayers following
matins 71/23.
laumpe, *n.* lamp 82/24.
lay, *see* ly.
leccherie, leccherye, *n.* lechery
7/25, 95/3.
lech, leche, *n.* leech, doctor 34/11,
60/10.
lede, *v. t. inf.* lead 29/15; led, *v. t.*
1 *s. p.* 30/2; ledde, *pp.* led
2/35.
lederes, *np.* leaders 50/23.
ledir, *n.* leather 38/22.
leed, *n.* lead 17/32.
lefte, *v. t. inf.* lift 48/33; lyft, *v. t.*
3 *pl. p.* 32/6; lift, lyfte, *pp.*
108/28, 116/8.
lefully, *adv.* lawfully 67/21.
legge, *n.* leg 126/20.
lendes, *np.* loins 38/31, 120/2.
lened, *v. i.* 3 *s. p.* leant 122/20;
lenyng, *pres. p.* leaning 32/2.
lenger, *adj. comp.* longer 51/16.
Lenton̄, *n.* Lent 70/13.
leones, *n. gen.* lion's 85/23.
leprosite, *n.* leprosy 133/27.
lerned, *pp.* taught 29/4.
lernyng, *n.* learning 4/14.
lese, *v. t. inf.* lose 51/10.
lesingis, *np.* lies 33/16.
lest, *v. i. inf.* last 93/9.
lestith, *v. i.* 3 *s. pres.* 7/22; lestid,
v. i. 3 *s. p.* lasted 42/6.
lest, *adj.* least 61/3.
lette, *v. t. inf.* prevent, obstruct
88/15; lete, *v. t.* 3 *s. p.* let, allowed
101/22; lettid, lettyd, *pp.* hin-
dered 13/15, 45/15.
lettered, letteryd, · *pp.* lettered,
learned 5/9, 40/26, 67/15.
letteris, *np.* letters 3/27.
letting, *n.* stop, cessation 11/10.
lettirur̃, *n.* learning 1/9.
letuse, *n.* lettuce 47/12.
leue, lyue, *v. i. inf.* live 4/12, 20/33;
leued, lyued, *v. i.* 3 *s. p.* lived
26/29, 98/2; leued, *v. i.* 3 *pl. p.*
lived 6/17, 34/20; leuand, liuand,
lyuand, lyuyng, *pres. p.* living
19/27, 28, 54/9, 130/11, 137/10.

leue, *n.* leave 45/31.
leue, *v. t. inf.* leave 23/8.
leuer, *adv.* liefer 73/4.
lewid, *adj.* lewd, unlearned 40/7.
ley, *v. t.* 2 *pl. imper.* lay! 32/23.
leyseᵹ, *n.* leisure 12/1, 21/31.
lich, *adv.* like 2/12, 28/20.
licorous, *adj.* voluptuous, gluttonous 47/30.
lif, lyue, *n.* life 1/17, 20/32, 62/33; lyues, *np.* 71/24.
lift, *see* lefte.
likly, *adv.* likely 13/24.
likne, *v. t. inf.* liken 145/heading; likned, *pp.* likened 2/10.
liknesse, *n.* likeness 19/12.
likouᵹ, *n.* liquor 125/11.
lippis, *np.* lips 33/15.
list, *v. i.* 2 *s. pres.* listest 28/30; list, *v. i.* 3 *s. p.* listed 66/5.
lith, *adj.* light, easy 27/28.
lith, *n.* light 9/25.
lithnesse, *n.* lightness 119/19.
litigious, *adj.* 17/25.
litil, *adv.* little 8/23.
litil, *n.* little (time) 32/29.
litly, *adv.* lightly 47/14.
liuand. *See* leue.
loggid, *pp.* lodged 89/19.
loke, *v. t. inf.* look 7/15, 17/34, 47/30; loke, *v. i.* 2 *pl. imper.* 38/25; lokid, *v. i.* 3 *s. p.* looked 32/21.
lond, *n.* land 16/5, 41/6.
londyd, *pp.* landed 104/10.
longith, *v. i.* 3 *s. pres.* belongeth 1/4; longid, *v. i.* 3 *pl. p.* belonged 34/19; longing, *pres. p.* belonging 6/32, 20/8.
lordchip, lordschip, *n.* lordship 2/7, 33/16.
lordis, *n. gen.* lord's 4/15.
losed, *pp.* loosed 33/2.
loth, *adj.* 18/28.
loue, *n.* love 1/28.
low, *v. i.* 3 *s. p.* laughed 8/28.
lowed, *v. t.* 3 *s. p.* humbled 68/17.
loy, *see* ly.
ly, *v. i. inf.* lie down 32/29, 71/7; liggest, *v. i.* 2 *s. pres.* 119/9; lith, *v. i.* 3 *s. pres.* 141/11; lay, loy, *v. i.* 3 *s. p.* 20/6, 51/15, 98/10.
Lyban, *n.* Lebanon 50/22.
lyft, *see* lefte.
lylyis, *np.* lilies 55/18.
lynand, *n.* linen 70/31, 123/32.
lyue, lyuand, *see* leue, lif.
lyuysch, *adj.* living 98/32.

M

magᵹ, *prep.* maugre, *malgré,* in spite of, 15/7.
makitȝ, *v. t.* 3 *s. pres.* maketh 7/13; mad, *pp.* 1/27, 20/37.
mal, *adj.* male 26/13.
malandrynes, *np.* highwaymen 109/8.
malencolie, *n.* melancholy 5/25.
Mandauris, *n.* Madaura 8/8.
maneᵹ, *n.* manner 6/8.
manhod, *n.* manhood 72/26.
Manicheis, Maniches, *np.* Manichaeans 9/27, 31/11.
mannes, *n. gen.* man's 5/4; mennys, *np. gen.* men's 66/19.
marchaunt, *n.* merchant 30/11.
marteres, *np.* martyrs 16/24.
masse, *n.* mass 117/14; messis, missis, *np.* 59/1.
matrimonial, *adj.* 6/9.
maydenes, *np.* maidens 6/26.
maydenhed, *n.* maidenhood 21/4.
maystires, *np.* masters, great authors 11/25.
mech, *adj.* much 18/31.
mede, *n.* reward 71/1.
medeled, *pp.* mingled, mixed 47/10, 63/10.
mediacioñ, *n.* 61/18.
medycyne, *n.* 33/21.
meked, *v. t.* 3 *s. p.* humbled 96/18.
meknesse, *n.* meekness 19/8.
mel, *n.* meal 47/20.
membres, *np.* members (of the body) 21/22.
mene, *adj.* mean, poor 46/33.
mene, *n.* mean, compromise 39/29; menes, *np.* means 10/7.
meny, *n.* company 30/28.
merciable, *adj.* capable of mercy 18/28.
merie, mery, myri, *adj.* merry 16/9, 13, 70/2.
merk, *n.* mark 6/5; merkys, *np.* marks 6/1.
merour, *n.* mirror 39/3.
meruayle, merveile, *n.* marvel 6/10, 68/28.
merueling, *pres. p.* marvelling 21/26; meruelyng, *pres. p.* marvelling, causing to marvel 12/4.
messageris, *np.* messengers 51/34.
messis, *see* masse.
mesurable, *adj.* measurable, moderate 46/21.
mette, *n.* measure 136/11.

meued, *v. t.* 3 *s. p.* moved, induced 1/15; meued, mevid, *pp.* moved 34/13, 44/13, 72/30.

mevyngis, *np.* movements 66/7.

meynteyn, *v. t. inf.* maintain 140/15.

meyr, *n.* mayor 14/23.

misellis, *np.* lepers 67/31.

moder, modir, modyr, *n.* mother 4/20, 5/3, 62/32; moderis, *n. gen.* 63/11.

molten, *pp.* molten, melted 48/3.

monasteriis, *np.* monasteries 64/20.

mony, *n.* money, coin 82/6.

moo, *adj.* more 24/11.

moost, *adv.* most 1/15.

mor, *adv.* more 1/11, 26/10.

morer, *n.* increaser, one who increases 1/6, 2/32.

moring, *n.* increasing 139/8.

mornyng, *n.* mourning 79/8.

morow, *adj.* morrow 77/22.

morownyng, *n.* morning 71/21.

motiues, motyues, *np.* motives 12/25, 13/6.

mountes, *np.* mountains 112/14.

munkys, *np.* monks 29/22.

myddis, *n.* midst 37/26.

mydwey, *n.* midway 70/31.

myschef, *n.* trouble, harm 48/6.

myth, *v. i.* 3 *s. p.* might 4/16; myte, myth, *v. i.* 3 *pl. p.* 21/27, 67/13.

myte, *n.* might 116/19.

N

Nabugodonosor, *n.* Nebuchadnezzar 112/18.

namely, namelych, *adv.* specially 6/20, 36/34, 61/19.

narratyf, *n.* narrative, a form of writing 31/20.

nase, *n.* nose 105/29.

nawt, nowt, *adv.* not, naught 7/17, 9/11, 21/20.

ne, *conj.* nor 3/25.

neoligense, *n.* negligence 66/18.

neoys, *np.* nieces 50/13.

nedis, *adv.* needs 118/15.

neophites, *np.* 85/20.

ner, *adv.* nearly 2/7.

neuer-pe-lasse, neuyrpelasse, *conj.* nevertheless 3/25, 89/12.

neuly, *adv.* newly 20/12.

neuyr, *adv.* never 5/28.

nite, nyth, *n.* night 10/8, 27/25, 77/19.

nobil, *adj.* noble 42/20.

Noe, *n.* Noah, 3/5.

non, *pron.* none 6/5.

nonas, *np.* nones 141/33.

norche, *v. t. inf.* nourish 102/17; norchid, *pp.* 4/21.

norcher, *n.* nourisher 46/6.

norching, *n.* nourishing 6/32.

notwithstand, *conj.* notwithstanding, 6/6.

notyfied, *pp.* 61/5.

noueltes, *np.* novelties, 11/14; noueltes, *np.* news, new things 122/15.

nowle, *n.* navel 106/16.

nowt, *see* nawt.

noyhous, *adj.* hurtful 100/33.

Numedie, Numedye, *n.* Numidia 3/20.

Nussie, *n.* ? Russie *or* Tussie, *for* Russia *or* Tuscany 8/15

ny, *adv.* nearly 20/36, 52/29; ny, *adv.* nigh 10/1; ny, *prep.* nigh 18/1.

nyher, *adv. comp.* nigher 38/19, 44/12.

O

o, *adj.* one 6/12, 20/23.

o, *prep.* on 55/20.

obeyen, *v. t.* 3 *pl. pres.* 103/13.

obliuious, *adj.* oblivious 147/15

off, *prep.* of 4/8, 19/30.

offense, *n.* 33/15.

oft-tyme, often-tyme, *adv.* 19/13, 14.

omelies, *np.* homilies 57/3.

on, *pron.* one 1/27, 19/10.

on = of them? 7/7.

on-certeyn, *adj.* uncertain 23/25.

onclennesse, *n.* uncleanliness 7/25.

on-corupte, *adj.* uncorrupted 75/2.

on-defensed, *adj.* undefended 94/16.

ondirstood, *v. t.* 3 *s. p.* understood 11/30.

ongilty, *adj.* unguilty, innocent 18/13.

onknowe, on-knowyn, *adj.* unknown 20/19, 68/21.

onlerned, *adj.* unlearned 21/15, 68/1.

on-mouled, *adj.* unmouldered 75/2.

opresonable, *adj.* unreasonable 5/31.

onstabilnesse, *n.* unstableness 23/23.

onthrifty, *adj.* unthrifty 65/22.

on-to, *prep.* unto 13/17.

on-wetyng, *adj.* unknowing 52/23.

on-wise, *adj.* unwise 1/3.

ony, *adj.* any 1/21.

onyment, *n.* ointment 93/18.

onys, *adv.* once 60/30.

ope, *adj.* open 84/20.

opinyones, *np.* opinions 23/6.

opposicion, *n.* opposition 61/12.
or, *adv.* ere 16/14, 141/5.
or, *v. i.* 3 *pl. pres.* ought 7/7.
orarium, *n.* border (Latin. *See note*, p. 157) 91/24.
oratorie, *n.* oratory 13/29.
ordeyn, *v. t. inf.* ordain 27/28.
ordres, *np.* orders (religious) 34/23.
oth, *n.* oath 51/9 ; othis, *np.* 51/8.
opir, *adj.* other 1/11, 20/23.
ouer-say, *v. t.* 3 *s. p.* revised 58/12.
our, *poss. pron.* ours 18/20.
our, *n.* hour 64/22.
ouyr-lokid, *v. t.* 3 *s. p.* revised 57/10.
ouyr-nyth, *adv.* overnight 97/5.
ouyrsailed, *v. t.* 3 *pl. p.* oversailed, passed at sea 135/18.
ouyrspred, *pp.* overspread 132/9.
owt, *n.* aught 18/19.
owt, *adv.* out 17/30, 40/7.
Oxenford, *n.* Oxford 99/12.
oyle, *n.* oil 82/25.

P

paciens, *n.* patience 6/17.
paganite, *n.* paganism 145/6.
palesye, *n.* palsy 73/17.
paleys, *n.* palace 19/34.
papate, *n.* papacy 142/14.
parceyue, *v. t. inf.* perceive 127/6.
parchemyn, *n.* parchment 60/5.
parfit, parfite, parfith, *adj.* perfect 29/24, 45/25, 66/14.
parfithly, *adv.* perfectly 16/8.
parfithnesse, *n.* perfection 29/18.
parischones, *np.* parishioners 65/28.
partie, partye, *n.* part 3/8, 31/4 ; parties, *np.* 2/31.
partye, *adv.* partly 95/27.
pase-tyme, *n.* Easter 25/30.
passe, *np.* paces 126/8.
passyng, *adj.* 25/22.
patrimonie, *n.* 37/32.
pauyment, *n.* pavement 120/23.
paynem, *adj.* pagan 4/30.
pencifnesse, *n.* pensiveness 147/24.
Pers, *n.* Persia, 3/13.
perseuering, *pres. p.* persevering 21/2.
perseyue, *v. t. inf.* perceive 39/3.
pertinent, *adj.* 62/29.
pes, *n.* peace 6/15, 24/30.
pesibily, *adv.* 37/12.
petites, *np.* little children 64/14.
petous, *adj.* piteous 129/21.
petycion, *np.* petitions 61/17.

peyre, *n.* pair 25/9.
peysed, *v. t.* 3 *s. p.* poised 53/29.
philisophr, *n.* philosopher 19/11.
pinsones, *np.* sort of thin shoes 99/25.
pipes, *np.* pipes, the trachea and gullet, 127/13.
pite, *n.* pity 125/3.
pitte, *n.* pit 62/4.
plat, *adv.* flat 101/17.
playes, *np.* games 64/17.
pleasauns, *n.* pleasance, 1/24.
plener, *adj.* plenary 75/25.
plente, *n.* plenty 37/31.
plenteuously, *adv.* plenteously 21/30.
plete, pleten, *v. i. inf.* plead 17/25, 28.
pley, pleye, *v. i. inf.* play 20/5, 31/15 ; played, *v. i.* 3 *pl. p.* 31/15.
plite, plith, *n.* plight 16/22, 122/25.
plowmen, *np.* 86/31.
podagra, *n.* podagra, gout 99/16.
Poncian, *n.* Pontitianus 19/30.
pored, *v. t.* 3 *s. p.* poured 69/2.
postcomun, *n.* post-communion 112/6.
postulacion, *n.* postulation, solicitation 138/14.
pouert, pouerte, *n.* poverty 30/2, 68/9, 77/8.
poynaunt, *adj.* poignant 93/22.
practik, *n.* practice 42/3.
praisen, *v. t.* 2 *pl. imper.* praise 77/22.
preamble, *n.* 62/24.
prechid, *v. i.* 3 *s. p.* preached 27/24.
prees, pres, *n.* press, crowd 32/3, 43/32.
preest, *n.* priest 5/4 ; prestis, *np.* 34/24.
preisable, *adj.* to be praised, praiseworthy 136/18.
prerogatif, *n.* prerogative 68/28.
presens, *n.* presence 27/7.
pressur, *n.* 128/1.
presthod, *n.* priesthood 65/11.
presumpcion, *n.* 80/32.
preuylegis, *np.* privileges 38/7.
prey, *v. i. inf.* pray 23/17.
prikkid, *pp.* pricked 118/22.
priuyth, *v. t.* 3 *s. pres.* depriveth 99/18.
proferen, *v. t.* 3 *pl. pres.* proffer 7/16 ; profered, *v. t* 3 *s. p.* 30/16.
profete, *n.* prophet 74/21.
profiten, *v. i. inf.* 88/22.
profith, *n.* profit 66/19.
progenie, *n.* 78/26.

progenitouris, *np.* progenitors 4/8.
propicius, *adj.* propitious 75/11.
propirly, *adv.* 54/33.
proporcioned, *v. t.* 3 *s. p.* 10/24.
prouentis, *np.* revenues 66/31.
proues, *np.* proofs 95/29.
prouost, *n.* 113/5 ; prouostis, *np.*
  76/19.
prouynces, *np.* provinces 3/14.
prys, *n.* price 33/27.
pryse, *n.* price, value 40/31.
pryuy, *adj.* privy 15/13.
pryuyly, *adv.* privily 31/7.
psalmys, *np. gen.* 72/11.
puericia, *n.* boyhood 7/21, 22.
puple, *n.* people 2/18.
puplysoh, *v. t. inf.* publish 107/23.
pupplicacion, *n.* publication 107/26.
purpos, *n.* purpose 20/37.
purpos, *v. t. inf.* propose 11/8 ; purpose, *v. t.* 1 *s. pres.* purpose 20/29.
pursewed, *v. t.* 3 *s. p.* 52/8.
purveyid, *v. t.* 3 *s. p.* purveyed 36/18.
purueyed, *v. t.* 3 *pl. p.* 114/17.
puruyaunce, *n.* purveyance 86/27.
putte, *v. t. inf.* put 2/31.
pyned, *v. t.* 3 *s. p.* pined, wasted 97/21.

Q

qwaked, *v. i.* 3 *s. p.* quaked 73/16.
qwech, *pron.* which 12/17.
qweer, *n.* choir 106/14.
I-qwenchid, *pp.* quenched 9/25.
quod, *v. t.* 3 *s. p.* quoth, said 10/27.

R

ragyn, *n.* raging 64/2.
rankour, *n.* rancour 120/3.
rankyd, *pp.* became rank 126/21.
ransake, *v. t. inf.* ransack 66/2.
rase, *v. t. inf.* raze 47/26.
rauyschid, *pp.* ravished 32/8.
rawt, *see* rowt.
Rebaptizatores, *np.* Rebaptizers
  52/30.
receyue, *v. t. inf.* receive 11/9 ; receyued, *v. t.* 1 *s. p.* received 1/14 ;
  receuyed, *v. t.* 2 *pl. p.* 2/24.
receynour, *n.* receiver 9/1.
receytis, *np.* receipts 50/1.
recors, *n.* recourse 28/15.
recure, *v. t.* 3 *pl. p.* recover 103/5.
recuryng, *n.* recovery 98/10.
red, *v. t. inf.* read 61/21 ; rede, *v. t.*
  1 *s. pres.* 89/14 ; rede, *v. t.* 2 *pl.*
  pres. 3/26 ; redith, *v. t.* 3 *s. pres.*
  54/20 ; red, *v. t.* 3 *s. p.* 11/29,

24/26 ; red, redde, *pp.* read 2/11,
  11/27, 61/14.
redact, *v. t.* 3 *pl. p.* arranged in
  writing 79/29.
rederes, *np.* readers 33/30.
redyer, *adj.* readier 11/8.
redyly, *adv.* readily 29/33.
redyng, *n.* reading 11/11, 20/27.
refelle, *v. t.* 3 *s. p.* refel, refute 41/26.
refresch, *v. t. inf.* 20/5 ; refreschid,
  pp. 31/5.
reherse, *v. t. inf.* 33/24.
reise, *v. t. inf.* 33/1.
reles, *n.* release 122/22.
remissiones, *n.* remissions 66/4.
renne, *v. i. inf.* run 18/14, 36/17 ;
  rennyth, *v. i.* 3 *s. pres.* 31/32 ; ran,
  v. i. 3 *s. p.* 41/5 ; runne, *v. i.* 3 *pl. p.*
  53/1 ; rennyng, *pres. p.* 85/2.
renneres, *np.* runners 38/27.
renounsid, *v. t.* 3 *s. p.* renounced
  25/15.
repayr, *v. t. inf.* 100/5.
repe, *v. t. inf.* reap 81/17 ; repe, *v. i.*
  3 *pl. pres.* 55/16.
replecchid, repleschid, *pp.* re-
  plenished 72/13, 145/18.
replet, *adj.* replete 76/28.
repreuyth, *v. t.* 3 *s. pres.* reproveth
  56/20.
reprobat, *adj.* reprobate 62/19.
rered, *pp.* reared 19/17.
reson, reson̄, *n.* reason 2/32, 7/12.
rest, *pp.* wrested 76/29.
rethorician, *n.* rhetorician 19/11.
rethorik, *n.* rhetoric 8/21.
retorne, *v. i. inf.* return 72/19.
Retractaciones, *np.* Retractations (by
  Augustine) 31/27.
retribuciones, *np.* rewards 1/25.
reuel, *n.* revel 13/15.
reuers, *n.* reverse 7/8, 52/6.
reule, *n.* rule 1/1 ; reule, *n.* rule,
  level board 10/18.
richesse, rychesse, *n.* riches 30/1,
  68/11.
ripening, *adj.* 2/16.
risyn, *see* roos.
ritefulmen, *np.* rightful men 136/25.
rith, *adj.* level, flat 10/11 ; rith, *adj.*
  right 2/35, 29/1.
rith, *adv.* right, just 20/1.
rithwysnesse, *n.* righteousness 72/21.
rof, *n.* roof 115/26.
rood, *v. i.* 3 *s. p.* rode 8/24.
roop, *n.* rope 118/33.
roos, *v. i.* 3 *s. p.* rose 21/31 ; risyn,
  pp. risen 127/9.

rote, *n.* root 62/23.
roted, *pp.* grounded, learned 45/31.
roted, *pp.* rooted 68/9.
rotes, *np.* roots 87/24.
rowt, *v. i.* 3 *s. p.* raught 40/31 ; **rawt,** *pp.* 7/9.
rubrich, *n.* rubric ; dedication of a book 5/12.
rudenesse, *n.* 74/28.
ryp, *adj.* ripe 24/26, 76/9.

S

Sabat-day, *n.* Sabbath-day 77/16.
saciat, *adj.* satiate 27/5.
sacramental, *adj.* 25/34.
sadeled, *pp.* saddled 104/1.
saf, *adj.* safe 52/22.
Sarsines, *np.* Saracens 147/13.
Sattirday, *n.* Saturday 77/15.
saue, *prep.* save, except 15/11, 24/10.
sauely, *adv.* safely 1/11.
sauoured, *v. i.* 3 *s. p.* savoured, cared 1/8.
say, sey, seyn, seyne, *v. t. inf.* say 1/17, 7/1, 49/16, 65/8, 86/2, 87/25 ; **seith, seyth,** *v. t.* 3 *s. pres.* saith 2/12, 35/8, 49/8 ; **sey,** *v. t.* 2 *pl. pres.* 7/7 ; **sei, sey, seye,** *v. t.* 3 *pl. pres.* say 2/28, 3/5, 99/16 ; **seid,** *v. t.* 1 *s. p.* 5/16 ; **saide, seid,** *v. t.* 3 *s. p.* 1/6, 2/23, 19/21 ; **saide,** *v. t.* 1 *pl. p.* 5/5 ; **sayde,** *v. t.* 2 *pl. p.* 61/14 ; **saide,** *v. t.* 3 *pl. p.* 9/27.
sayle, *v. i. inf.* sail 32/1.
scalis, *np.* scales, 134/26.
I-schake, *pp.* roused, moved 84/7.
schal, *v. aux.* 2 *s. pres.* shalt 11/11 ; **schul,** 2 *pl. pres.* shall 3/3 ; **schal, schul,** 3 *pl. pres.* 5/19, 6/29 ; **schul,** 1 *pl. pres.* 16/4 ; **schulde,** 3 *s. p.* should 19/24.
schalful, *adj.* 22/20. *See note* p. 152.
schape, *pp.* shapen 28/20.
scharp, *adv.* sharp 2/25.
schaue, *pp.* shaven 48/27.
sche, *pron.* she 1/20, 10/27.
schepis, *n. gen.* sheep's 85/22.
schew, *v. t. inf.* show 11/4 ; **schewid,** *pp.* 3/23.
schidis, *np.* strips of wood 80/28.
schipmen, *np.* sailors 16/2.
schippard, *n.* shepherd 79/11.
schippe, *v. i. inf.* ship 29/21.
schippis, *np.* 34/8.
schon, *np.* shoes 45/18.

schortly, *adv.* 74/13.
schrine, soryne, *n.* shrine 115/19, 34.
schryue, *v. i. inf.* shrive 41/10 ; **schryuyth,** *v. t.* 3 *s. pres.* shriveth 9/5, 54/16 ; **schryue,** *pp.* shriven 133/10.
schyne, *v. i. inf.* shine 74/16 ; **schynyth,** *v. i.* 3 *s. pres.* shineth 2/12 ; **schone, schyned,** *v. i.* 3 *s. p.* shone 83/19.
sciens, *n.* science, learning 1/10, 19/12 ; **sciens,** *np.* 3/26.
scisme, *n.* schism 75/28.
scorne, *n.* 19/18.
scrowes, *np.* scrolls 30/12.
se, see, *n.* sea 15/28, 29/20, 30/28.
se, *n.* see 58/2.
se, *v. t. inf.* see 11/11, 15/29 ; **se,** *v.* 1 *s. pres.* 19/17 ; **se,** *v. t.* 3 *pl. pres.* 18/3 ; **say, sey,** *v. t.* 3 *s. p.* 6/33, 12/12, 19/27, 29/30 ; **sey,** *v. t.* 2 *pl. p.* 96/27 ; **sey,** *v. t.* 3 *pl. p.* 20/34 ; **seand,** *pres. p.* seeing 76/27 ; **sen, sene, seyn,** *pp.* seen 6/19, 65/27, 137/35, 138/1.
sealis, *np.* seals 139/5.
secretaries, *np.* 97/7.
secrete, *n.* secret, a prayer 112/5.
seculer, *adj.* secular 20/7.
sedes, *np.* seeds 81/17.
seid, seyn, *pp.* 7/8, 28/20 ; **seying,** *pres. p.* saying 16/26.
seke, *n.* sick 66/29.
sekenesse, *n.* sickness 8/11 ; **seknesse,** *np.* 75/5.
sekyng, *pres. p.* seeking 10/1.
seld, *seldom, adv.* 34/21, 47/12.
selle, *v. t. inf.* sell 81/10 ; **seld,** *v. t.* 3 *s. p.* sold 76/33, 77/6.
selue, *n.* self 64/6.
semeth, *v. i.* 3 *s. pres.* seems 4/23 ; **sempt,** *v. i.* 3 *s. p.* seemed 65/19.
semly, *adv.* seemly 51/1.
sengil, *adj.* single, unmarried 26/6.
ser, *n.* sir 112/20 ; **seres,** *np.* 16/4.
sercle, *n.* circle 77/30.
sere, *adj.* sere 118/26.
sered, *pp.* sered 118/16.
seruage, *n.* servitude 63/19.
seruauntis, *np.* servants 6/21.
seruyse, *n.* service 6/14.
seruyse, *n.* dinner 51/10.
seruyseable, *adj.* serviceable 30/32.
sesed, *v. t.* 3 *s. p.* ceased 96/9.
se-side, *n.* sea-side 13/23.
sete, *n.* seat 77/32.
sette, *v. t.* 3 *s. p.* set 17/1 ; **sette,** *pp.* set 1/1, 19/27.

seuene, *adj.* seven 7/22.

sewe, sewid, *v. t.* 3 *s. p.* pursued, followed, 26/9, 69/33.

sewirer, *adj. comp.* surer 90/7.

sexte, *adj.* sixth 35/3.

sextenesse, *n.* female sexton 121/1.

seying, *n.* seeing 67/14.

seyn, *n.* saint 17/1.

sikir, *adj.* certain 26/25.

sikirly, *adv.* certainly 13/23.

sikirnesse, sikyrnesse, *n.* certainty, safety 11/20, 35/11, 89/22.

silens, *n.* silence 20/20.

siluyr, *n.* silver 17/29, 100/2.

similitude, *n.* 82/2.

simpil, *adj.* simple 1/11.

sistir, *n.* sister 5/9.

sith, sithe, *adv.* since 15/17, 56/4.

sith, *n.* sight 21/28, 38/27, 73/21.

sithe, *n.* time 40/21.

Sithia, *n.* Scythia, 58/20.

sitte, *v. i. inf.* sit 21/27; satte, *v. i.* 3 *s. p.* sat 20/19; sat, soten, *v. i.* 3 *pl. p.* 21/26, 70/20.

skape, *v. t. inf.* escape 8/1; skaped, *v. t.* 3 *pl. p.* 134/31.

skil, *n.* reason, cause 57/27.

skole, *n.* school 4/13, 23/3.

skole mater, *n.* divinity, doctrine 56/4.

skoleres, skoleris, *np.* scholars 13/17, 23/10.

skoleward, *n.* schoolward 118/14.

slaundir, *n.* slaunder 16/35.

slauth, *n.* sloth 21/28.

slep, *n.* sleep 71/12.

slitte, *pp.* slit 34/12.

sluttynesse, *n.* sluttishness 46/23.

sly, *adj.* 53/7.

smale, *adj.* small 8/6.

smet, *pp.* smitten 95/32.

snybbe, *v. t. inf.* snub, rebuke 6/26.

snybbyng, *n.* rebuking 73/11.

sobbyng, *n.* 24/27.

sobir, *adj.* sober 21/14.

socour, *n.* succour 92/17.

sodeynly, *adv.* suddenly 7/9, 19/21.

soke, *n.* suck 89/36.

sokkys, *np.* socks 99/25.

solace, *n.* 27/10, 73/1.

solacious, *adj.* 70/3.

solemply, *adv.* solemnly 23/12.

solempne, *adj.* solemn 1/22.

solempnyȝed, *pp.* solemnized 80/4.

solitarie, *adj.* solitary 20/34.

solitarily, *adv.* 23/17.

somyr, *n.* summer 70/25.

sond, *n.* sending 118/10; sondes, *np.* messages 139/24.

sone, *adv.* soon 5/25.

soner, *adv. comp.* sooner 108/33.

sones, *np.* sons 3/6.

songe, songen, sunge, *pp.* 27/1, 27/13, 28/5.

sonner, *adv. comp.* sooner 49/28.

soo, *adv.* so 7/6, 19/21.

soor, *n.* sore 100/13.

sophisticacion, *n.* 10/31.

sor, *adv.* sorely 21/25.

sory, *adj.* sorry, worthless 8/26.

soten, *see* sitte.

soth, *n.* sooth, truth 95/6.

sotil, sotitt, *adj.* subtle, delicate 9/25, 26/16, 35/12, 47/28.

sotilly, *adv.* subtly 26/19.

souered, *see* suffir.

souereynis, *np.* sovereigns 76/18.

soundeth, *v. i.* 3 *s. pres.* 23/25.

soute, *v. t.* 1 *s. p.* sought 36/23; soute, sowt, *v. t.* 3 *s. p.* 15/27, 37/2, 81/2; sout, *v. t.* 3 *pl. p.* 20/35; sout, *pp.* sought 4/24.

sowe, *v. t. inf.* sew 112/35; sowe, *v. t.* 2 *s. imper.* sew 113/10.

sowe, *v. t. inf.* sow 81/16; sowe, *v. i.* 3 *pl. pres.* 55/16; sowyn, *pp.* sown 81/22.

spatil, *n.* spittle 131/5.

specialte, *n.* speciality, importance 32/25.

speks, *v. i. inf.* speak 12/19, 20/15, 25/6; spekith, *v. i.* 3 *s. pres.* 28/24; spak, *v. i.* 3 *s. p.* 1/5, 12/14, 76/28.

sperd, *v. t.* 3 *s. p.* closed 83/5; sperd, *pp.* closed 67/10.

spirith, *n.* spirit 16/13.

sprad, *v. t.* 3 *s. p.* spread 134/16.

spryngin, *v. i.* 3 *pl. pres.* spring 56/30; sprange, *v. i.* 3 *pl. p.* 62/24.

spynne, *v. i.* 3 *pl. pres.* spin 55/18.

stabil, *adj.* stable 10/30.

stale, *see* stele.

stant, *v. i.* 3 *s. pres.* stands 3/18, 33/20, 37/15; stant, *v. i.* 3 *pl. pres.* stand 3/13; stant, stood, *v. i.* 3 *s. p.* stood 10/11, 114/9.

statua, *n.* statue. Used as a Latin word by Capgrave. Latin *statua* = image, statue 19/12.

stedfast, *adj.* steadfast 20/12.

stele, *v. t. inf.* steal 18/1; stelist, *v. t.* 2 *s. pres.* stealest 30/27; stale, *v. t.* 3 *pl. p.* stole 14/1.

steppis, *np.* steps 19/24.

step-modiꝛ, *n.* step-mother 55/29.
steꝛ, *v. t. inf.* stir, incite 54/21;
stered, *pp.* 6/16, 35/28.
sterres, *np.* stars 2/10, 77/23.
stert, stirt, *v. i. 3 s. p.* started 21/23,
25, 47/30.
stewis, *np.* stews, brothels 8/26.
stile, *n.* style 25/23.
stille, *adv.* 21/2.
stilled, *v. i. 3 pl. p.* distilled 132/32.
stodie, *n.* study 11/11.
stodied, *v. i. 3 s. p.* studied 80/28;
stodiand, stodying, *pres. p.* studying 17/23, 111/13.
stombeled, *v. i. 3 s. p.* stumbled
123/13.
stood, *see* stant.
stoon, *n.* stone 118/24.
straungeris, *np.* strangers 36/34.
strawe, stre, *n.* straw 71/20, 111/22.
streit, streitn, *adv.* straitly 34/4,
95/24.
stretes, *np.* streets 101/6.
streyned, *v. i. 3 pl. p.* strained
120/30.
streyt, *adj.* straight 67/18, 108/24.
strokis, strokys, *np.* strokes, blows
53/2.
stuf, *n.* material 60/28.
stuffid, *pp.* stocked, filled 69/35.
stynkyng, *adj.* stinking 64/2.
suasiones, *np.* suasions 95/12.
subieccioñ, *n.* subjection 6/13.
substauns, *n.* substance 4/17.
subucula (Latin), undergarment
125/30.
suffir, *v. t. 1 s. pres.* suffer 6/10;
suffir, *v. t. 2 pl. pres.* 21/15;
souered, *v. t. 3 s. p.* 33/21.
summe, *pron.* some 6/1.
sumtyme, *adv.* sometimes 5/32.
Sunamite, *n.* Shunammite 102/9.
sunne, *n.* sun 20/34.
supplanteꝛ, *n.* 145/3.
supplicacioñ, *n.* 25/7.
Surre, Surry, *n.* Syria 3/13, 109/12.
suspecte, *adj.* suspect 36/28.
suspense, *adj.* undecided, unbiased
13/8; suspense, *adj.* raised up
72/10.
sustentacle, *n.* sustainment 71/11.
swames, *np.* scales (Latin *squama*)
134/25.
sweoh, *adj.* such 1/13, 20/14.
swem, *n.* swoon, sorrow 29/30.
swete, *adj.* sweet 2/18.
swete, *n.* sweat 132/30.
swetith, *v. i. 3 s. pres.* sweateth

132/31; swette, *v. i. 3 s. p.* sweated
119/10.
swynesye, *n.* quinsy 127/10.
swynys, *n. gen.* swine's 94/9.
syluyr, *n.* silver 48/3.
synne, *n.* sin 21/9.

T

tables, *np.* written agreements 6/9.
Tagatenses, *n.* Tagaste 3/22.
tak, *v. t. inf.* take 85/23; take, *pp.*
taken 21/12, 56/10.
talent, *n.* talent, piece of money
87/17.
talkyng, *n.* 5/2.
tariing, tary, taryying, *n.* tarrying
24/27, 113/16, 115/19.
tast, *v. t. inf.* taste 25/2.
tecches, *np.* characteristics 78/29.
tech, *v. t. inf.* teach 14/19; techith,
v. t. 3 s. pres. 11/13; taute, *v. t.
3 s. p.* 12/4; tawt, *v. i. 3 s. p.*
23/26; taute, *v. t. 3 pl. p.* 27/23.
techer, *n.* teacher 63/34.
tedious, *adj.* 63/10.
telle, *v. t. inf.* tell 1/15, 30/12; telle,
v. 3 s. subj. pres. tell 4/24; tellet3,
tellith, tellit, tell3, *v. i. 3 s. pres.*
4/26, 7/8, 16/31, 17/22, 26/16;
teld, *v. t. 3 s. p.* told 19/5.
tempir, *v. t. inf.* temper 95/23; tempered, *v. t. 3 s. p.* tempered, mode-
rated 51/37.
temporal, *adj.* 27/11.
teres, *np.* tears 11/20.
tete, *n.* teat 9/19; tetes, *np.* 89/35.
teth, *np.* teeth 7/16, 25/5.
tewnys, *np.* tunes 27/14.
Tewysday, *n.* Tuesday 78/28.
teyhid, *v. t. 3 s. p.* tied 118/33.
than, *adv.* then 1/22, 9/21.
theef, *n.* thief 17/31.
tho, thoo, *adv.* then 9/26, 20/14,
21/13.
tilleres, *np.* tillers 63/16.
tilth, *n.* 101/5.
to-gidir, to-gidyr, *adv.* together
2/31, 19/32.
tokne, *n.* token 87/6; toknes, tokenes, *np.* 30/13, 107/11.
tong, tonge, tunge, *n.* tongue 2/34,
3/30, 21/21; tonge, *n.* tongue,
used for nation or country 3/16;
tongis, *np.* tongues 3/31.
too, *pron.* two 17/3, 20/24.
too, *adj.* two 3/12, 16/10.
toos, *np.* toes 118/29.

touchith, *v. t.* 3 *s. pres.* 33/9.

touȝ, *n.* tower 111/19.

tow, *adj.* tough 73/12.

trad, *v. i.* 3 *s. p.* trod 119/12.

translat, *v. t.* 1 *s. p.* translated 61/7; translat, translate, *pp.* translated 33/6, 80/6.

transumpciones, *np.* transumptions 85/27.

trauase, *v. t. inf.* traverse 135/1.

trauayle, *v. i. inf.* travail, work 37/28; trauayled, *v. i.* 3 *s. p.* laboured, suffered 6/33.

trauns, *n.* trance 128/20.

trayled, *v. i.* 3 *s. p.* trailed 118/32.

tre, *n.* tree 10/11, 21/32; tre, *n.* wood 100/2.

tremel, *v. i. inf.* tremble 15/14; tremuled, *v. i.* 3 *pl. p.* trembled 94/27.

tresoȝ, tresouȝ, *n.* treasure 1/13, 50/3.

trespas, *n.* 33/22.

tretith, *v. i.* 3 *s. pres.* 23/31; tretith, *v. t.* 3 *s. pres.* treateth 25/21.

tretys, *n.* treatise 56/2.

treuly, *adv.* truly 1/17.

tribus, *np.* tribes 145/20.

trost, *n.* trust 15/19.

trostand, trosting, trostyng, *pres. p.* 90/32, 94/30, 99/4, 126/24.

trowe, *v. t.* 1 *s. pres.* trow 47/13.

Tussie, *n.* Tuscany 31/2.

tuycioñ, *n.* tuition 27/26.

twyes, *adv.* twice 14/13.

tydannes, tydyngis, tytandis, *np.* tidings 35/27, 72/34, 115/4.

tyl, *adv.* till 17/18.

Tyrington, *n.* West Torrington 81/28.

Þ

þai, *pron.* 48/19.

þan, þanñ, þanne, *adv.* then 19/17, 20/28, 21/6.

þankyng, *n.* thanking, thanks 20/10; þankinggis, *np.* 187/2.

þankyng, *pres. p.* 21/1.

þat, *conj.* that 1/2.

þat, *rel. pron.* who 18/6.

þedir, þedyr, þidir, *adv.* thither 14/8, 31/13, 111/20.

þei, *pron.* they 6/17.

þem, *pron.* them 96/32.

þenne, *adv.* thence 102/21.

þeȝ, *adv.* there 5/18.

þese, *pron.* these 1/7.

þi, *pron.* thy 111/33.

þidir, *see* þedir.

þing, þingis, *np.* things, 1/27, 103/6.

þink, *v. t. inf.* 28/6.

þird, *adj.* third 1/29.

þirknesse, *n.* darkness 16/17, 77/27. (*Also* dirknes.)

þirled, *pp.* pierced 115/26.

þo, *adj.* those 16/32.

þoo, *pron.* those 9/17, 12/13.

þolyd, *pp.* endured 75/15.

þongis, *np.* thongs 38/30.

þorw, *prep.* through 11/14.

þorw-oute, *prep.* throughout 2/17, 15/3.

þouȝ, *conj.* though 30/31.

þouȝt, *v. t.* 3 *s. p.* thought 10/11, 36/8, 67/6, 88/27; þout, þouȝt, *v. t.* 3 *pl. p.* 32/9, 76/10.

þoutes, *np.* thoughts 15/13, 86/11.

þouȝ, *conj.* though 1/8.

þretis, *np.* threats 48/19.

þretyng, *n.* threatening 95/11.

þrew, *v. t. inf.* 21/32; þrew, *v. t.* 3 *s. p.* 81/7.

þries, *adv.* thrice 64/33.

þrote, *n.* throat 95/14.

V

vacaunt, *adj.* vacant, unemployed 61/21.

vanite, *n.* vanity 9/6; vanytees, *np.* 23/6.

venemhous, *adj.* venemous 27/17.

veniauns, *n.* vengeance 7/17.

vers, *n.* verse 24/28; vers, *np.* verses 47/21.

vertu, *np.* virtues 67/6.

very, *adj.* true 30/13.

veryly, *adv.* verily 1/20.

vexid, *pp.* vexed 49/2.

veyn, *adj.* vain 8/6, 14/14.

veynglorie, *n.* vainglory 70/33.

vhanne, *adv.* when 8/19.

viage, *n.* voyage 91/17, 135/20.

vikeȝ, vykeȝ, *n.* vicar 40/22, 90/30.

vis, *n.* vice 47/20; vices *np.* 47/19.

visite, *v. t.* 3 *s. p.* visited 31/4, 49/1.

vitaile, *n.* victuals 69/35.

vnce, *n.* ounce 82/7.

vnch, *np.* inches 132/19.

vndir-fote, *adv.* underfoot 81/7.

vndirtake, *v. t. inf.* take charge of 8/27.

vnkunnyng, *n.* ignorance 114/19.

vnneth, *adv.* scarcely 61/20.

vnsperd, *v. t.* 3 *s. p.* unclasped, opened 20/7.

vomyte, *n.* vomiting 133/22.

voyde, *v. t. inf.* dismiss 11/18.

voys, *n.* voice 21/14; voyses, *np.* cries 22/1.

up-hap, vphap, *adv.* 20/25, 46/32.

vsetȝ, *v. t.* 3 *s. pres.* useth 88/19; vsed, *pp.* habituated 41/11.

vttyr, *v. t. inf.* utter 32/9; vttered, vttir, *v. t.* 3 *s. p.* 34/27, 43/11.

W

wallid, *pp.* walled 83/28.

wallis, *np.* walls 19/18.

Wandali, *np.* Vandals 58/18 (Latin *Vandali*).

war, *adj.* ware 48/15.

Wardon, *n.* Watton 109/17.

warned, *pp.* forbidden, refused 47/17.

was, wast, *see* be.

wasch, *pp.* washed 62/10.

wast, *n.* waste 47/28.

water, *v. t. inf.* wash 112/27.

watirside, *n.* 64/30.

wauntown, *adj.* wanton 8/25, 64/2.

wawe, *n.* wave, sea 103/21.

wecch, *n.* watch 27/28.

wecchid, *pp.* 121/20.

weddid, *pp.* 5/26, 21/3.

wedyr, *n.* weather 103/24.

welde, *v. t. inf.* possess, rule 83/21.

welfar, *n.* 20/2.

well, *adv.* well 3/28, 14/24, 43/31.

wenest, *v. t.* 2 *s. pres.* 105/12.

wenyng, *pres. p.* weening, causing to ween 42/28.

wengis, *np.* wings 85/23.

wepe, *v. i. inf.* weep 21/30.

wepun, *np.* weapons 53/2.

were, *v. t. inf.* wear 47/4; wered, *v. t.* 3 *s. p.* wore 46/19. μ.μμ. 99/26

werk, *n.* work 1/23.

werre, *n.* war 50/31.

weuer, *n.* weaver 129/31.

weuyng, *n.* weaving 129/32.

wex, *v. i.* 3 *s. p.* waxed, grew 96/2.

weye, *n.* way 2/35.

weyk, *adj.* weak 34/12.

whan, *adv.* when 4/13.

whech, *pron.* which, who 1/6, 16/2, &c.

wheither, *conj.* whether 15/2.

whens, *adv.* whence 32/34.

wher-so-euyr, *adv.* wheresoever 17/1.

whil, whill, *adv.* while 4/30, 16/23.

while, *n.* 32/9.

who, *adv.* how 5/18. 36/30

wicchis, *np.* witches 137/30.

widowis, *np.* 66/29.

wil, *n.* will 1/20.

wildyrnesse, *n.* wilderness 20/16.

wilful, *adj.* voluntary 30/2.

wite, *v. t. inf.* blame 51/5.

withdrawe, *v. t. inf.* diminish 45/16; with-drow, *v. t.* 3 *s. p.* withdrew 39/19.

withinne, *prep.* within 19/17.

with-outen, *conj.* without 4/16; witȝ-outen, *prep.* 99/22.

witnes, *n.* evidence 113/24; witnesseres, *np.* witnesses 110/9.

witte, *n.* wit, understanding 26/15; wittes, wittis, *np.* wits 32/20, 93/27.

witȝ, *prep.* with 10/7, 112/24.

wode, *adj.* mad 128/15.

wode, *n.* wood 20/23; wodes, wodis, *np.* woods 20/22, 81/2.

wodnesse, *n.* madness 79/20.

womannes, *n. gen.* woman's 15/31.

womennes, *np. gen.* 86/27.

wone, *adj.* wont 21/20.

wonyng, *n.* dwelling 122/28.

wook, *v. i.* 3 *s. p.* woke 66/10.

worchep, worchip, *n.* worship 1/23, 74/22.

worchipid, *v. t.* 3 *s. p.* worshipt 19/2.

wordes, wordis, wordys, *np.* words 2/24, 10/28, 11/19.

wortes, wortys, *np.* worts, herbs, roots 47/12, 70/14.

wot, wote, *v. t.* 1 *s. pres.* know 4/3, 32/13; wist, wost, *v. t.* 3 *s. p.* 14/5, 29/13.

wounde, wounden, woundyn, *pp.* wound 116/7, 117/15, 18.

wrastillingis, *np.* wrestlings 65/22.

wrecched, *adj.* wretched 46/21.

wrestiling, *pres. p.* wrestling 58/17.

wroth, *adj.* 30/19.

wrout, *v. t.* 3 *s. p.* wrought 34/33; wroute, *v. t.* 3 *pl. p.* 17/30.

wrytith, *v. i.* 3 *s. pres.* writeth 28/26; wroot, wrot, *v. t.* 3 *s. p.* wrote 25/10, 60/21; wrytyn, *v. i.* 3 *pl. p.* 95/5; wretyn, writin, writyn, wrytin, *pp.* written 5/12, 7/26, 135/27, 136/7.

wyis, *adj.* wise 50/19.

wyndown, wyndown, *n.* window 32/2, 84/1.

wynne, *v. t.* 3 *pl. p.* win 21/16.

Wyntir, *n.* Winter 70/24.

12

wyte, *n.* imposition, burden 90/10.
wyues, wyuys, *np.* wives 6/12, 26/9.

Y

ydiotes, ydiotis, *np.* unlearned, ignorant people 1/4, 85/16.
ydropesey, *n.* dropsy 122/10.
ylde, *n.* island 76/5.
ympne, *n.* hymne 25/34; **ympnis, ympnys,** *np.* 27/1, 11; **ympnis,** *np. gen.* 72/11.
Ynde, *n.* India 3/13.
Ynglond, *n.* England 3/17, 68/21.
Ypone, *n.* Hippo 3/21.
Ytaile, *n.* Italy 3/16.

ȝ

ȝa, *adv.* yes 18/19.
ȝald, *v. t. 3 s. p.* yielded 60/15.
ȝe, *pron.* ye 6/8.
ȝel, *n.* zeal 65/10.

ȝelow, *adj.* yellow 132/32.
ȝere, *n.* year 33/2; **ȝer, ȝere,** *np.* years 7/6, 8/19, 33/5, 75/2; **ȝeris,** *n. gen.* year's 49/36.
ȝet, ȝit, *adv.* yet 1/9, 111/9.
ȝeue, *v. t. inf.* 16/27, 46/24; **ȝeueth,** *v. t. 3 s. pres.* 26/28; **ȝyue,** *v. t. 3 s. pres. subj.* 46/27; **gaf, ȝaue,** *v. t. 3 s. p.* 14/12, 18/17, 19/8, 50/1; **ȝoue,** *v. t. 3 pl. p.* gave 13/13; **ȝeuyng,** *pres. p.* giving 46/10; **goue, ȝoue, ȝouen,** *pp.* 2/4, 13/17, 20/14, 56/21, 136/14.
ȝeueres, *np.* givers 88/15.
ȝeugis, *n.* Zeugitana 3/18.
ȝiftis, *np.* gifts 68/8.
ȝok, *n.* yoke 90/19.
ȝondir, *adv.* yonder 105/14.
ȝong, *adj.* young 6/20, 21/3.
ȝonger, *adj. comp.* younger 49/20.
ȝou, ȝow, *pron.* you 3/23, 6/9, 29/1, 37/29.
ȝour, *pron.* your 6/8.

SUBJECT INDEX

A

Achademia, explanation of 23/25.

Achaia 3/15.

Acharius, abbot of Peterborough 79/28, 142/9.

Adeodatus, son of Augustine, baptized with him 26/4 ; cause of *de Quantitate Animae* 26/26, 31/17.

Ad fratres in heremo, a sermon 146/22.

Africa 3/10.

Ages, the seven 7/4.

Alans 58/18.

Albyne, a canon of St. Gilbert's 98/4.

Alexander, Bishop of Lincoln, 83/32, 87/34.

Alypius, goes to Augustine 17/4; convicted of theft 17/20 ; goes to Africa with Augustine 29/20, 37/6.

Anagnia 111/2, 142/3.

Anastasius, a monk of Augustine's 30/3, 37/7.

Ancelme, a priest 135/5.

Anna 89/32.

Antichrist 137/31.

Antioch, Council of 43/21.

Apollo 56/12.

Apostolus Petrus, a sermon 49/13.

Arabia 3/13.

Arian heresy 27/16.

Arillus, a monk 30/4.

Aristotle, his *Categories* 4/2, 11/27.

Asher 147/3.

Asia 3/8.

Augustine, his life translated from Latin at the request of a gentle woman 1/15; virtues of his name 1/26; significance of his name 2/25 ; born at Tagaste 3/22 ; hated Greek 3/27; knew both Greek and Latin 3/31; translated Aristotle's *Categories* 4/2; position of his parents 4/9 ; goes to school at Carthage 4/13 ; born on St. Brice's day 4/28; his brother, Navigius

5/6 ; his monasteries 5/16 ; his childhood 7/3; at school 7/27 ; studies Scripture unprofitably 9/21 ; at Madaura 8/8; study at Carthage 8/20, 11/25 ; robs an apple-tree 9/7 ; reads Cicero 9/12 ; becomes a Manichaean 9/27 ; teaching rhetoric at Carthage 12/7 ; doubts the Manichaean heresy 12/20 ; writes against Manichaean heresy 12/18 ; argues with Faustus 12/30 ; goes to Rome 13/11 ; goes to Milan to teach rhetoric 14/21 ; meets St. Ambrose 14/28 ; converted by the preaching of St. Ambrose 15/12 ; goes to Simplicianus 18/25; Simplicianus and 19/24 ; Pontitianus visits him 19/30 ; hears a voice: 'Take up and read !' 22/8 ; leaves Milan 23/17; lives in a field (villa) belonging to Verecundus 23/19 ; asks advice of St. Ambrose 25/14 ; helps Ambrose compose *Te Deum* 25/35 ; adopts a habit from Simplicianus 28/11 ; gets twelve hermits from Simplicianus 29/8 ; names of his first monks 30/3 ; goes to Ostia 30/28, 31/31 ; goes to Rome 31/1; writes against Manichaeans 31/9, 34/32 ; communes with Monica 32/4; goes to Carthage 34/1; returns to his heritage at Tagaste 34/19 ; goes to Hippo 36/5 ; builds a monastery near Hippo 36/30; elected priest 39/4 ; his second monastery 40/2; preaching under Valerius 40/29 ; argues with Fortunatus 41/20 ; chosen bishop 42/23 ; his third monastery 43/29 ; increase of his order 46/2; his manner at table 47/8 ; casts out spirits 49/2; conduct of worldly affairs 50/2; in danger from heretics 52/16; writes his *Retractations* 57/18 ; in the siege of Hippo 58/16 ; miracle before death 59/21 ; death 60/15 ; rule of 67/23 ; St. Jerome and

The manufacturer's authorised representative in the EU for product
safety is Oxford University Press España S.A. of El Parque Empresarial
San Fernando de Henares, Avenida de Castilla, 2 - 28830 Madrid
(www.oup.es/en or product.safety@oup.com). OUP España S.A. also acts
as importer into Spain of products made by the manufacturer.
Printed and bound by CPI Group (UK) Ltd, Croydon, CR0 4YY

05/05/2026

02102998-0002